Step-by-Step Spanish

From Alphabet to Conversation

Valeria S.

My First Picture Book Inc.

Copyright © 2024 by My First Picture Book Inc.

All rights reserved.

No portion of this book may be reproduced in any form without written permission from the publisher or author, except as permitted by U.S. copyright law.

Contents

1. Introduction to Spanish — 1
2. The Spanish Alphabet and Pronunciation — 4
3. Basic Greetings and Introductions — 9
4. Numbers and Counting — 14
5. Days of the Week — 19
6. Months of the Year — 23
7. Seasons and Weather — 28
8. Colors in Spanish — 34
9. Basic Phrases for Everyday Use — 39
10. Asking Questions in Spanish — 45
11. Telling Time — 51
12. Family and Relationships — 56
13. Describing People: Physical Appearance — 61
14. Describing People: Personality Traits — 67
15. Basic Verbs: To Be and To Have (Ser, Estar, Tener) — 73
16. Common Nouns and Articles — 79
17. Food and Drink Vocabulary — 84
18. Shopping Vocabulary — 89
19. Navigating Directions and Places — 95
20. Around the House: Rooms and Objects — 101
21. Basic Adjectives and Their Agreement — 107
22. School and Education Vocabulary — 111
23. Work and Professions — 117

24. Animals in Spanish — 121
25. Basic Sentence Structure — 126
26. The Present Tense: Regular Verbs — 130
27. The Present Tense: Irregular Verbs — 135
28. Reflexive Verbs — 140
29. Expressing Likes and Dislikes — 144
30. Talking About the Past: Preterite Tense — 148
31. Talking About the Past: Imperfect Tense — 153
32. The Future Tense — 159
33. Expressing Obligations: Tener que, Deber, and More — 164
34. Making Comparisons — 168
35. The Subjunctive Mood: Introduction — 172
36. Expressing Wishes and Desires — 176
37. Giving Commands: The Imperative Mood — 180
38. Expressing Feelings and Emotions — 185
39. Talking About Health and the Body — 190
40. Travel Vocabulary — 195
41. Expressing Opinions — 201
42. The Conditional Tense — 206
43. Understanding and Using Prepositions — 210
44. Indirect and Direct Object Pronouns — 216
45. The Passive Voice — 221
46. Discussing the Future: Plans and Predictions — 225

Chapter 1

Introduction to Spanish

Welcome to the Wonderful World of Spanish! Imagine being able to greet someone from Spain with a warm "¡Hola!" or ordering your favorite taco in perfect Spanish. Doesn't that sound exciting? Spanish is one of the most beautiful and widely spoken languages in the world. By learning it, you're opening the door to new cultures, people, and experiences. In this book, we're going to take a fun and easy journey to learn Spanish, starting from the very basics and gradually moving to more complex conversations. Whether you're talking to a friend or exploring a new country, knowing Spanish will help you connect with others in a way you never thought possible.

But first, let's talk about why learning Spanish is so important.

Why Learn Spanish?

Did you know that Spanish is the second most spoken language in the world? Over 460 million people speak Spanish as their first language, and it's the official language in 21 countries! That means when you learn Spanish, you're not just learning a language—you're gaining the ability to communicate with millions of people across the globe. Here are a few reasons why learning Spanish is a great idea:

- **Global Communication:** Spanish is spoken in Europe, Latin America, Africa, and even parts of the United States. Learning Spanish allows you to talk to people in places like Spain, Mexico, Argentina, and many more.

- **Cultural Understanding:** Spanish-speaking countries have rich histories and traditions. By learning the language, you'll be able to understand and appreciate the culture, music, food, and festivals of these countries.

- **Travel:** If you ever travel to a Spanish-speaking country, knowing the language will make your trip much more enjoyable. You'll be able to ask for directions, order food, and make friends easily.

- **Educational Opportunities:** Many schools and universities offer programs in Spanish-speaking countries. Knowing Spanish could open up exciting study abroad opportunities.

- **Job Opportunities:** Many companies are looking for people who can speak more than one language. By learning Spanish, you'll have a skill that can help you in your future career.

Now that you know why learning Spanish is so valuable, let's talk about what you'll be learning in this book.

What Will You Learn?

We're going to start from the very beginning, so don't worry if you don't know any Spanish yet. This book is designed for beginners, and by the time you finish, you'll be able to have conversations in Spanish, read and write simple sentences, and understand much of what you hear in Spanish. Here's a quick look at some of the exciting things you'll learn:

- **The Alphabet:** The first step in learning Spanish is understanding the alphabet and how to pronounce the letters. Spanish pronunciation is quite different from English, but don't worry—we'll practice it together!

- **Basic Words and Phrases:** You'll learn how to say hello, introduce yourself, ask for directions, and much more. These phrases will be your building blocks for conversation.

- **Numbers and Counting:** From "uno" (one) to "cien" (a hundred), you'll learn how to count in Spanish and use numbers in everyday situations.

- **Days, Months, and Seasons:** You'll be able to talk about the days of the week, months of the year, and the different seasons in Spanish. For example, "lunes" (Monday), "abril" (April), and "invierno" (winter).

- **Describing People and Things:** You'll learn how to describe people, like saying someone is "alto" (tall) or "simpático" (nice), and how to talk about objects around you.

- **Verbs and Actions:** Verbs are action words like "correr" (to run) or "leer" (to read). You'll learn how to use verbs to describe what you or others are doing.

- **Telling Time:** Knowing how to tell time is important in any language. You'll learn how to ask and tell the time in Spanish, such as "¿Qué hora es?" (What time is it?) and how to respond.

And that's just the beginning! As you move through the book, you'll gradually learn more complex things like talking about the past and future, expressing your feelings, and even discussing your hobbies and interests in Spanish.

How Will You Learn?

This book is designed to be as easy and fun as possible. Each chapter will introduce you to new words and phrases, and then show you how to use them in sentences. We'll also provide plenty of examples and practice activities to help you remember what you've learned. Don't worry if you don't get everything right away—it's normal to make mistakes when you're learning something new. The important thing is to keep practicing!

Transcriptions for Non-English Words

Whenever we introduce a new Spanish word, we'll provide a transcription to help you pronounce it correctly. For example, the word "hola" (pronounced OH-lah) means "hello" in Spanish. This way, you'll always know how to say the words you're learning.

Let's Get Started!

Now that you have an idea of what we're going to learn, it's time to jump in! Remember, learning a language is like solving a puzzle—it can be challenging at times, but it's also incredibly rewarding. By the end of this book, you'll have the tools you need to start speaking Spanish and exploring a whole new world of possibilities. ¡Vamos! (Let's go!)

Chapter 2

The Spanish Alphabet and Pronunciation

Welcome to your first step in learning Spanish! Before we dive into speaking, writing, and understanding Spanish, we need to start with the basics—the alphabet and pronunciation. Just like in English, knowing the alphabet is the foundation of everything you'll learn. But don't worry, the Spanish alphabet is quite similar to the English one, with just a few differences. By the end of this chapter, you'll be able to recognize, pronounce, and understand each letter of the Spanish alphabet.

The Spanish Alphabet

The Spanish alphabet, known as el abecedario (pronounced ah-bay-say-DAH-ryoh), has 27 letters. That's one more than the English alphabet! Most of the letters are the same, but there's one special letter that makes the Spanish alphabet unique—ñ (pronounced EH-nyeh). Let's take a look at all the letters:

- **A** - pronounced ah
- **B** - pronounced bay
- **C** - pronounced say
- **D** - pronounced day
- **E** - pronounced eh
- **F** - pronounced eh-fay
- **G** - pronounced hay
- **H** - pronounced AH-chay

- **I** - pronounced ee
- **J** - pronounced HO-tah
- **K** - pronounced kah
- **L** - pronounced EH-lay
- **M** - pronounced EH-may
- **N** - pronounced EH-nay
- **Ñ** - pronounced EH-nyeh
- **O** - pronounced oh
- **P** - pronounced pay
- **Q** - pronounced koo
- **R** - pronounced EH-ray
- **S** - pronounced EH-say
- **T** - pronounced tay
- **U** - pronounced oo
- **V** - pronounced bay
- **W** - pronounced DOH-blay bay
- **X** - pronounced EH-kees
- **Y** - pronounced ee-gree-AY-gah
- **Z** - pronounced SAY-tah

As you can see, most of the letters in Spanish are pronounced similarly to English, but there are some key differences. For example, the letter **H** is always silent in Spanish, so the word "hola" (which means "hello") is pronounced OH-lah, without any "h" sound.

The Special Letter: Ñ

The letter **Ñ** (pronounced EH-nyeh) is unique to the Spanish language. It's not just an N with a squiggly line on top; it has its own sound, like the "ny" in the English word "canyon." For example, the word "niño" (which means "boy") is pronounced NEE-nyoh. This letter is very important in Spanish and appears in many words, so it's important to recognize and pronounce it correctly.

Vowels in Spanish

Vowels in Spanish are straightforward and always pronounced the same way, which makes learning them a bit easier than in English. Here's how each vowel is pronounced:

- **A** - pronounced ah as in "father"
- **E** - pronounced eh as in "bed"
- **I** - pronounced ee as in "see"
- **O** - pronounced oh as in "go"
- **U** - pronounced oo as in "food"

Notice that there are no tricky vowel sounds like in English. Once you learn the sounds, you can apply them to any word in Spanish!

Pronouncing Consonants

Consonants in Spanish are mostly similar to English, but there are some differences you need to know:

- **B and V:** Both of these letters are pronounced the same in Spanish, which can be a bit confusing at first. They both make a sound similar to the English "b." For example, "bien" (which means "well") is pronounced BYEN.

- **C:** The letter C can make two different sounds. When it comes before "e" or "i," it sounds like an "s," as in "centro" (center), pronounced SEN-troh. Before "a," "o," or "u," it sounds like a "k," as in "casa" (house), pronounced KAH-sah.

- **G:** Like C, the letter G can make two sounds. Before "e" or "i," it sounds like the English "h," as in "gente" (people), pronounced HEN-tay. Before "a," "o," or "u," it sounds like the "g" in "go," as in "gato" (cat), pronounced GAH-toh.

- **J:** The letter J is always pronounced like the English "h," so the word "jamón" (ham) is pronounced hah-MOHN.

- **LL:** The double L (ll) is usually pronounced like the English "y." For example, "llama" (which means both "flame" and "llama" the animal) is pronounced YAH-mah.

- **R:** The letter R is pronounced with a tap of the tongue against the roof of the mouth, like a quick "d" sound. For example, "pero" (but) is pronounced PEH-doh. When you see a double R (rr), it's pronounced with a strong rolling sound, as in "perro" (dog), pronounced PEH-rroh.

- **X:** The letter X is pronounced like the English "ks," as in "taxi" (taxi), pronounced TAHK-see. But in some words, like "México," it's pronounced like an "h," so "México" is pronounced MEH-hee-koh.

- **Y:** The letter Y can be pronounced like the English "y" as in "yes," or like the Spanish vowel "i," depending on where it is in the word. For example, "yo" (I) is pronounced YOH, and "y" (and) is pronounced ee.

- **H:** The letter H is always silent in Spanish. So "hola" (hello) is pronounced OH-lah and not "HOH-lah."

- **Z:** The letter Z is pronounced like the "s" in "see" in most Spanish-speaking countries. For example, "zapato" (shoe) is pronounced sah-PAH-toh.

Putting It All Together

Now that you know the Spanish alphabet and how to pronounce each letter, you're ready to start putting it all together. Let's practice by saying a few simple words:

- **Hola** - Pronounced OH-lah, this means "hello."

- **Casa** - Pronounced KAH-sah, this means "house."

- **Amigo** - Pronounced ah-MEE-goh, this means "friend."

- **Familia** - Pronounced fah-MEE-lee-ah, this means "family."

- **Gracias** - Pronounced GRAH-syahs, this means "thank you."

With these words, you're already starting to speak Spanish!

Key Points to Remember

1. **The Spanish Alphabet:** The Spanish alphabet has 27 letters, including the unique letter "ñ" (pronounced EH-nyeh), which is important for many Spanish words.

2. **Vowels in Spanish:** Spanish vowels (a, e, i, o, u) have consistent pronunciations, making them easier to learn compared to English vowels.

3. **Silent "H":** The letter "H" is always silent in Spanish, as in the word "hola" (pronounced OH-lah).

4. **Special Consonant Sounds:** Letters like "C," "G," "J," and "R" have different sounds depending on their placement in a word. For example, "C" can sound like "s" or "k" depending on the following vowel.

5. **Practice Words:** Words like "hola," "casa," "amigo," "familia," and "gracias" help you practice the Spanish alphabet and pronunciation.

Chapter 3

Basic Greetings and Introductions

Now that you've learned the Spanish alphabet and how to pronounce the letters, it's time to start speaking! One of the first things you'll need to know in any language is how to greet people and introduce yourself. Whether you're meeting someone for the first time or just saying "hello" to a friend, these basic greetings and introductions will help you start conversations in Spanish with confidence.

Greetings: Saying Hello and Goodbye

Let's start with the most common way to say "hello" in Spanish: **Hola** (pronounced OH-lah). "Hola" is a simple and friendly way to greet someone, and it's used at any time of day. You can use it when you meet someone in the morning, afternoon, or evening. Just like in English, a friendly "hola" can go a long way in making someone feel welcome.

But what if you want to say something more specific, like "good morning" or "good night"? Spanish has special greetings for different times of the day:

- **Buenos días** - Pronounced BWAY-nohs DEE-ahs, this means "good morning." You can use "buenos días" from when you wake up until around noon.

- **Buenas tardes** - Pronounced BWAY-nahs TAR-days, this means "good afternoon." You can use "buenas tardes" from around noon until the sun starts to set.

- **Buenas noches** - Pronounced BWAY-nahs NOH-chays, this means "good evening" or "good night." You can use "buenas noches" when it's dark outside or when you're saying goodbye at night.

Just like in English, there are also different ways to say goodbye in Spanish. Here are a few common ways to bid someone farewell:

- **Adiós** - Pronounced ah-DYOHSS, this means "goodbye." It's the most common way to say goodbye in Spanish, and it can be used in almost any situation.

- **Hasta luego** - Pronounced AHS-tah LWAY-goh, this means "see you later." You can use this phrase when you expect to see the person again soon.

- **Hasta mañana** - Pronounced AHS-tah mah-NYAH-nah, this means "see you tomorrow." Use it when you know you'll see the person the next day.

- **Chao** - Pronounced CHOW, this is a more casual way to say "bye," similar to "see ya!" in English.

By using these greetings, you'll be able to start and end conversations politely and naturally, just like a native Spanish speaker!

Introducing Yourself

Once you've said hello, the next step is to introduce yourself. Introducing yourself in Spanish is easy, and there are just a few phrases you need to know to get started. Here's how to do it:

To say "My name is [your name]," you use the phrase **Me llamo** (pronounced may YAH-moh). For example, if your name is Maria, you would say:

Me llamo Maria. - Pronounced may YAH-moh mah-REE-ah, this means "My name is Maria."

Another way to introduce yourself is by saying "I am [your name]," which in Spanish is **Soy** (pronounced soh-ee). So if your name is Alex, you would say:

Soy Alex. - Pronounced soh-ee AH-lehx, this means "I am Alex."

After introducing yourself, it's polite to ask the other person for their name. You can do this by asking **¿Cómo te llamas?** (pronounced KOH-moh tay YAH-mahs), which means "What's your name?" The person might respond by saying "Me llamo [their name]" or "Soy [their name]."

Here's an example of a simple conversation when you meet someone for the first time:

- **Tú:** Hola. Me llamo Maria. (Hello. My name is Maria.)

- **Otra persona:** ¡Hola! Soy Alex. ¿Cómo te llamas? (Hello! I'm Alex. What's your name?)

- **Tú:** Me llamo Maria. (My name is Maria.)

- **Otra persona:** ¡Mucho gusto! (Nice to meet you!)

Polite Expressions

Being polite is important in any language, and Spanish is no different. After you've introduced yourself, it's nice to say "nice to meet you." In Spanish, you can say **Mucho**

gusto (pronounced MOO-choh GOO-stoh), which literally means "much pleasure" but is used just like "nice to meet you" in English.

Another polite expression to know is **Por favor** (pronounced pohr fah-VOHR), which means "please." You can use this whenever you're asking for something. For example, if you want to ask someone to help you, you could say:

¿Me ayudas, por favor? - Pronounced may ah-YOO-dahs pohr fah-VOHR, this means "Can you help me, please?"

And when someone helps you or does something nice for you, it's important to say "thank you." In Spanish, you say **Gracias** (pronounced GRAH-syahs). If you want to say "thank you very much," you can say **Muchas gracias** (pronounced MOO-chahs GRAH-syahs).

Here's how a polite conversation might look:

- **Tú:** Hola. ¿Cómo te llamas? (Hello. What's your name?)

- **Otra persona:** Me llamo Ana. (My name is Ana.)

- **Tú:** ¡Mucho gusto, Ana! (Nice to meet you, Ana!)

- **Otra persona:** ¡Mucho gusto! (Nice to meet you!)

Introducing Others

Sometimes, you might need to introduce someone else, like a friend or family member. In Spanish, you can introduce someone by saying **Te presento a** (pronounced tay preh-SEN-toh ah), which means "I introduce you to." For example:

Te presento a mi amiga, Laura. - Pronounced tay preh-SEN-toh ah mee ah-MEE-gah LAH-oo-rah, this means "I introduce you to my friend, Laura."

After you introduce someone, the person you introduced them to might say "Mucho gusto" or "Encantado" (if they are male) or "Encantada" (if they are female). "Encantado/Encantada" (pronounced en-kahn-TAH-doh for males or en-kahn-TAH-dah for females) means "pleased to meet you" and is another polite way to greet someone.

Here's an example of introducing a friend:

- **Tú:** Hola, Ana. Te presento a mi amigo, Carlos. (Hello, Ana. I introduce you to my friend, Carlos.)

- **Ana:** ¡Mucho gusto, Carlos! (Nice to meet you, Carlos!)

- **Carlos:** ¡Encantado, Ana! (Pleased to meet you, Ana!)

Greetings for Different Situations

In Spanish, the way you greet someone can change depending on the situation. For example, when you're talking to someone older than you or someone you don't know well, it's polite to use a more formal greeting. Instead of just saying "Hola," you can say **Buenos días** (good morning), **Buenas tardes** (good afternoon), or **Buenas noches** (good evening).

If you're talking to someone your own age or someone you know well, you can be more informal. You might just say "Hola" or even "¿Qué tal?" (pronounced kay TAHL), which means "How's it going?"

Here's how a formal greeting might look:

- **Tú:** Buenos días, señor. ¿Cómo está usted? (Good morning, sir. How are you?)
- **Señor:** Buenos días. Estoy bien, gracias. ¿Y usted? (Good morning. I'm fine, thank you. And you?)

And here's how an informal greeting might look:

- **Tú:** ¡Hola, María! ¿Qué tal? (Hi, María! How's it going?)
- **María:** ¡Hola! Bien, gracias. ¿Y tú? (Hi! Good, thanks. And you?)

Remembering Names

One of the most important parts of meeting someone new is remembering their name. In Spanish, if you forget someone's name or didn't catch it the first time, you can politely ask **¿Cómo te llamas, otra vez?** (pronounced KOH-moh tay YAH-mahs, OH-trah vehz), which means "What's your name, again?"

If someone asks you this, just repeat your name with a smile. Don't worry if you forget a name—it happens to everyone!

Key Points to Remember

1. **Basic Greetings:** Use "Hola" to say "hello" in Spanish. For specific times of the day, use "Buenos días" (good morning), "Buenas tardes" (good afternoon), or "Buenas noches" (good evening).

2. **Saying Goodbye:** Common ways to say goodbye include "Adiós" (goodbye), "Hasta luego" (see you later), and "Hasta mañana" (see you tomorrow). "Chao" is a casual way to say "bye."

3. **Introducing Yourself:** You can introduce yourself by saying "Me llamo [Your Name]" (My name is [Your Name]) or "Soy [Your Name]" (I am [Your Name]).

4. **Polite Expressions:** Use "Mucho gusto" (nice to meet you) when meeting someone, "Por favor" (please) when asking for something, and "Gracias" (thank you) to express gratitude.

5. **Introducing Others:** Introduce someone by saying "Te presento a [Name]" (I introduce you to [Name]). The person introduced might reply with "Mucho gusto" or "Encantado/Encantada" (pleased to meet you).

Chapter 4

Numbers and Counting

Numbers are everywhere! Whether you're telling someone your age, counting your money, or just saying how many apples you want, numbers are a big part of everyday life. In this chapter, we're going to learn how to count in Spanish, from 0 all the way up to 100 and beyond. By the end of this chapter, you'll be able to count like a pro and use numbers in all kinds of situations.

Counting from 0 to 10

Let's start with the basics: the numbers from 0 to 10. These are the most important numbers to learn first, because they are the building blocks for all the other numbers. Here they are:

- **0** - Cero (pronounced SEH-roh)
- **1** - Uno (pronounced OO-noh)
- **2** - Dos (pronounced DOHSS)
- **3** - Tres (pronounced TRESS)
- **4** - Cuatro (pronounced KWAH-troh)
- **5** - Cinco (pronounced SEEN-koh)
- **6** - Seis (pronounced SAYSS)
- **7** - Siete (pronounced SYEH-tay)
- **8** - Ocho (pronounced OH-choh)
- **9** - Nueve (pronounced NWAY-vay)
- **10** - Diez (pronounced DYESS)

Practice saying these numbers out loud. Notice how some of the numbers, like "uno" and "tres," might sound a little like their English counterparts "one" and "three." This will make them easier to remember!

Counting from 11 to 20

Once you've got 0 to 10 down, the next step is to learn the numbers from 11 to 20. These numbers have their own unique names, but don't worry—they're not too difficult. Here they are:

- **11** - Once (pronounced OHN-say)
- **12** - Doce (pronounced DOH-say)
- **13** - Trece (pronounced TRAY-say)
- **14** - Catorce (pronounced kah-TOR-say)
- **15** - Quince (pronounced KEEN-say)
- **16** - Dieciséis (pronounced dyay-see-SAYSS)
- **17** - Diecisiete (pronounced dyay-see-SYEH-tay)
- **18** - Dieciocho (pronounced dyay-see-OH-choh)
- **19** - Diecinueve (pronounced dyay-see-NWAY-vay)
- **20** - Veinte (pronounced VAYN-tay)

You might notice that the numbers 16 through 19 all start with "dieci-," which comes from "diez" (10). This pattern makes it easier to learn these numbers, as they're like saying "ten and six" (dieciséis) and so on. This pattern will continue as we learn even bigger numbers.

Counting from 21 to 30

Now that you've got the basics down, let's move on to the numbers from 21 to 30. Starting with 21, you'll see that Spanish numbers become a little more regular. Here's how they go:

- **21** - Veintiuno (pronounced VAYN-tee-OO-noh)
- **22** - Veintidós (pronounced VAYN-tee-DOHSS)
- **23** - Veintitrés (pronounced VAYN-tee-TRAYSS)
- **24** - Veinticuatro (pronounced VAYN-tee-KWAH-troh)

- **25** - Veinticinco (pronounced VAYN-tee-SEEN-koh)
- **26** - Veintiséis (pronounced VAYN-tee-SAYSS)
- **27** - Veintisiete (pronounced VAYN-tee-SYEH-tay)
- **28** - Veintiocho (pronounced VAYN-tee-OH-choh)
- **29** - Veintinueve (pronounced VAYN-tee-NWAY-vay)
- **30** - Treinta (pronounced TRAYN-tah)

The numbers 21 to 29 all start with "veinti-," which is similar to "veinte" (20), followed by the number from 1 to 9. Once you learn the pattern, counting in Spanish becomes easier and more predictable.

Counting by Tens: 30 to 100

Now that you've learned to count up to 30, you're ready to tackle the bigger numbers! The numbers from 30 to 100 in Spanish are built by combining the multiples of ten with the smaller numbers. Here are the multiples of ten:

- **30** - Treinta (pronounced TRAYN-tah)
- **40** - Cuarenta (pronounced kwah-REN-tah)
- **50** - Cincuenta (pronounced seen-KWEN-tah)
- **60** - Sesenta (pronounced say-SEN-tah)
- **70** - Setenta (pronounced say-TEN-tah)
- **80** - Ochenta (pronounced oh-CHEN-tah)
- **90** - Noventa (pronounced noh-VEN-tah)
- **100** - Cien (pronounced SYEN)

To form numbers like 31, 42, or 58, you just say the multiple of ten followed by the smaller number. For example:

- **31** - Treinta y uno (pronounced TRAYN-tah ee OO-noh)
- **42** - Cuarenta y dos (pronounced kwah-REN-tah ee DOHSS)
- **58** - Cincuenta y ocho (pronounced seen-KWEN-tah ee OH-choh)

Notice how you use the word "y" (pronounced ee), which means "and," to connect the tens with the units. So "42" is literally "forty and two," or "cuarenta y dos" in Spanish.

Beyond 100

Once you're comfortable counting up to 100, you can go even higher! The word for "hundred" in Spanish is **cien** (pronounced SYEN) when it's exactly 100, and **ciento** (pronounced SYEN-toh) when it's part of a larger number, like 101. Here's how to count by hundreds up to 1,000:

- **100** - Cien (pronounced SYEN)
- **101** - Ciento uno (pronounced SYEN-toh OO-noh)
- **200** - Doscientos (pronounced dohs-SYEN-toss)
- **300** - Trescientos (pronounced tray-SYEN-toss)
- **400** - Cuatrocientos (pronounced kwah-troh-SYEN-toss)
- **500** - Quinientos (pronounced kee-NYEN-toss)
- **600** - Seiscientos (pronounced say-SYEN-toss)
- **700** - Setecientos (pronounced say-tay-SYEN-toss)
- **800** - Ochocientos (pronounced oh-choh-SYEN-toss)
- **900** - Novecientos (pronounced noh-vay-SYEN-toss)
- **1,000** - Mil (pronounced MEEL)

To form numbers like 215, 376, or 999, you combine these hundreds with the tens and units, just as you did before. For example:

- **215** - Doscientos quince (pronounced dohs-SYEN-toss KEEN-say)
- **376** - Trescientos setenta y seis (pronounced tray-SYEN-toss say-TEN-tah ee SAYSS)
- **999** - Novecientos noventa y nueve (pronounced noh-vay-SYEN-toss noh-VEN-tah ee NWAY-vay)

Numbers in Everyday Life

Now that you know how to count, let's talk about how numbers are used in everyday life. Here are some common situations where you'll need to use numbers:

- **Telling Your Age:** When someone asks how old you are, you can say **Tengo [number] años** (pronounced TEN-goh [number] AHN-yohs), which means "I am [number] years old." For example, if you are 12 years old, you would say "Tengo doce años."

- **Talking About Money:** If you're buying something, you'll need to know how much it costs. For example, if something costs $20, you would say **Cuesta veinte dólares** (pronounced KWES-tah VAYN-tay DOH-lah-rehs), which means "It costs twenty dollars."

- **Giving Your Phone Number:** In Spanish, phone numbers are usually given in pairs of digits. For example, if your phone number is 123-4567, you would say **Uno-dos-tres, cuatro-cinco-seis-siete** (pronounced OO-noh-dohs-trays, KWAH-troh-SEEN-koh-SAYSS-SYEH-teh).

Numbers are also used for telling time, saying dates, counting objects, and much more. The more you practice, the more comfortable you'll become with using numbers in all kinds of situations!

Key Points to Remember

1. **Counting from 0 to 10:** Learn the basics with numbers like "cero" (0), "uno" (1), and "diez" (10). These are the foundation for all other numbers.

2. **Counting from 11 to 20:** Numbers like "once" (11) and "veinte" (20) are essential as they introduce new patterns, especially with "dieci-" for numbers 16-19.

3. **Counting by Tens:** Numbers like "treinta" (30), "cuarenta" (40), and "cien" (100) help you build higher numbers by adding smaller units with "y" (and), e.g., "treinta y uno" (31).

4. **Beyond 100:** Understand how to use "ciento" for numbers above 100, like "ciento uno" (101) and "doscientos" (200). This forms the basis for even larger numbers.

5. **Using Numbers in Everyday Life:** Apply your counting skills in real-world situations like telling your age, discussing prices, or sharing your phone number.

Chapter 5

Days of the Week

One of the first things you'll want to know in any language is how to talk about the days of the week. Whether you're making plans with friends, scheduling an appointment, or just talking about what you did last weekend, knowing the days of the week in Spanish will come in handy every day. In this chapter, we're going to learn the names of the days, how to pronounce them, and how to use them in sentences.

The Days of the Week in Spanish

In Spanish, the days of the week are pretty straightforward. There are seven days, just like in English, and they're used in the same way. Here are the names of the days of the week:

- **Lunes** (pronounced LOO-ness) - Monday

- **Martes** (pronounced MAR-tess) - Tuesday

- **Miércoles** (pronounced MYER-coh-less) - Wednesday

- **Jueves** (pronounced HWEH-vess) - Thursday

- **Viernes** (pronounced BYER-ness) - Friday

- **Sábado** (pronounced SAH-bah-doh) - Saturday

- **Domingo** (pronounced doh-MEEN-goh) - Sunday

As you can see, some of these words might look a little similar to their English counterparts. For example, "sábado" looks like "Saturday," and "domingo" is similar to "Sunday." This can help you remember them more easily.

Pronunciation Tips

Pronouncing the days of the week in Spanish is not too difficult, but there are a few things to keep in mind. First, remember that the letter "h" is always silent in Spanish, so "jueves"

(Thursday) is pronounced HWEH-vess, not "JWEH-vess." Also, the letter "v" in Spanish is often pronounced like a soft "b," so "viernes" (Friday) might sound like BYER-ness.

It's also important to stress the right syllable in each word. In Spanish, the stress usually falls on the second-to-last syllable unless there's an accent mark telling you otherwise. So for "lunes," the stress is on the first syllable: LOO-ness. For "miércoles," the stress is on the second syllable: MYER-coh-less.

Practice saying the days of the week out loud, paying attention to the pronunciation and the stress in each word. The more you practice, the more natural it will feel!

Using the Days of the Week in Sentences

Now that you know the names of the days of the week, let's talk about how to use them in sentences. Just like in English, you can use the days of the week to talk about when something happens. Here are a few simple examples:

- **Hoy es lunes.** (Pronounced OY ess LOO-ness) - "Today is Monday."

- **Mañana es martes.** (Pronounced mah-NYAH-nah ess MAR-tess) - "Tomorrow is Tuesday."

- **El miércoles tengo clase.** (Pronounced el MYER-coh-less TEN-goh KLAH-say) - "On Wednesday, I have class."

- **Nos vemos el viernes.** (Pronounced NOHS VAY-mohs el BYER-ness) - "See you on Friday."

Notice that in Spanish, the days of the week are not capitalized like they are in English. So "lunes" (Monday) stays lowercase even when it's at the beginning of a sentence.

Also, when you want to say something happens on a certain day, you usually use the word "el" (which means "the") before the day. For example, "el lunes" means "on Monday," and "el jueves" means "on Thursday."

Talking About Repeated Actions

What if you want to say that something happens every week on a certain day? In Spanish, you can simply use the plural form of the day of the week. For example:

- **Los lunes voy al gimnasio.** (Pronounced lohs LOO-ness BOY ahl heem-NASS-yoh) - "On Mondays, I go to the gym."

- **Los sábados juego al fútbol.** (Pronounced lohs SAH-bah-dohs HWAY-goh ahl

FOOT-bol) - "On Saturdays, I play soccer."

Here, "los" (which means "the" in plural form) is used before the day of the week to indicate that the action happens regularly on that day.

Asking Questions About the Days

If you want to ask someone about the days of the week, like what day it is or when something is happening, you can use a few simple questions. Here are some examples:

- **¿Qué día es hoy?** (Pronounced kay DEE-ah ess OY) - "What day is it today?"

- **¿Cuándo es la reunión?** (Pronounced KWAN-doh ess lah ray-oo-NEE-ohn) - "When is the meeting?"

- **¿Qué día es tu cumpleaños?** (Pronounced kay DEE-ah ess too koom-play-AHN-yohss) - "What day is your birthday?"

These questions can help you find out what day it is, make plans, or ask about special events. When you respond, you can use the day of the week in your answer, like "Es lunes" (It's Monday) or "Es el sábado" (It's on Saturday).

Days of the Week in Culture

In Spanish-speaking cultures, just like in the United States, the days of the week are used to mark important events, holidays, and traditions. For example, in many Spanish-speaking countries, "el domingo" (Sunday) is a day for rest and family gatherings, much like in the U.S.

There are also special celebrations that happen on certain days of the week. For example, in some parts of Spain and Latin America, "el miércoles de ceniza" (Ash Wednesday) marks the beginning of Lent, a religious season of fasting and reflection. Another example is "el viernes santo" (Good Friday), which is an important day in the Christian calendar.

Understanding the days of the week in Spanish will help you not only communicate better but also understand and appreciate the cultural significance of these days.

Combining Days with Dates

Sometimes, you might want to say a specific date along with the day of the week. For example, if you want to say "Monday, August 2nd," in Spanish, you would say **Lunes, dos de agosto** (pronounced LOO-ness DOHSS day ah-GOHS-toh). Notice that the day of the week comes first, followed by the number (which we learned in the previous chapter), and then the month.

This is a common way to refer to specific dates in Spanish, and it's important to remember the order of the words when putting it all together.

Key Points to Remember

1. **Days of the Week:** The Spanish days are "lunes" (Monday), "martes" (Tuesday), "miércoles" (Wednesday), "jueves" (Thursday), "viernes" (Friday), "sábado" (Saturday), and "domingo" (Sunday). These are not capitalized in Spanish.

2. **Pronunciation Tips:** Remember the silent "h" in "jueves" and the soft "b" sound in "viernes." Stress usually falls on the second-to-last syllable unless there's an accent.

3. **Using Days in Sentences:** Use "el" before the day to specify when something happens, e.g., "el lunes" (on Monday). Example: "Hoy es lunes" (Today is Monday).

4. **Talking About Repeated Actions:** To express a repeated action, use the plural form, e.g., "Los lunes voy al gimnasio" (On Mondays, I go to the gym).

5. **Cultural Significance:** Days of the week in Spanish-speaking cultures are important for marking events, holidays, and traditions, such as "el domingo" (Sunday) for rest and family time.

Chapter 6

Months of the Year

Now that you know how to talk about the days of the week in Spanish, it's time to learn about the months of the year. Knowing the months is important for talking about birthdays, holidays, seasons, and even school events. In this chapter, we'll learn the names of the months in Spanish, how to pronounce them, and how to use them in sentences.

The Months of the Year in Spanish

There are 12 months in a year, just like in English, and they follow the same order. Here are the names of the months in Spanish:

- **Enero** (pronounced eh-NEH-roh) - January

- **Febrero** (pronounced feh-BRAY-roh) - February

- **Marzo** (pronounced MAR-soh) - March

- **Abril** (pronounced ah-BREEL) - April

- **Mayo** (pronounced MY-oh) - May

- **Junio** (pronounced HOO-nyoh) - June

- **Julio** (pronounced HOO-lyoh) - July

- **Agosto** (pronounced ah-GOHS-toh) - August

- **Septiembre** (pronounced sep-tyem-bray) - September

- **Octubre** (pronounced ohk-TOO-bray) - October

- **Noviembre** (pronounced noh-VYEM-bray) - November

- **Diciembre** (pronounced dee-SYEM-bray) - December

As you can see, many of the months in Spanish look very similar to their English counterparts. For example, "marzo" is very close to "March," and "diciembre" is almost the same as "December." This similarity can make it easier to learn and remember the months in Spanish.

Pronunciation Tips

Let's go over how to pronounce the months in Spanish. Remember that in Spanish, each letter is usually pronounced the same way every time. Here are some tips for pronouncing the months correctly:

- **Enero:** The "e" is pronounced like the "e" in "bed." Stress the second syllable: eh-NEH-roh.

- **Febrero:** The "r" sound is rolled, and the stress is on the second syllable: feh-BRAY-roh.

- **Marzo:** The "z" is pronounced like an "s." Stress the first syllable: MAR-soh.

- **Abril:** The "i" sounds like "ee," and the stress is on the second syllable: ah-BREEL.

- **Mayo:** The "y" sounds like the English "y" in "yes." Stress the first syllable: MY-oh.

- **Junio:** The "j" is pronounced like the English "h." Stress the first syllable: HOO-nyoh.

- **Julio:** Similar to "junio," but with a different ending: HOO-lyoh.

- **Agosto:** The "g" sounds like a soft "g," as in "go." Stress the second syllable: ah-GOHS-toh.

- **Septiembre:** The "p" is pronounced clearly, and the stress is on the second syllable: sep-TYEM-bray.

- **Octubre:** The "o" sounds like "oh," and the stress is on the second syllable: ohk-TOO-bray.

- **Noviembre:** The "v" is pronounced like a soft "b," and the stress is on the second syllable: noh-VYEM-bray.

- **Diciembre:** The "d" is pronounced softly, almost like a "th" sound in English. Stress the second syllable: dee-SYEM-bray.

Practice saying each month out loud, paying attention to the pronunciation and the stress on the correct syllable. The more you practice, the more natural it will sound!

Using the Months in Sentences

Now that you know the names of the months, let's talk about how to use them in sentences. Just like in English, you can use the months to talk about when things happen. Here are some examples:

- **Mi cumpleaños es en mayo.** (Pronounced mee koom-play-AHN-yohs ess en MY-oh) - "My birthday is in May."

- **La escuela empieza en septiembre.** (Pronounced lah ess-KWEH-lah em-PYAY-sah en sep-TYEM-bray) - "School starts in September."

- **Voy de vacaciones en julio.** (Pronounced voy day vah-kah-SYOH-nays en HOO-lyoh) - "I go on vacation in July."

In Spanish, when you talk about something happening in a particular month, you use the word "en" (pronounced en), which means "in." So "en enero" means "in January," and "en diciembre" means "in December."

Asking Questions About the Months

If you want to ask someone about when something happens or which month something takes place, you can use a few simple questions. Here are some examples:

- **¿En qué mes es tu cumpleaños?** (Pronounced en keh mess ess too koom-play-AHN-yohs) - "In which month is your birthday?"

- **¿Cuándo es la fiesta?** (Pronounced KWAN-doh ess lah FYEH-stah) - "When is the party?"

- **¿En qué mes empieza el verano?** (Pronounced en keh mess em-PYAY-sah el veh-RAH-noh) - "In which month does summer begin?"

These questions can help you find out important dates, make plans, or just learn more about someone's schedule. When you respond, you can use the month in your answer, like "Es en abril" (It's in April) or "Es en octubre" (It's in October).

Combining Months with Days

Sometimes, you might want to say a specific date, including both the month and the day. For example, if you want to say "July 4th" in Spanish, you would say **el cuatro de julio** (pronounced el KWAH-troh day HOO-lyoh). Notice that in Spanish, the day comes before the month.

Here are a few more examples:

- **El veinte de enero** (Pronounced el VAYN-tay day eh-NEH-roh) - "January 20th"

- **El quince de febrero** (Pronounced el KEEN-say day feh-BRAY-roh) - "February 15th"

- **El primero de mayo** (Pronounced el pree-MEH-roh day MY-oh) - "May 1st"

When talking about the first day of a month, you use "primero" (first) instead of "uno" (one). So "May 1st" is "el primero de mayo," not "el uno de mayo."

Months and Seasons

In Spanish-speaking countries, just like in the U.S., the months of the year are often associated with the seasons. Here's how the seasons line up with the months:

- **La primavera** (pronounced lah pree-mah-VEH-rah) - Spring (March, April, May)

- **El verano** (pronounced el veh-RAH-noh) - Summer (June, July, August)

- **El otoño** (pronounced el oh-TOH-nyoh) - Fall (September, October, November)

- **El invierno** (pronounced el een-VYEHR-noh) - Winter (December, January, February)

When you want to talk about what happens in each season, you can use the months to describe it. For example:

- **En primavera, las flores empiezan a crecer en marzo.** (Pronounced en pree-mah-VEH-rah, lahs FLOH-rehs em-PYAY-san ah kreh-SER en MAR-soh) - "In spring, the flowers start to grow in March."

- **El verano empieza en junio.** (Pronounced el veh-RAH-noh em-PYAY-sah en HOO-nyoh) - "Summer begins in June."

- **En otoño, las hojas caen en octubre.** (Pronounced en oh-TOH-nyoh, lahs OH-hahs KAH-en en ohk-TOO-bray) - "In fall, the leaves fall in October."

- **En invierno, nieva en diciembre.** (Pronounced en een-VYEHR-noh, NYEH-vah en dee-SYEM-bray) - "In winter, it snows in December."

Understanding the months of the year will help you talk about all sorts of things, from your favorite holiday to when you go on vacation. Plus, knowing the months is key to understanding the calendar and keeping track of important events.

Key Points to Remember

1. **Months of the Year:** The 12 months in Spanish are similar to their English counterparts, making them easier to remember. Examples include "enero" (January) and "diciembre" (December).

2. **Pronunciation Tips:** Each month has a specific pronunciation pattern, such as stressing the correct syllable. For example, "febrero" (February) is stressed on the second syllable.

3. **Using Months in Sentences:** To indicate something happening in a particular month, use "en," as in "en mayo" (in May) or "en diciembre" (in December).

4. **Combining Months with Days:** When stating a specific date, the day comes before the month, such as "el cuatro de julio" (July 4th).

5. **Months and Seasons:** The months are associated with seasons: "primavera" (spring), "verano" (summer), "otoño" (fall), and "invierno" (winter), helping to describe seasonal events.

Chapter 7

Seasons and Weather

The weather and the seasons play a big part in our everyday lives. Whether it's sunny, rainy, or snowy, the weather affects what we wear, what we do, and how we feel. In this chapter, you're going to learn how to talk about the seasons and the weather in Spanish. By the end of this chapter, you'll be able to describe the weather, talk about your favorite season, and even discuss the forecast with your friends.

The Four Seasons

Just like in English, there are four seasons in Spanish. Here are the names of the seasons:

- **La primavera** (pronounced lah pree-mah-VEH-rah) - Spring

- **El verano** (pronounced el veh-RAH-noh) - Summer

- **El otoño** (pronounced el oh-TOH-nyoh) - Fall/Autumn

- **El invierno** (pronounced el een-VYEHR-noh) - Winter

Each of these seasons comes with its own kind of weather. In the next sections, we'll talk about the different kinds of weather you might experience during each season and how to describe them in Spanish.

Talking About the Weather

One of the most common things people talk about is the weather. In Spanish, there are several ways to describe what the weather is like. Let's start with some basic phrases:

- **Hace sol.** (Pronounced AH-say sohl) - "It's sunny."

- **Hace calor.** (Pronounced AH-say kah-LOR) - "It's hot."

- **Hace frío.** (Pronounced AH-say FREE-oh) - "It's cold."

- **Hace viento.** (Pronounced AH-say BYEN-toh) - "It's windy."

- **Está nublado.** (Pronounced es-TAH noo-BLAH-doh) - "It's cloudy."

- **Está lloviendo.** (Pronounced es-TAH yoh-BYEN-doh) - "It's raining."

- **Está nevando.** (Pronounced es-TAH nay-VAHN-doh) - "It's snowing."

Notice that the phrases for describing the weather usually start with "hace" (pronounced AH-say) or "está" (pronounced es-TAH). "Hace" is used for conditions like sun, heat, cold, and wind, while "está" is used for conditions like clouds, rain, and snow.

Seasons and Their Weather

Now, let's look at each season and the kind of weather you might expect during that time of year.

La Primavera (Spring)

In spring, the weather starts to warm up after the cold winter. Flowers begin to bloom, and the days get longer. In many places, spring is known for its mild weather, with a mix of sunny days and rain showers. Here are some phrases you might use to describe the weather in spring:

- **En primavera, hace buen tiempo.** (Pronounced en pree-mah-VEH-rah, AH-say bwen TYEHM-poh) - "In spring, the weather is nice."

- **En abril, llueve mucho.** (Pronounced en ah-BREEL, YWEH-veh MOO-choh) - "In April, it rains a lot."

- **El sol brilla en primavera.** (Pronounced el sohl BREE-yah en pree-mah-VEH-rah) - "The sun shines in spring."

Spring is a beautiful time of year when nature comes back to life, and you might find yourself spending more time outdoors enjoying the pleasant weather.

El Verano (Summer)

Summer is the hottest season of the year. The days are long and sunny, and it's a great time for going to the beach, swimming, or just relaxing in the sun. Here are some ways to talk about the weather in summer:

- **En verano, hace mucho calor.** (Pronounced en veh-RAH-noh, AH-say MOO-choh kah-LOR) - "In summer, it's very hot."

- **Hace sol todos los días en verano.** (Pronounced AH-say sohl TOH-dohs lohs DEE-ahs en veh-RAH-noh) - "It's sunny every day in summer."

- **En julio, el clima es muy caluroso.** (Pronounced en HOO-lyoh, el KLEE-mah ess MOO-ee kah-loo-ROH-soh) - "In July, the weather is very warm."

Summer is often the time for vacations and outdoor activities. Whether you're at the beach or just enjoying the sunshine, summer is a season full of fun and energy.

El Otoño (Fall/Autumn)

Fall, also known as autumn, is a time when the weather starts to cool down after the hot summer. The leaves change color, and the air becomes crisp and cool. Here are some phrases to describe fall weather:

- **En otoño, hace fresco.** (Pronounced en oh-TOH-nyoh, AH-say FRES-koh) - "In fall, it's cool."

- **Las hojas caen en otoño.** (Pronounced lahs OH-hahs KAH-en en oh-TOH-nyoh) - "The leaves fall in autumn."

- **En noviembre, está nublado y hace viento.** (Pronounced en noh-VYEM-bray, es-TAH noo-BLAH-doh ee AH-say BYEN-toh) - "In November, it's cloudy and windy."

Fall is a time for enjoying the changing colors of nature, wearing cozy sweaters, and getting ready for the winter ahead.

El Invierno (Winter)

Winter is the coldest season of the year. Depending on where you live, winter might bring snow, ice, and freezing temperatures. It's a season for bundling up in warm clothes and enjoying winter activities like sledding and building snowmen. Here are some phrases to describe winter weather:

- **En invierno, hace mucho frío.** (Pronounced en een-VYEHR-noh, AH-say MOO-choh FREE-oh) - "In winter, it's very cold."

- **Está nevando en diciembre.** (Pronounced es-TAH nay-VAHN-doh en dee-SYEM-bray) - "It's snowing in December."

- **En enero, el clima es muy frío.** (Pronounced en eh-NEH-roh, el KLEE-mah ess MOO-ee FREE-oh) - "In January, the weather is very cold."

Winter can be a magical time of year, especially if you enjoy playing in the snow or sitting by a warm fire. It's also a time when people come together to celebrate holidays and enjoy the coziness of the season.

Talking About Your Favorite Season

Now that you know the names of the seasons and how to describe the weather in each one, you can talk about your favorite season in Spanish. Here's how you might do that:

- **Mi estación favorita es el verano porque me gusta el sol y el calor.** (Pronounced mee es-tah-SYOHN fah-boh-REE-tah ess el veh-RAH-noh pohr-keh may GOOS-tah el sohl ee el kah-LOR) - "My favorite season is summer because I like the sun and the heat."

- **Me encanta el invierno porque me gusta la nieve.** (Pronounced may en-KAHN-tah el een-VYEHR-noh pohr-keh may GOOS-tah lah NYEH-veh) - "I love winter because I like the snow."

- **Prefiero la primavera porque las flores empiezan a crecer.** (Pronounced preh-FYEH-roh lah pree-mah-VEH-rah pohr-keh lahs FLOH-rehs em-PYAY-sahn ah kreh-SER) - "I prefer spring because the flowers start to grow."

When talking about your favorite season, you can use the word "porque" (pronounced pohr-keh), which means "because," to explain why you like that season. You can talk about the weather, activities you enjoy, or anything else that makes that season special to you.

Weather Expressions

In addition to describing the weather, there are also some common expressions and sayings related to weather in Spanish. These phrases can be fun to learn and use in conversation. Here are a few examples:

- **Llueve a cántaros.** (Pronounced YWEH-veh ah KAHN-tah-rohs) - "It's raining cats and dogs." (This means it's raining very hard.)

- **Hace un frío que pela.** (Pronounced AH-say oon FREE-oh keh PEH-lah) - "It's freezing cold." (Literally, "It's a cold that peels.")

- **Hace un sol de justicia.** (Pronounced AH-say oon sohl day hoos-TEE-syah) - "It's scorching hot." (Literally, "It's a sun of justice.")

These expressions can add color to your conversations and help you sound more like a native Spanish speaker.

Asking About the Weather

If you want to ask someone about the weather, there are a few simple questions you can use. Here are some examples:

- **¿Qué tiempo hace?** (Pronounced keh TYEHM-poh AH-say) - "What's the weather like?"

- **¿Hace frío o calor?** (Pronounced AH-say FREE-oh oh kah-LOR) - "Is it cold or hot?"

- **¿Va a llover mañana?** (Pronounced vah ah yoh-BER mah-NYAH-nah) - "Is it going to rain tomorrow?"

These questions can help you find out what the weather is like or what it's going to be like in the future. When you respond, you can use the weather phrases we've learned in this chapter.

Weather and Culture

In many Spanish-speaking countries, the weather and seasons are closely tied to cultural events and traditions. For example, in Spain, the arrival of spring is celebrated with "Las Fallas" (pronounced lahs FYEH-yahs), a festival in March where people build and burn large sculptures to welcome the new season.

In Mexico, "El Día de los Muertos" (pronounced el DEE-ah day lohs MWEHR-tohs), or the Day of the Dead, takes place in the fall, during the first days of November. This is a time when families remember and honor their loved ones who have passed away.

Understanding how the weather and seasons are celebrated in different cultures can help you appreciate the diversity and richness of Spanish-speaking countries.

Key Points to Remember

1. **The Four Seasons:** The seasons in Spanish are "la primavera" (spring), "el verano" (summer), "el otoño" (fall/autumn), and "el invierno" (winter). Each season has its own characteristic weather.

2. **Weather Phrases:** Use "hace" (it is) or "está" (it is) to describe the weather, such as "hace sol" (it's sunny) or "está lloviendo" (it's raining).

3. **Describing Seasonal Weather:** Each season has typical weather patterns, like "hace calor" (it's hot) in summer and "hace frío" (it's cold) in winter.

4. **Talking About Your Favorite Season:** You can express your preference for a season

by saying "Mi estación favorita es..." (My favorite season is...), followed by the reason using "porque" (because).

5. **Weather and Culture:** Weather and seasons are often linked to cultural events, like "Las Fallas" in Spain during spring or "El Día de los Muertos" in Mexico during the fall.

Chapter 8

Colors in Spanish

Colors are everywhere! They add life to the world around us, and they're a big part of how we describe things. Whether you're talking about your favorite shirt, describing a beautiful sunset, or picking out a new backpack, knowing how to talk about colors in Spanish is really useful. In this chapter, you'll learn the names of the most common colors in Spanish, how to describe things using colors, and even how to talk about your favorite color.

Basic Colors in Spanish

Let's start with the basic colors. These are the colors you see every day, and they're the ones you'll use most often when talking about the world around you. Here are the basic colors in Spanish:

- **Rojo** (pronounced ROH-hoh) - Red

- **Azul** (pronounced ah-SOOL) - Blue

- **Amarillo** (pronounced ah-mah-REE-yoh) - Yellow

- **Verde** (pronounced VER-day) - Green

- **Negro** (pronounced NAY-groh) - Black

- **Blanco** (pronounced BLAHN-koh) - White

- **Marrón** or **Café** (pronounced mah-ROHN or kah-FAY) - Brown

- **Rosa** (pronounced ROH-sah) - Pink

- **Morado** or **Púrpura** (pronounced moh-RAH-doh or POOR-poo-rah) - Purple

- **Gris** (pronounced GREESS) - Gray

- **Anaranjado** or **Naranja** (pronounced ah-nah-rahn-HAH-doh or nah-RAHN-hah) -

Orange

These colors are the foundation for describing almost anything. Some of these words might look or sound similar to their English counterparts, which makes them easier to remember. For example, "rojo" sounds a bit like "red," and "verde" sounds like "verdant," a word related to green in English.

Pronunciation Tips

Pronouncing colors in Spanish is pretty straightforward once you know the basic rules of Spanish pronunciation. Here are a few tips to help you get it right:

- **Rojo:** The "j" in "rojo" is pronounced like the English "h." So, "rojo" sounds like ROH-hoh.

- **Azul:** The "z" in "azul" is pronounced like an "s," so it sounds like ah-SOOL.

- **Amarillo:** The "ll" in "amarillo" is pronounced like the English "y," so it sounds like ah-mah-REE-yoh.

- **Verde:** The "r" in "verde" is rolled or tapped lightly with your tongue, and it sounds like VER-day.

- **Marrón:** The "rr" in "marrón" is rolled, making it sound like mah-ROHN.

Practice saying these colors out loud, paying attention to how each word sounds. With a little practice, you'll be able to pronounce them like a native speaker!

Describing Objects with Colors

Now that you know the names of the basic colors, let's talk about how to use them to describe things. In Spanish, colors usually come after the noun they describe. This is different from English, where the color comes before the noun. Here are some examples:

- **Una camisa roja** (Pronounced OO-nah kah-MEE-sah ROH-hah) - "A red shirt"

- **Un coche azul** (Pronounced oon KOH-chay ah-SOOL) - "A blue car"

- **Una casa blanca** (Pronounced OO-nah KAH-sah BLAHN-kah) - "A white house"

- **Un gato negro** (Pronounced oon GAH-toh NAY-groh) - "A black cat"

Notice how the color comes after the noun in Spanish. So instead of saying "red shirt" like we do in English, you say "camisa roja" (shirt red) in Spanish.

Also, the color word needs to match the gender and number of the noun it describes. For example, "rojo" becomes "roja" when describing a feminine noun like "camisa" (shirt). If you're describing something plural, like "shoes," you'd say "zapatos rojos" (red shoes) for masculine or "camisas rojas" (red shirts) for feminine.

Talking About Your Favorite Color

One of the most common questions people ask each other is, "What's your favorite color?" In Spanish, you can ask and answer this question like this:

- **¿Cuál es tu color favorito?** (Pronounced kwahl ess too koh-LOR fah-boh-REE-toh) - "What's your favorite color?"

- **Mi color favorito es azul.** (Pronounced mee koh-LOR fah-boh-REE-toh ess ah-SOOL) - "My favorite color is blue."

You can use any color word to answer this question. Just remember that "color" in Spanish is masculine, so the adjective "favorito" also stays masculine, even if the color is a feminine word. For example:

- **Mi color favorito es rosa.** (Pronounced mee koh-LOR fah-boh-REE-toh ess ROH-sah) - "My favorite color is pink."

It's that simple! Now you can tell people all about your favorite color in Spanish.

Shades and Tints

Sometimes, you might want to be more specific about a color. Maybe you want to talk about light blue or dark green. In Spanish, you can do this by adding the words "claro" (light) or "oscuro" (dark) to the color. Here are some examples:

- **Azul claro** (Pronounced ah-SOOL KLAH-roh) - Light blue

- **Verde oscuro** (Pronounced VER-day ohs-KOO-roh) - Dark green

- **Rosa claro** (Pronounced ROH-sah KLAH-roh) - Light pink

- **Morado oscuro** (Pronounced moh-RAH-doh ohs-KOO-roh) - Dark purple

Adding "claro" or "oscuro" to a color is a great way to be more descriptive and talk about exactly the shade you're thinking of.

Fun with Colors

Colors aren't just about describing things—they're also a big part of culture, art, and even expressions in language. Here are some fun ways that colors are used in Spanish-speaking cultures:

- **Rojo** (Red) is often associated with passion, love, and energy. It's a powerful color that you'll see in many flags, decorations, and celebrations.

- **Blanco** (White) represents purity, peace, and cleanliness. It's a color often used in weddings and religious ceremonies.

- **Negro** (Black) can represent elegance and formality, but it's also used to symbolize mystery or even mourning.

- **Verde** (Green) is the color of nature and is often linked to growth, health, and harmony.

Colors can also be part of common expressions or idioms. For example:

- **Estar verde** (Pronounced es-TAR VER-day) - Literally "to be green," this expression means to be inexperienced or not ready.

- **Verlo todo de color de rosa** (Pronounced VER-loh TOH-doh day koh-LOR day ROH-sah) - "To see everything in pink," meaning to see things in an overly optimistic way.

Learning these expressions can be a fun way to add some color (pun intended!) to your Spanish conversations.

Colors and Art

In many Spanish-speaking countries, art plays a big role in the culture, and colors are a huge part of that. For example, in Mexico, you might see bright colors like "rojo" (red), "amarillo" (yellow), and "verde" (green) used in traditional crafts and decorations, especially during celebrations like "El Día de los Muertos" (The Day of the Dead).

Artists like Frida Kahlo and Pablo Picasso used bold colors in their paintings to express emotions and tell stories. Understanding the names of colors in Spanish can help you appreciate and talk about art in a new way.

Colors in Nature

Colors are all around us in nature, too! Whether you're talking about a green tree ("un árbol verde"), a blue sky ("un cielo azul"), or a red flower ("una flor roja"), knowing the names of colors in Spanish will help you describe the beauty of the world around you.

Here are some examples of how you might describe colors in nature:

- **Las hojas son verdes en primavera.** (Pronounced lahs OH-hahs sohn VER-days en pree-mah-VEH-rah) - "The leaves are green in spring."

- **El cielo es azul en verano.** (Pronounced el SYEH-loh ess ah-SOOL en veh-RAH-noh) - "The sky is blue in summer."

- **Las flores son rojas y amarillas.** (Pronounced lahs FLOH-rehs sohn ROH-hahs ee ah-mah-REE-yahs) - "The flowers are red and yellow."

Being able to talk about colors in nature can help you share your experiences and observations with others, whether you're describing a beautiful sunset or a colorful garden.

Key Points to Remember

1. **Basic Colors:** Learn the basic colors in Spanish like "rojo" (red), "azul" (blue), "verde" (green), and more. These are the foundation for describing objects around you.

2. **Pronunciation Tips:** Pay attention to pronunciation, especially for letters like "j" in "rojo" (ROH-hoh) and "ll" in "amarillo" (ah-mah-REE-yoh). Practice saying the colors out loud.

3. **Describing Objects:** In Spanish, the color comes after the noun, like "una casa blanca" (a white house). Also, match the color's gender and number with the noun it describes.

4. **Talking About Preferences:** To say your favorite color, use "Mi color favorito es..." (My favorite color is...). Remember, "color" is masculine, so adjectives like "favorito" stay masculine.

5. **Shades and Tints:** Use "claro" (light) or "oscuro" (dark) to describe different shades, such as "azul claro" (light blue) or "verde oscuro" (dark green).

Chapter 9

Basic Phrases for Everyday Use

When you're learning a new language, one of the most important things to know is how to use basic phrases in everyday situations. These are the phrases you'll use all the time, whether you're greeting someone, asking for help, or just being polite. In this chapter, you'll learn some essential Spanish phrases that will help you get through common situations with confidence. By the end of this chapter, you'll be able to greet people, ask simple questions, and use polite expressions in Spanish.

Greetings

Let's start with greetings. Knowing how to say "hello" and "goodbye" is one of the first things you'll need to do when you meet someone. Here are some basic greetings in Spanish:

- **Hola** (Pronounced OH-lah) - Hello

- **Buenos días** (Pronounced BWAY-nohs DEE-ahs) - Good morning

- **Buenas tardes** (Pronounced BWAY-nahs TAR-days) - Good afternoon

- **Buenas noches** (Pronounced BWAY-nahs NOH-chess) - Good evening/Good night

- **Adiós** (Pronounced ah-DYOHSS) - Goodbye

- **Hasta luego** (Pronounced AHS-tah LWAY-goh) - See you later

- **Nos vemos** (Pronounced NOHS VAY-mohss) - See you

- **Chao** (Pronounced CHOW) - Bye (informal)

These phrases are easy to remember and can be used in almost any situation. For example, you might say "Hola" when you see a friend, "Buenos días" when you greet someone in the morning, and "Adiós" when you're leaving.

Asking Simple Questions

Being able to ask questions is another important skill in any language. In Spanish, there are a few basic questions that you'll use often. Here are some examples:

- **¿Cómo estás?** (Pronounced KOH-moh es-TAHSS) - How are you?

- **¿Qué tal?** (Pronounced KEH tahl) - How's it going?

- **¿Cómo te llamas?** (Pronounced KOH-moh tay YAH-mahss) - What's your name?

- **¿Dónde está...?** (Pronounced DOHN-deh es-TAH) - Where is...?

- **¿Qué es esto?** (Pronounced KEH ess ES-toh) - What is this?

- **¿Cuánto cuesta?** (Pronounced KWAN-toh KWEH-stah) - How much does it cost?

These questions are useful in many different situations. For example, you can ask "¿Cómo estás?" to see how someone is doing, "¿Dónde está...?" to ask where something is, and "¿Cuánto cuesta?" when you want to know the price of something.

When you're asking questions in Spanish, remember that the question mark comes at the beginning and the end of the sentence. The first question mark is upside down: ¿

Polite Expressions

Being polite is important in any language, and Spanish is no different. Here are some basic phrases that will help you be polite in Spanish:

- **Por favor** (Pronounced pohr fah-VOHR) - Please

- **Gracias** (Pronounced GRAH-syahss) - Thank you

- **De nada** (Pronounced deh NAH-dah) - You're welcome

- **Perdón** (Pronounced pehr-DOHN) - Sorry/Excuse me

- **Disculpe** (Pronounced dees-KOOL-peh) - Excuse me

- **Lo siento** (Pronounced loh SYEN-toh) - I'm sorry

These phrases are very useful in everyday conversations. For example, you might say "Por favor" when you're asking for something, "Gracias" when someone helps you, and "Perdón" if you accidentally bump into someone.

Using polite expressions will make your conversations in Spanish more respectful and friendly.

Introducing Yourself

When you meet someone new, it's important to know how to introduce yourself. Here's how you can do that in Spanish:

- **Me llamo [your name]** (Pronounced may YAH-moh) - My name is [your name]
- **Soy [your name]** (Pronounced soy) - I am [your name]
- **¿Cómo te llamas?** (Pronounced KOH-moh tay YAH-mahss) - What's your name?

For example, if your name is Alex, you would say "Me llamo Alex" or "Soy Alex" when introducing yourself. If you want to ask someone else's name, you can say "¿Cómo te llamas?"

Here's a simple conversation you might have when meeting someone for the first time:

- **Tú:** Hola, ¿cómo te llamas? (Hello, what's your name?)
- **Otra persona:** Me llamo Maria. ¿Y tú? (My name is Maria. And you?)
- **Tú:** Soy Alex. Mucho gusto. (I'm Alex. Nice to meet you.)
- **Otra persona:** Mucho gusto. (Nice to meet you.)

Introducing yourself and asking someone's name is a great way to start a conversation and make new friends.

Expressing Needs and Wants

When you're in a new place, it's important to know how to express your needs and wants. Here are some basic phrases that can help you do that in Spanish:

- **Quiero...** (Pronounced kee-EH-roh) - I want...
- **Necesito...** (Pronounced neh-seh-SEE-toh) - I need...
- **Tengo hambre** (Pronounced TEN-goh AHM-bray) - I'm hungry
- **Tengo sed** (Pronounced TEN-goh sed) - I'm thirsty
- **Tengo frío** (Pronounced TEN-goh FREE-oh) - I'm cold
- **Tengo calor** (Pronounced TEN-goh kah-LOR) - I'm hot

For example, if you're hungry, you can say "Tengo hambre," or if you want something specific, you can say "Quiero [item]." If you need something, you can say "Necesito [item]."

Knowing these phrases will help you communicate your needs in Spanish, whether you're at a restaurant, in a store, or just talking with friends.

Making Requests

If you need to ask someone to do something, you can use these basic request phrases in Spanish:

- **¿Puedes ayudarme?** (Pronounced PWAY-dess ah-yoo-DAR-may) - Can you help me?

- **¿Me puedes dar...?** (Pronounced may PWAY-dess dar) - Can you give me...?

- **¿Puedo ir al baño?** (Pronounced PWAY-doh eer ahl BAH-nyoh) - Can I go to the bathroom?

- **¿Puedo tener...?** (Pronounced PWAY-doh teh-NER) - Can I have...?

These phrases are very useful when you need to ask for help, permission, or something specific. For example, if you're in class and need to use the restroom, you can say "¿Puedo ir al baño?"

Using these polite request phrases will help you communicate your needs effectively and respectfully.

Understanding and Responding

When someone speaks to you in Spanish, it's important to understand what they're saying and know how to respond. Here are some helpful phrases for understanding and responding:

- **No entiendo** (Pronounced noh en-TYEN-doh) - I don't understand

- **¿Puedes repetir eso?** (Pronounced PWAY-dess reh-peh-TEER ESS-oh) - Can you repeat that?

- **¿Qué significa...?** (Pronounced KEH seeg-nee-FEE-kah) - What does ... mean?

- **Sí** (Pronounced SEE) - Yes

- **No** (Pronounced NOH) - No

- **Está bien** (Pronounced es-TAH BYEN) - It's okay

If you don't understand something, you can say "No entiendo" or ask the person to repeat what they said with "¿Puedes repetir eso?" If you're not sure what a word means, you can ask "¿Qué significa [word]?"

These phrases will help you navigate conversations in Spanish, especially when you're still learning the language.

Expressing Likes and Dislikes

It's also useful to know how to talk about things you like or don't like. Here's how you can do that in Spanish:

- **Me gusta...** (Pronounced may GOOS-tah) - I like…

- **No me gusta...** (Pronounced noh may GOOS-tah) - I don't like…

- **Me encanta...** (Pronounced may en-KAHN-tah) - I love…

For example, if you like ice cream, you can say "Me gusta el helado" (I like ice cream). If you love something, you can say "Me encanta" (I love it). If there's something you don't like, you can say "No me gusta" (I don't like it).

These phrases are great for sharing your opinions and talking about your favorite things in Spanish.

Farewell Phrases

Finally, when you're ending a conversation or saying goodbye, it's important to know a few farewell phrases in Spanish:

- **Hasta luego** (Pronounced AHS-tah LWAY-goh) - See you later

- **Adiós** (Pronounced ah-DYOHSS) - Goodbye

- **Nos vemos** (Pronounced NOHS VAY-mohss) - See you

- **Cuídate** (Pronounced KWEE-dah-tay) - Take care

These phrases are a nice way to end a conversation politely. For example, you can say "Hasta luego" if you'll see the person later, or "Cuídate" to tell them to take care.

Key Points to Remember

1. **Basic Greetings:** Learn essential greetings like "Hola" (Hello) and "Adiós" (Goodbye) to start and end conversations in Spanish.

2. **Asking Questions:** Use simple questions like "¿Cómo estás?" (How are you?) and "¿Dónde está...?" (Where is...?) to communicate effectively in different situations.

3. **Polite Expressions:** Remember to use polite phrases such as "Por favor" (Please) and "Gracias" (Thank you) to show respect in conversations.

4. **Introducing Yourself:** Know how to introduce yourself with "Me llamo [your name]" (My name is...) and ask others "¿Cómo te llamas?" (What's your name?).

5. **Expressing Needs and Wants:** Use phrases like "Quiero..." (I want...) and "Tengo hambre" (I'm hungry) to express your needs and desires in everyday situations.

Chapter 10

Asking Questions in Spanish

Asking questions is an important part of learning any language. Questions help you get information, start conversations, and understand what's going on around you. In this chapter, you'll learn how to ask questions in Spanish. By the end of this chapter, you'll be able to ask about people, places, things, and more. You'll also learn how to use question words and form questions in different ways.

Basic Question Words

Let's start with some basic question words in Spanish. These words are the key to asking questions about almost anything. Here they are:

- **¿Qué?** (Pronounced KEH) - What?

- **¿Quién?** (Pronounced kee-YEN) - Who?

- **¿Dónde?** (Pronounced DOHN-deh) - Where?

- **¿Cuándo?** (Pronounced KWAN-doh) - When?

- **¿Por qué?** (Pronounced pohr KEH) - Why?

- **¿Cómo?** (Pronounced KOH-moh) - How?

- **¿Cuál?** (Pronounced KWAL) - Which?

- **¿Cuánto?** (Pronounced KWAN-toh) - How much?/How many?

These question words will help you ask about all kinds of things. For example, you can use "¿Qué?" to ask "What?" or "¿Dónde?" to ask "Where?" Let's look at how to use these question words in sentences.

Using "¿Qué?" (What?)

"¿Qué?" is one of the most common question words in Spanish. You can use it to ask about things, actions, or explanations. Here are some examples:

- **¿Qué es esto?** (Pronounced KEH ess ES-toh) - What is this?
- **¿Qué haces?** (Pronounced KEH AH-sess) - What are you doing?
- **¿Qué quieres comer?** (Pronounced KEH kee-EH-res koh-MER) - What do you want to eat?

When using "¿Qué?" in a question, remember to place it at the beginning of the sentence. In Spanish, questions often start with the question word, followed by the verb and then the subject.

Using "¿Quién?" (Who?)

"¿Quién?" is used to ask about people. It's the Spanish word for "Who?" Here are some examples:

- **¿Quién es él?** (Pronounced kee-YEN ess el) - Who is he?
- **¿Quiénes son ellos?** (Pronounced kee-YEN-ess sohn EH-yohs) - Who are they?
- **¿Quién está en la puerta?** (Pronounced kee-YEN ess-TAH en lah PWEHR-tah) - Who is at the door?

When asking about more than one person, "¿Quién?" becomes "¿Quiénes?" Notice how the verb changes depending on whether you're talking about one person or more than one.

Using "¿Dónde?" (Where?)

If you want to ask about a place or location, you use "¿Dónde?" Here are some examples:

- **¿Dónde estás?** (Pronounced DOHN-deh es-TAHS) - Where are you?
- **¿Dónde vives?** (Pronounced DOHN-deh VEE-ves) - Where do you live?
- **¿Dónde está la tienda?** (Pronounced DOHN-deh es-TAH lah TYEHN-dah) - Where is the store?

"¿Dónde?" is always followed by a verb and then the subject or object you're asking about. This structure helps keep your questions clear and easy to understand.

Using "¿Cuándo?" (When?)

To ask about time or when something happens, use "¿Cuándo?" Here are some examples:

- **¿Cuándo es tu cumpleaños?** (Pronounced KWAN-doh ess too koom-play-AHN-yohs) - When is your birthday?

- **¿Cuándo vamos al cine?** (Pronounced KWAN-doh VAH-mohs ahl SEE-neh) - When are we going to the movies?

- **¿Cuándo empieza la clase?** (Pronounced KWAN-doh em-PYAY-sah lah KLAH-say) - When does the class start?

Just like the other question words, "¿Cuándo?" comes at the beginning of the sentence. It's followed by the verb and then the subject or object.

Using "¿Por qué?" (Why?)

If you want to know the reason for something, you ask "¿Por qué?" It's the Spanish word for "Why?" Here are some examples:

- **¿Por qué estás triste?** (Pronounced pohr KEH es-TAHS TREES-teh) - Why are you sad?

- **¿Por qué no viniste ayer?** (Pronounced pohr KEH noh vee-NEES-teh ah-YEHR) - Why didn't you come yesterday?

- **¿Por qué quieres aprender español?** (Pronounced pohr KEH kee-EH-res ah-pren-DAIR es-pah-NYOL) - Why do you want to learn Spanish?

When answering a question with "¿Por qué?" you might start your response with "Porque..." (because...), which explains the reason.

Using "¿Cómo?" (How?)

"¿Cómo?" is used to ask about the manner or way something is done. It's the Spanish word for "How?" Here are some examples:

- **¿Cómo estás?** (Pronounced KOH-moh es-TAHS) - How are you?

- **¿Cómo se dice... en español?** (Pronounced KOH-moh seh DEE-seh... en es-pah-NYOL) - How do you say... in Spanish?

- **¿Cómo llego a la escuela?** (Pronounced KOH-moh YEH-goh ah lah es-KWEH-lah) - How do I get to the school?

Use "¿Cómo?" when you want to know the method, manner, or condition of something.

Using "¿Cuál?" (Which?)

If you need to choose between options, use "¿Cuál?" It's the Spanish word for "Which?" Here are some examples:

- **¿Cuál es tu color favorito?** (Pronounced KWAL ess too koh-LOR fah-boh-REE-toh) - Which is your favorite color?

- **¿Cuál prefieres, chocolate o vainilla?** (Pronounced KWAL preh-FYEH-res, cho-koh-LAH-teh oh vy-NEE-yah) - Which do you prefer, chocolate or vanilla?

- **¿Cuál es tu libro favorito?** (Pronounced KWAL ess too LEE-broh fah-boh-REE-toh) - Which is your favorite book?

When asking with "¿Cuál?" you're usually choosing between two or more specific options. If you're asking about something more general, you might use "¿Qué?" instead.

Using "¿Cuánto?" (How much?/How many?)

To ask about quantity, use "¿Cuánto?" It can mean either "How much?" or "How many?" depending on the context. Here are some examples:

- **¿Cuánto cuesta?** (Pronounced KWAN-toh KWEH-stah) - How much does it cost?

- **¿Cuántos años tienes?** (Pronounced KWAN-tohss AHN-yohs tee-EH-ness) - How old are you? (Literally, "How many years do you have?")

- **¿Cuánta agua necesitas?** (Pronounced KWAN-tah AH-gwah neh-seh-SEE-tahss) - How much water do you need?

"¿Cuánto?" changes to match the gender and number of the noun it's asking about. For example, "¿Cuántos?" is used with masculine plural nouns, and "¿Cuánta?" is used with feminine singular nouns.

Yes/No Questions

Not all questions in Spanish need a question word. Sometimes, you just need a simple yes or no answer. To ask a yes/no question, you usually just change the order of the words. Here's how:

- **¿Estás cansado?** (Pronounced es-TAHS kahn-SAH-doh) - Are you tired?

- **¿Vas al parque?** (Pronounced VAHSS ahl PAR-kay) - Are you going to the park?

- **¿Tienes hambre?** (Pronounced tee-EH-ness AHM-bray) - Are you hungry?

To make a statement into a question, just switch the subject and the verb. For example, "Tienes hambre" (You are hungry) becomes "¿Tienes hambre?" (Are you hungry?).

Forming Negative Questions

If you want to ask a question in the negative, just add "no" before the verb. Here are some examples:

- **¿No te gusta?** (Pronounced noh tay GOOS-tah) - Don't you like it?

- **¿No vienes con nosotros?** (Pronounced noh VYEH-ness kohn noh-SOH-trohss) - Aren't you coming with us?

- **¿No tienes tiempo?** (Pronounced noh tee-EH-ness TYEM-poh) - Don't you have time?

Negative questions are a way to express surprise or check if something is true. They're formed just like yes/no questions, but with "no" added before the verb.

Using "¿Verdad?" (Right?)

Sometimes, you might want to ask for confirmation or make sure that what you're saying is correct. In Spanish, you can do this by adding "¿Verdad?" (Right?) to the end of a statement. Here are some examples:

- **Estás cansado, ¿verdad?** (Pronounced es-TAHS kahn-SAH-doh, vehr-DAHD) - You're tired, right?

- **Vamos al cine, ¿verdad?** (Pronounced VAH-mohss ahl SEE-neh, vehr-DAHD) - We're going to the movies, right?

- **Te gusta la pizza, ¿verdad?** (Pronounced tay GOOS-tah lah PEET-sah, vehr-DAHD) - You like pizza, right?

Adding "¿Verdad?" to the end of a sentence is an easy way to turn a statement into a question that asks for confirmation.

Understanding Questions and Responding

Now that you know how to ask questions, it's also important to understand how to respond. Here are some basic ways to answer questions in Spanish:

- **Sí** (Pronounced SEE) - Yes

- **No** (Pronounced NOH) - No

- **No sé** (Pronounced noh say) - I don't know

- **Claro** (Pronounced KLAH-roh) - Of course

- **Tal vez** (Pronounced tahl VESS) - Maybe

- **Por supuesto** (Pronounced pohr soo-PWAY-stoh) - Of course

When answering questions, you can simply say "sí" or "no," but sometimes you might need to add more information. For example:

- **¿Tienes hambre?** - "Sí, tengo mucha hambre." (Yes, I'm very hungry.)

- **¿Vas al parque?** - "No, no voy al parque." (No, I'm not going to the park.)

Practice asking and answering questions to become more comfortable using Spanish in everyday conversations.

Key Points to Remember

1. **Basic Question Words**: Learn essential question words like ¿Qué? (What?), ¿Quién? (Who?), ¿Dónde? (Where?), ¿Cuándo? (When?), ¿Por qué? (Why?), ¿Cómo? (How?), ¿Cuál? (Which?), and ¿Cuánto? (How much/How many?).

2. **Using Question Words in Sentences**: Place the question word at the beginning of the sentence, followed by the verb and then the subject. For example, ¿Dónde vives? (Where do you live?).

3. **Yes/No Questions**: Form yes/no questions by inverting the subject and verb. For example, ¿Estás cansado? (Are you tired?).

4. **Negative Questions**: Add no before the verb to form negative questions, such as ¿No te gusta? (Don't you like it?).

5. **Responding to Questions**: Use simple responses like Sí (Yes), No (No), and No sé (I don't know) to answer questions.

Chapter 11

Telling Time

Being able to tell time is a really important skill, no matter what language you're speaking. Whether you're meeting friends, going to school, or catching a bus, knowing how to ask and tell the time in Spanish will help you manage your day. In this chapter, you'll learn how to ask for the time, tell the time, and talk about different parts of the day in Spanish.

How to Ask for the Time

If you want to ask someone what time it is, you can use the phrase **¿Qué hora es?** (Pronounced KEH OH-rah ess). This means "What time is it?" It's a simple question that you can use anytime you need to know the time.

Here's an example of how you might use it:

- **Tú:** ¿Qué hora es? (What time is it?)

- **Otra persona:** Son las tres. (It's three o'clock.)

Notice that in Spanish, the word "hora" (pronounced OH-rah) means "hour" or "time." So when you're asking "¿Qué hora es?" you're literally asking "What hour is it?"

Telling the Time: Full Hours

To tell the time in Spanish, you start with the phrase **Es la...** or **Son las...** depending on the hour. You use "Es la..." for one o'clock and "Son las..." for any other hour. Here's how it works:

- **Es la una.** (Pronounced ess lah OO-nah) - It's one o'clock.

- **Son las dos.** (Pronounced sohn las DOHS) - It's two o'clock.

- **Son las tres.** (Pronounced sohn las TRESS) - It's three o'clock.

- **Son las cuatro.** (Pronounced sohn las KWAH-troh) - It's four o'clock.

As you can see, the pattern is the same for all the hours. Just change the number at the end to match the hour. For example, "Son las cinco" means "It's five o'clock," and "Son las seis" means "It's six o'clock."

Adding Minutes to the Time

What if the time isn't exactly on the hour? To tell the time with minutes, you simply add the minutes after saying the hour. Here's how:

- **Son las dos y cinco.** (Pronounced sohn las DOHS ee SEEN-koh) - It's 2:05.
- **Son las tres y diez.** (Pronounced sohn las TRESS ee DYESS) - It's 3:10.
- **Son las cuatro y quince.** (Pronounced sohn las KWAH-troh ee KEEN-say) - It's 4:15.
- **Son las cinco y veinte.** (Pronounced sohn las SEEN-koh ee VAYN-tay) - It's 5:20.

In Spanish, the word "y" (pronounced ee) means "and." So when you say "Son las dos y cinco," you're literally saying "It's two and five," which means "It's 2:05."

Telling Time with "Quarter" and "Half"

In Spanish, there are special ways to talk about quarter hours and half hours. Instead of saying "Son las dos y quince" for 2:15, you can say **Son las dos y cuarto** (Pronounced sohn las DOHS ee KWAHR-toh), which means "It's a quarter past two." The word "cuarto" means "quarter."

Here are some more examples:

- **Son las tres y cuarto.** (Pronounced sohn las TRESS ee KWAHR-toh) - It's 3:15.
- **Son las cuatro y media.** (Pronounced sohn las KWAH-troh ee MEH-dyah) - It's 4:30.
- **Son las cinco menos cuarto.** (Pronounced sohn las SEEN-koh MEH-nohs KWAHR-toh) - It's a quarter to five (4:45).

Notice that "media" (pronounced MEH-dyah) means "half." So "Son las cuatro y media" means "It's four and a half," which is how you say "It's 4:30."

If you want to say it's a certain number of minutes before the hour, you can use "menos" (pronounced MEH-nohs), which means "minus" or "less." For example, "Son las cinco menos cuarto" means "It's five minus a quarter," or 4:45.

Asking About Specific Times

If you want to ask about a specific time, you can use the question word "¿A qué hora...?" (Pronounced ah KEH OH-rah), which means "At what time...?" Here are some examples:

- **¿A qué hora empieza la clase?** (Pronounced ah KEH OH-rah em-PYAY-sah lah KLAH-say) - What time does the class start?

- **¿A qué hora es la película?** (Pronounced ah KEH OH-rah ess lah peh-LEE-koo-lah) - What time is the movie?

- **¿A qué hora llegas a casa?** (Pronounced ah KEH OH-rah YEH-gahs ah KAH-sah) - What time do you get home?

When answering these questions, you can start with "Es a la..." or "Es a las..." For example, "Es a las seis" means "It's at six o'clock."

Talking About Parts of the Day

In addition to telling the time, it's also important to know how to talk about different parts of the day. Here are some common phrases you can use:

- **Por la mañana** (Pronounced pohr lah mah-NYAH-nah) - In the morning

- **Por la tarde** (Pronounced pohr lah TAR-day) - In the afternoon

- **Por la noche** (Pronounced pohr lah NOH-chay) - In the evening/At night

- **Mediodía** (Pronounced MEH-dyoh-DEE-ah) - Noon

- **Medianoche** (Pronounced MEH-dyah-NOH-chay) - Midnight

Here's how you might use these phrases in sentences:

- **Voy a la escuela por la mañana.** (Pronounced BOY ah lah ess-KWEH-lah pohr lah mah-NYAH-nah) - I go to school in the morning.

- **Comemos por la tarde.** (Pronounced koh-MEH-mohs pohr lah TAR-day) - We eat in the afternoon.

- **La fiesta es por la noche.** (Pronounced lah FYEHS-tah ess pohr lah NOH-chay) - The party is in the evening.

Using these phrases will help you describe when things happen during the day. Whether you're talking about your daily routine or planning an event, these expressions will be very useful.

24-Hour Clock vs. 12-Hour Clock

In Spanish-speaking countries, people often use the 24-hour clock, especially in formal situations like schedules, timetables, and official events. Here's how it works:

- **13:00** - 1:00 PM (Trece horas)
- **14:00** - 2:00 PM (Catorce horas)
- **15:00** - 3:00 PM (Quince horas)
- **16:00** - 4:00 PM (Dieciséis horas)

To convert the 24-hour clock to the 12-hour clock, just subtract 12 from any hour after 12:00. For example, 14:00 becomes 2:00 PM.

If you're telling time in a more casual setting, you can use the 12-hour clock and add "de la mañana" (in the morning), "de la tarde" (in the afternoon), or "de la noche" (in the evening) to clarify when something is happening. For example:

- **Es la una de la tarde.** (Pronounced ess lah OO-nah deh lah TAR-day) - It's 1:00 PM.
- **Son las ocho de la mañana.** (Pronounced sohn las OH-choh deh lah mah-NYAH-nah) - It's 8:00 AM.
- **Son las nueve de la noche.** (Pronounced sohn las NWEH-veh deh lah NOH-chay) - It's 9:00 PM.

Expressions Related to Time

Here are some common expressions and phrases in Spanish that are related to time:

- **A tiempo** (Pronounced ah TYEM-poh) - On time
- **Tarde** (Pronounced TAR-day) - Late
- **Temprano** (Pronounced tem-PRAH-noh) - Early
- **A las tres en punto** (Pronounced ah las TRESS en POON-toh) - At three o'clock sharp
- **De vez en cuando** (Pronounced deh VESS en KWAN-doh) - From time to time

These expressions can help you talk about being on time, arriving late, or doing something occasionally. For example:

- **Llegamos a tiempo a la escuela.** (Pronounced yeh-GAH-mohs ah TYEM-poh ah lah es-KWEH-lah) - We arrive at school on time.

- **Siempre llegas tarde.** (Pronounced SYEM-preh YEH-gahs TAR-day) - You always arrive late.

- **Nos encontramos a las tres en punto.** (Pronounced nohs en-kohn-TRAH-mohs ah las TRESS en POON-toh) - We'll meet at three o'clock sharp.

Key Points to Remember

1. **Asking for the Time**: Use the phrase ¿Qué hora es? (What time is it?) to ask for the current time.

2. **Telling Time**: Start with Es la… for one o'clock or Son las… for any other hour, and add minutes after the hour using y. For example, Son las dos y cinco (It's 2:05).

3. **Quarter and Half Hours**: Use y cuarto for a quarter past, y media for half past, and menos cuarto for a quarter to the hour. For example, Son las cuatro y media (It's 4:30).

4. **Talking About Parts of the Day**: Use phrases like por la mañana (in the morning), por la tarde (in the afternoon), and por la noche (in the evening) to specify times of day.

5. **24-Hour Clock**: In formal settings, the 24-hour clock is used. For example, 14:00 is 2:00 PM. Subtract 12 from the hour to convert to the 12-hour clock.

Chapter 12

Family and Relationships

Family is one of the most important parts of our lives. Knowing how to talk about your family and relationships in Spanish will help you share more about yourself and understand others better. In this chapter, you'll learn the words for different family members, how to describe relationships, and some common phrases that you can use when talking about your family in Spanish.

Family Members

Let's start by learning the basic words for family members in Spanish. Here are the names for the most common family members:

- **Padre** (Pronounced PAH-dray) - Father
- **Madre** (Pronounced MAH-dray) - Mother
- **Hermano** (Pronounced ehr-MAH-noh) - Brother
- **Hermana** (Pronounced ehr-MAH-nah) - Sister
- **Abuelo** (Pronounced ah-BWAY-loh) - Grandfather
- **Abuela** (Pronounced ah-BWAY-lah) - Grandmother
- **Tío** (Pronounced TEE-oh) - Uncle
- **Tía** (Pronounced TEE-ah) - Aunt
- **Primo** (Pronounced PREE-moh) - Cousin (male)
- **Prima** (Pronounced PREE-mah) - Cousin (female)
- **Sobrino** (Pronounced soh-BREE-noh) - Nephew
- **Sobrina** (Pronounced soh-BREE-nah) - Niece

These words will help you talk about your immediate family and extended family. Notice that for some family members, like "hermano" (brother) and "hermana" (sister), the ending changes depending on whether you're talking about a male or female relative. This is a common pattern in Spanish.

Talking About Your Family

Now that you know the names of different family members, let's talk about how to describe your family in Spanish. Here are some basic sentences you can use:

- **Mi familia es grande.** (Pronounced mee fah-MEE-lee-ah ess GRAHN-day) - My family is big.

- **Tengo dos hermanos y una hermana.** (Pronounced TEN-goh dohs ehr-MAH-nohs ee OO-nah ehr-MAH-nah) - I have two brothers and one sister.

- **Mis abuelos viven cerca de nosotros.** (Pronounced mees ah-BWAY-lohs VEE-ven SEHR-kah day noh-SOH-trohss) - My grandparents live close to us.

- **Mi madre es profesora.** (Pronounced mee MAH-dray ess proh-feh-SOH-rah) - My mother is a teacher.

These sentences give you a simple way to talk about your family members and where they live or what they do. You can change the number of siblings or other details to fit your own family situation.

Describing Relationships

In addition to talking about who is in your family, you might want to describe your relationships with them. Here are some useful phrases to help you do that:

- **Me llevo bien con mi hermano.** (Pronounced may YEH-voh byehn kohn mee ehr-MAH-noh) - I get along well with my brother.

- **No me llevo bien con mi primo.** (Pronounced noh may YEH-voh byehn kohn mee PREE-moh) - I don't get along well with my cousin.

- **Mi hermana y yo somos muy cercanos.** (Pronounced mee ehr-MAH-nah ee yoh SOH-mohss MOO-ee sehr-KAH-nohss) - My sister and I are very close.

- **Mi padre es muy estricto.** (Pronounced mee PAH-dray ess MOO-ee ess-TREEK-toh) - My father is very strict.

These phrases can help you describe how you feel about your family members and what your relationships with them are like. Whether you get along well with your siblings or you have a strict parent, these phrases will help you express that in Spanish.

Extended Family Members

Beyond your immediate family, you might also want to talk about your extended family. Here are some words for extended family members:

- **Bisabuelo** (Pronounced bee-sah-BWAY-loh) - Great-grandfather

- **Bisabuela** (Pronounced bee-sah-BWAY-lah) - Great-grandmother

- **Suegro** (Pronounced SWEH-groh) - Father-in-law

- **Suegra** (Pronounced SWEH-grah) - Mother-in-law

- **Yerno** (Pronounced YEHR-noh) - Son-in-law

- **Nuera** (Pronounced NWEH-rah) - Daughter-in-law

These words are useful when talking about your larger family, especially when you're describing family gatherings or special occasions where your extended family might be involved.

Common Phrases About Family

Here are some common phrases that you can use when talking about your family in everyday conversations:

- **¿Tienes hermanos?** (Pronounced tee-EH-ness ehr-MAH-nohss) - Do you have siblings?

- **¿Cómo se llaman tus padres?** (Pronounced KOH-moh seh YAH-mahn tooss PAH-dress) - What are your parents' names?

- **Mi abuelo tiene ochenta años.** (Pronounced mee ah-BWAY-loh tee-EH-neh oh-CHEN-tah AHN-yohss) - My grandfather is eighty years old.

- **Mi prima vive en otra ciudad.** (Pronounced mee PREE-mah VEE-veh en OH-trah see-you-DAHD) - My cousin lives in another city.

These questions and statements are helpful for talking about your family in different situations. Whether you're asking someone about their family or sharing information about your own, these phrases will come in handy.

Talking About Pets

Pets are often considered part of the family, so it's useful to know how to talk about them in Spanish as well. Here are some common words and phrases related to pets:

- **Perro** (Pronounced PEH-rroh) - Dog

- **Gato** (Pronounced GAH-toh) - Cat

- **Mi perro se llama Max.** (Pronounced mee PEH-rroh seh YAH-mah Max) - My dog's name is Max.

- **Tengo un gato negro.** (Pronounced TEN-goh oon GAH-toh NEH-groh) - I have a black cat.

- **Nosotros queremos mucho a nuestro perro.** (Pronounced noh-SOH-trohss keh-REH-mohss MOO-choh ah nweh-STROH PEH-rroh) - We love our dog very much.

These phrases allow you to talk about your pets just like you would your family members. Whether you're introducing your pet to someone or describing what kind of pet you have, these sentences will be useful.

Cultural Notes on Family

Family is very important in Spanish-speaking cultures, just as it is in many other cultures. In many Spanish-speaking countries, families are often large, and it's common for multiple generations to live close to each other or even in the same household. Family gatherings and celebrations are important events, and respect for elders is a key value.

When talking about family in Spanish, you might notice that people are very close with their extended family members, such as aunts, uncles, and cousins. These relationships are often as important as those with immediate family members.

Talking About Family Traditions

Many families have special traditions or celebrations that they enjoy together. Here are some phrases to help you talk about family traditions in Spanish:

- **En mi familia, celebramos la Navidad juntos.** (Pronounced en mee fah-MEE-lee-ah, seh-leh-BRAH-mohss lah nah-vee-DAHD HOON-tohss) - In my family, we celebrate Christmas together.

- **Siempre vamos a la casa de mis abuelos para el Día de Acción de Gracias.** (Pronounced SYEM-preh VAH-mohss ah lah KAH-sah day mees ah-BWAY-lohss PAH-rah el DEE-ah day ahk-see-OHN day GRAH-syahss) - We always go to my grandparents' house for Thanksgiving.

- **Nosotros hacemos una cena especial para el cumpleaños de mi madre.** (Pronounced noh-SOH-trohss ah-SEH-mohss OO-nah SEH-nah ess-peh-SYAL PAH-rah el koom-play-AHN-yohs day mee MAH-dray) - We make a special dinner for my mother's birthday.

Talking about traditions is a great way to share more about your family and learn about other people's families as well.

Introducing Your Family

If you want to introduce your family members to someone, here are some simple phrases you can use:

- **Este es mi padre.** (Pronounced ESS-teh ess mee PAH-dray) - This is my father.

- **Esta es mi hermana.** (Pronounced ESS-tah ess mee ehr-MAH-nah) - This is my sister.

- **Ellos son mis abuelos.** (Pronounced EH-yohs sohn mees ah-BWAY-lohss) - These are my grandparents.

When introducing someone, you use "este" (this) for masculine nouns like "padre" and "esta" (this) for feminine nouns like "hermana." These phrases are perfect for introducing your family members in a conversation.

Key Points to Remember

1. **Basic Family Members**: Learn the Spanish names for common family members, like padre (father), madre (mother), hermano (brother), and hermana (sister).

2. **Describing Family Relationships**: Use phrases to describe your family, such as Mi familia es grande (My family is big) or Tengo dos hermanos (I have two brothers).

3. **Extended Family**: Familiarize yourself with terms for extended family members, like abuelo (grandfather), tía (aunt), and primo (cousin).

4. **Talking About Relationships**: Express how you relate to your family members with phrases like Me llevo bien con mi hermano (I get along well with my brother).

5. **Cultural Significance**: Understand that family is central in Spanish-speaking cultures, often involving close relationships with extended family members and strong traditions.

Chapter 13

Describing People: Physical Appearance

When you meet someone new or want to talk about a friend, it's helpful to know how to describe their physical appearance. In this chapter, you'll learn how to talk about what people look like in Spanish. You'll learn words and phrases to describe height, hair color, eye color, and more. By the end of this chapter, you'll be able to give a detailed description of someone's physical appearance in Spanish.

Talking About Height

One of the first things you might notice about someone is their height. Here are some words you can use to describe how tall or short someone is:

- **Alto/Alta** (Pronounced AHL-toh/AHL-tah) - Tall (masculine/feminine)

- **Bajo/Baja** (Pronounced BAH-hoh/BAH-hah) - Short (masculine/feminine)

- **De estatura media** (Pronounced deh ess-tah-TOO-rah MEH-dyah) - Medium height

Here's how you might use these words in a sentence:

- **Mi hermano es alto.** (Pronounced mee ehr-MAH-noh ess AHL-toh) - My brother is tall.

- **Mi hermana es baja.** (Pronounced mee ehr-MAH-nah ess BAH-hah) - My sister is short.

- **Soy de estatura media.** (Pronounced soy deh ess-tah-TOO-rah MEH-dyah) - I am medium height.

When describing someone's height, remember to match the adjective to the gender of the person you're describing. Use "alto" for a tall boy or man and "alta" for a tall girl or woman.

Describing Hair

Another important part of describing someone's appearance is talking about their hair. You can describe hair by its color, length, and texture. Here are some common words you can use:

- **Cabello/Pelo** (Pronounced kah-BEH-yoh/PEH-loh) - Hair

- **Rubio/Rubia** (Pronounced ROO-byoh/ROO-byah) - Blonde (masculine/feminine)

- **Castaño/Castaña** (Pronounced kahs-TAH-nyoh/kahs-TAH-nyah) - Brown (masculine/feminine)

- **Moreno/Morena** (Pronounced moh-REH-noh/moh-REH-nah) - Dark (masculine/feminine)

- **Negro/Negra** (Pronounced NEH-groh/NEH-grah) - Black (masculine/feminine)

- **Pelirrojo/Pelirroja** (Pronounced peh-lee-ROH-hoh/peh-lee-ROH-hah) - Redhead (masculine/feminine)

- **Largo/Larga** (Pronounced LAR-goh/LAR-gah) - Long (masculine/feminine)

- **Corto/Corta** (Pronounced KOR-toh/KOR-tah) - Short (masculine/feminine)

- **Rizado/Rizada** (Pronounced ree-SAH-doh/ree-SAH-dah) - Curly (masculine/feminine)

- **Liso/Lisa** (Pronounced LEE-soh/LEE-sah) - Straight (masculine/feminine)

Here are some examples of how you can use these words to describe someone's hair:

- **Ella tiene el cabello rubio.** (Pronounced EH-yah tee-EH-neh el kah-BEH-yoh ROO-byoh) - She has blonde hair.

- **Mi amigo tiene el pelo castaño.** (Pronounced mee ah-MEE-goh tee-EH-neh el PEH-loh kahs-TAH-nyoh) - My friend has brown hair.

- **Mi hermana tiene el pelo largo y rizado.** (Pronounced mee ehr-MAH-nah tee-EH-neh el PEH-loh LAR-goh ee ree-SAH-doh) - My sister has long, curly hair.

When describing hair in Spanish, "cabello" and "pelo" both mean "hair," but "cabello" is often used to refer to head hair specifically, while "pelo" can refer to hair anywhere on the body.

Talking About Eye Color

Eye color is another feature you might want to describe. Here are some common words to describe eye color in Spanish:

- **Ojos** (Pronounced OH-hohs) - Eyes

- **Azules** (Pronounced ah-SOO-less) - Blue

- **Verdes** (Pronounced VER-dess) - Green

- **Marrones** (Pronounced mah-ROH-ness) - Brown

- **Negros** (Pronounced NEH-grohs) - Black

- **Grises** (Pronounced GREE-sess) - Gray

Here's how you can use these words to describe someone's eye color:

- **Tengo ojos azules.** (Pronounced TEN-goh OH-hohs ah-SOO-less) - I have blue eyes.

- **Él tiene ojos marrones.** (Pronounced el tee-EH-neh OH-hohs mah-ROH-ness) - He has brown eyes.

- **Mi madre tiene ojos verdes.** (Pronounced mee MAH-dray tee-EH-neh OH-hohs VER-dess) - My mother has green eyes.

When describing eyes, remember that the adjective needs to agree with the noun "ojos," which is plural. So you'll use the plural form of the color, like "azules" or "verdes."

Describing Skin Color and Complexion

You might also want to describe someone's skin color or complexion. Here are some common words you can use:

- **Claro/Clara** (Pronounced KLAH-roh/KLAH-rah) - Light (masculine/feminine)

- **Oscuro/Oscura** (Pronounced ohs-KOO-roh/ohs-KOO-rah) - Dark (masculine/feminine)

- **Blanco/Blanca** (Pronounced BLAHN-koh/BLAHN-kah) - White (masculine/feminine)

- **Moreno/Morena** (Pronounced moh-REH-noh/moh-REH-nah) - Brown-skinned or tan (masculine/feminine)

Here's how you might use these words in a sentence:

- **Ella es morena.** (Pronounced EH-yah ess moh-REH-nah) - She is tan.

- **Tengo la piel clara.** (Pronounced TEN-goh lah PYEHL KLAH-rah) - I have light skin.

- **Él es de piel oscura.** (Pronounced el ess deh pyehl ohs-KOO-rah) - He has dark skin.

In Spanish, you can describe someone's skin color directly or talk about their "piel" (skin) and use an adjective to describe it.

Describing Body Type

You can also describe someone's body type. Here are some words you might use:

- **Delgado/Delgada** (Pronounced del-GAH-doh/del-GAH-dah) - Slim (masculine/feminine)

- **Gordo/Gorda** (Pronounced GOR-doh/GOR-dah) - Fat (masculine/feminine)

- **Fuerte** (Pronounced FWEHR-teh) - Strong

- **Débil** (Pronounced DEH-beel) - Weak

Here's how you can use these words in a sentence:

- **Mi primo es delgado.** (Pronounced mee PREE-moh ess del-GAH-doh) - My cousin is slim.

- **Ella es fuerte.** (Pronounced EH-yah ess FWEHR-teh) - She is strong.

- **El hombre es gordo.** (Pronounced el OHM-breh ess GOR-doh) - The man is fat.

These adjectives help you describe a person's body type in a simple way. As always, make sure the adjective agrees with the gender of the person you're describing.

Describing Facial Features

Facial features are another important aspect of physical appearance. Here are some words and phrases you can use:

- **Cara** (Pronounced KAH-rah) - Face

- **Bonito/Bonita** (Pronounced boh-NEE-toh/boh-NEE-tah) - Pretty (masculine/feminine)

- **Guapo/Guapa** (Pronounced GWAH-poh/GWAH-pah) - Handsome (masculine/feminine)

- **Feo/Fea** (Pronounced FEH-oh/FEH-ah) - Ugly (masculine/feminine)

- **Bigote** (Pronounced bee-GOH-teh) - Mustache

- **Barba** (Pronounced BAR-bah) - Beard

Here's how you can use these words in a sentence:

- **Ella es muy bonita.** (Pronounced EH-yah ess MOO-ee boh-NEE-tah) - She is very pretty.

- **Mi tío tiene un bigote grande.** (Pronounced mee TEE-oh tee-EH-neh oon bee-GOH-teh GRAHN-deh) - My uncle has a big mustache.

- **El hombre tiene barba.** (Pronounced el OHM-breh tee-EH-neh BAR-bah) - The man has a beard.

These words help you talk about someone's face and facial features. Whether you're describing someone as "bonito" (pretty) or "feo" (ugly), or talking about their "bigote" (mustache) or "barba" (beard), these words are very useful.

Putting It All Together

Now that you know how to describe height, hair, eyes, skin color, body type, and facial features, you can put it all together to give a complete description of someone. Here's an example:

Mi mejor amigo se llama Carlos. Es alto y delgado, y tiene el cabello castaño y rizado. Sus ojos son verdes, y tiene la piel clara. Carlos es muy guapo y siempre tiene una sonrisa en su cara. (Pronounced mee meh-HOR ah-MEE-goh seh YAH-mah CAR-lohs. ess AHL-toh ee del-GAH-doh, ee tee-EH-neh el kah-BEH-yoh kahs-TAH-nyoh ee ree-SAH-doh. sooss OH-hohs sohn VER-dess, ee tee-EH-neh lah PYEHL KLAH-rah. CAR-lohs ess MOO-ee GWAH-poh ee SYEM-preh tee-EH-neh OO-nah sohn-REE-sah en soo KAH-rah)

This sentence describes Carlos as a tall and slim friend with brown, curly hair, green eyes, light skin, and a handsome face. It's a detailed description that gives you a clear picture of what he looks like.

Key Points to Remember

1. **Describing Height**: Use words like alto/alta (tall), bajo/baja (short), and de estatura media (medium height) to describe someone's height, ensuring the adjective matches the person's gender.

2. **Talking About Hair**: Describe hair using terms like rubio/rubia (blonde), largo/larga (long), and rizado/rizada (curly), adjusting the endings for gender.

3. **Describing Eye Color**: Use ojos (eyes) along with colors like azules (blue), verdes (green), and marrones (brown) to talk about eye color.

4. **Describing Body Type**: Use adjectives like delgado/delgada (slim), fuerte (strong), and gordo/gorda (fat) to describe someone's body type, matching the gender as needed.

5. **Describing Facial Features**: Use words like bonito/bonita (pretty), bigote (mustache), and barba (beard) to describe facial features, ensuring the description is gender-appropriate.

Chapter 14

Describing People: Personality Traits

When you get to know someone, you don't just notice what they look like—you also learn about their personality. Describing someone's personality in Spanish can help you share more about who they are as a person. In this chapter, you'll learn how to talk about different personality traits in Spanish. By the end of this chapter, you'll be able to describe whether someone is friendly, shy, funny, and more.

Basic Personality Traits

Let's start with some basic words that you can use to describe someone's personality. These are common adjectives that can help you talk about what someone is like:

- **Amable** (Pronounced ah-MAH-blay) - Kind

- **Divertido/Divertida** (Pronounced dee-ver-TEE-doh/dee-ver-TEE-dah) - Fun (masculine/feminine)

- **Serio/Seria** (Pronounced SEH-ree-oh/SEH-ree-ah) - Serious (masculine/feminine)

- **Gracioso/Graciosa** (Pronounced grah-SYOH-soh/grah-SYOH-sah) - Funny (masculine/feminine)

- **Tímido/Tímida** (Pronounced TEE-mee-doh/TEE-mee-dah) - Shy (masculine/feminine)

- **Inteligente** (Pronounced een-teh-lee-HEN-teh) - Intelligent

- **Trabajador/Trabajadora** (Pronounced trah-bah-hah-DOR/trah-bah-hah-DOH-rah) - Hardworking (masculine/feminine)

- **Perezoso/Perezosa** (Pronounced peh-reh-SOH-soh/peh-reh-SOH-sah) - Lazy (masculine/feminine)

Here are some examples of how you can use these words in sentences:

- **Mi mejor amigo es muy amable.** (Pronounced mee meh-HOR ah-MEE-goh ess MOO-ee ah-MAH-blay) - My best friend is very kind.

- **Ella es muy divertida.** (Pronounced EH-yah ess MOO-ee dee-ver-TEE-dah) - She is very fun.

- **Mi hermano es un poco tímido.** (Pronounced mee ehr-MAH-noh ess oon POH-koh TEE-mee-doh) - My brother is a little shy.

When using adjectives to describe someone's personality, make sure the adjective agrees with the gender of the person. For example, "divertido" is used for a boy, and "divertida" is used for a girl.

Positive Personality Traits

Now, let's look at some more positive personality traits. These words can help you describe someone who is friendly, hardworking, and a good friend:

- **Simpático/Simpática** (Pronounced seem-PAH-tee-koh/seem-PAH-tee-kah) - Friendly (masculine/feminine)

- **Generoso/Generosa** (Pronounced heh-neh-ROH-soh/heh-neh-ROH-sah) - Generous (masculine/feminine)

- **Honesto/Honesta** (Pronounced oh-NESS-toh/oh-NESS-tah) - Honest (masculine/feminine)

- **Valiente** (Pronounced bah-LYEN-teh) - Brave

- **Creativo/Creativa** (Pronounced kreh-ah-TEE-voh/kreh-ah-TEE-vah) - Creative (masculine/feminine)

- **Optimista** (Pronounced op-tee-MEES-tah) - Optimistic

Here's how you might use these words in sentences:

- **Mi madre es muy simpática.** (Pronounced mee MAH-dray ess MOO-ee seem-PAH-tee-kah) - My mother is very friendly.

- **Mi profesor es generoso con su tiempo.** (Pronounced mee proh-feh-SOR ess heh-neh-ROH-soh kohn soo TYEHM-poh) - My teacher is generous with his time.

- **Ella es muy creativa y siempre tiene buenas ideas.** (Pronounced EH-yah ess MOO-ee kreh-ah-TEE-vah ee SYEM-preh tee-EH-neh BWEH-nahs ee-DEH-ahs) - She is very creative and always has good ideas.

These adjectives help you highlight the positive aspects of someone's personality. Whether they are friendly, generous, or creative, you can use these words to describe them.

Negative Personality Traits

Sometimes, you might need to describe someone who has less positive traits. Here are some adjectives that can be used to describe negative personality traits:

- **Antipático/Antipática** (Pronounced an-tee-PAH-tee-koh/an-tee-PAH-tee-kah) - Unfriendly (masculine/feminine)

- **Egoísta** (Pronounced eh-goh-EES-tah) - Selfish

- **Mentiroso/Mentirosa** (Pronounced men-tee-ROH-soh/men-tee-ROH-sah) - Liar (masculine/feminine)

- **Impaciente** (Pronounced eem-pah-SYEN-teh) - Impatient

- **Celoso/Celosa** (Pronounced seh-LOH-soh/seh-LOH-sah) - Jealous (masculine/feminine)

- **Terco/Terca** (Pronounced TEHR-koh/TEHR-kah) - Stubborn (masculine/feminine)

Here's how you might use these words in sentences:

- **Él es muy egoísta y no comparte con nadie.** (Pronounced el ess MOO-ee eh-goh-EES-tah ee noh kom-PAHR-teh kohn NAH-dyeh) - He is very selfish and doesn't share with anyone.

- **Mi primo es un poco impaciente.** (Pronounced mee PREE-moh ess oon POH-koh eem-pah-SYEN-teh) - My cousin is a little impatient.

- **Ella es mentirosa, no siempre dice la verdad.** (Pronounced EH-yah ess men-tee-ROH-sah, noh SYEM-preh DEE-seh lah vehr-DAHD) - She is a liar, she doesn't always tell the truth.

These adjectives can help you describe negative aspects of someone's personality, whether they are selfish, impatient, or stubborn. Remember, it's important to be kind when talking about others, even if you're describing a negative trait.

Talking About Personality in General

Sometimes, you might want to describe someone's overall personality without focusing on specific traits. Here are some phrases you can use to talk about someone's personality in general:

- **Tiene una gran personalidad.** (Pronounced tee-EH-neh OO-nah grahn per-soh-nah-lee-DAHD) - He/She has a great personality.

- **Es una persona muy interesante.** (Pronounced ess OO-nah per-SOH-nah MOO-ee een-teh-reh -SAHN-teh) - He/She is a very interesting person.

- **Es una persona difícil de conocer.** (Pronounced ess OO-nah per-SOH-nah dee-FEE-seel deh koh-noh-SER) - He/She is a difficult person to get to know.

These phrases are useful when you want to give a general description of someone's personality, whether they have a great personality or are more challenging to get to know.

Combining Personality Traits

Often, people have a mix of different personality traits. Here's how you can combine traits to give a more complete description of someone:

- **Mi amigo es inteligente, pero también es un poco perezoso.** (Pronounced mee ah-MEE-goh ess een-teh-lee-HEN-teh, PEH-roh tahm-BYEN ess oon POH-koh peh-reh-SOH-soh) - My friend is smart, but he's also a little lazy.

- **Mi hermana es muy amable y trabajadora.** (Pronounced mee ehr-MAH-nah ess MOO-ee ah-MAH-blay ee trah-bah-hah-DOH-rah) - My sister is very kind and hardworking.

- **Él es simpático, pero a veces puede ser un poco terco.** (Pronounced el ess seem-PAH-tee-koh, PEH-roh ah BEH-sess PWEH-deh ser oon POH-koh TEHR-koh) - He is friendly, but sometimes he can be a bit stubborn.

Combining traits in your descriptions can give a more complete picture of someone's personality. It shows that people are complex and can have both positive and negative traits.

Personality and Situations

Sometimes, a person's personality might change depending on the situation. Here's how you can talk about that in Spanish:

- **En la escuela, él es muy serio, pero con sus amigos, es muy

divertido. (Pronounced en lah es-KWEH-lah, el ess MOO-ee SEH-ree-oh, PEH-roh kohn sooss ah-MEE-gohss, ess MOO-ee dee-ver-TEE-doh) - At school, he is very serious, but with his friends, he is very fun.

- **Ella es tímida cuando conoce a gente nueva, pero después es muy simpática.** (Pronounced EH-yah ess TEE-mee-dah KWAHN-doh koh-NOH-seh ah HEN-teh NWEH-vah, PEH-roh dehs-PWEH-ess ess MOO-ee seem-PAH-tee-kah) - She is shy when she meets new people, but afterward, she is very friendly.

These sentences show how someone's behavior might change in different settings. It's important to remember that personality isn't always the same in every situation.

Talking About Yourself

Finally, it's important to know how to describe your own personality. Here are some phrases you can use to talk about yourself in Spanish:

- **Soy una persona optimista.** (Pronounced soy OO-nah per-SOH-nah op-tee-MEES-tah) - I am an optimistic person.

- **Soy muy trabajador/trabajadora.** (Pronounced soy MOO-ee trah-bah-hah-DOR/trah-bah-hah-DOH-rah) - I am very hardworking.

- **No soy muy sociable, pero me gusta estar con amigos cercanos.** (Pronounced noh soy MOO-ee soh-SYAH-blay, PEH-roh meh GOOS-tah ess-TAR kohn ah-MEE-gohss sehr-KAH-nohss) - I am not very sociable, but I like being with close friends.

These phrases can help you share more about who you are as a person. Whether you're talking about being hardworking, optimistic, or sociable, these sentences will help you express yourself in Spanish.

Key Points to Remember

1. **Basic Personality Traits**: Learn common adjectives like amable (kind), divertido/divertida (fun), and inteligente (intelligent) to describe someone's personality, ensuring the adjectives match the gender of the person.

2. **Positive Personality Traits**: Use words like simpático/simpática (friendly), generoso/generosa (generous), and creativo/creativa (creative) to highlight the positive aspects of someone's character.

3. **Negative Personality Traits**: Describe less favorable traits with adjectives like antipático/antipática (unfriendly), egoísta (selfish), and terco/terca (stubborn), being

mindful of the appropriate gender form.

4. **Combining Traits**: Combine different traits to give a more nuanced description, such as inteligente pero un poco perezoso (smart but a little lazy) to reflect the complexity of someone's personality.

5. **Talking About Yourself**: Learn to describe your own personality using phrases like soy una persona optimista (I am an optimistic person) and soy muy trabajador/trabajadora (I am very hardworking) to share more about who you are.

Chapter 15

Basic Verbs: To Be and To Have (Ser, Estar, Tener)

In Spanish, just like in English, there are some very important verbs that you'll use all the time. Three of the most important verbs are "ser," "estar," and "tener." These verbs are essential because they help you describe people, places, things, and conditions. In this chapter, you'll learn how to use these verbs and when to use each one. By the end of this chapter, you'll be able to say things like "I am a student," "She is happy," and "We have a dog" in Spanish.

Ser: The Verb "To Be"

The first verb we're going to learn is "ser." The verb "ser" is used to describe what something is—its essence or identity. You use "ser" to talk about things like names, professions, physical characteristics, and where someone is from. Here's how you conjugate "ser" for different subjects:

- **Yo soy** (Pronounced yoh soy) - I am

- **Tú eres** (Pronounced too EH-rehs) - You are (informal)

- **Él/Ella/Usted es** (Pronounced el/EH-yah/oo-STEHD ess) - He/She/You (formal) is

- **Nosotros/Nosotras somos** (Pronounced noh-SOH-trohs/noh-SOH-trahs SOH-mohs) - We are

- **Vosotros/Vosotras sois** (Pronounced voh-SOH-trohs/voh-SOH-trahs soys) - You all are (informal, used in Spain)

- **Ellos/Ellas/Ustedes son** (Pronounced EH-yohs/EH-yahs/oo-STEH-dehs sohn) - They/You all are

Let's look at some examples of how to use "ser" in a sentence:

- **Yo soy estudiante.** (Pronounced yoh soy ehs-too-dee-AHN-teh) - I am a student.

- **Tú eres mi amigo.** (Pronounced too EH-rehs mee ah-MEE-goh) - You are my friend.

- **Ella es doctora.** (Pronounced EH-yah ess dok-TOH-rah) - She is a doctor.

- **Nosotros somos hermanos.** (Pronounced noh-SOH-trohs SOH-mohs ehr-MAH-nohs) - We are siblings.

- **Ellos son de México.** (Pronounced EH-yohs sohn deh MEH-hee-koh) - They are from Mexico.

You use "ser" to talk about things that are permanent or that define someone or something. For example, if you're saying where someone is from, what their profession is, or what their name is, you'll use "ser."

Estar: The Verb "To Be"

The next verb we're going to learn is "estar." The verb "estar" is also used to mean "to be," but it's used differently from "ser." "Estar" is used to describe temporary states or conditions, such as emotions, physical states, or locations. Here's how you conjugate "estar" for different subjects:

- **Yo estoy** (Pronounced yoh es-TOY) - I am

- **Tú estás** (Pronounced too es-TAHS) - You are (informal)

- **Él/Ella/Usted está** (Pronounced el/EH-yah/oo-STEHD es-TAH) - He/She/You (formal) is

- **Nosotros/Nosotras estamos** (Pronounced noh-SOH-trohs/noh-SOH-trahs es-TAH-mohs) - We are

- **Vosotros/Vosotras estáis** (Pronounced voh-SOH-trohs/voh-SOH-trahs es-TAYS) - You all are (informal, used in Spain)

- **Ellos/Ellas/Ustedes están** (Pronounced EH-yohs/EH-yahs/oo-STEH-dehs es-TAHN) - They/You all are

Here are some examples of how to use "estar" in a sentence:

- **Yo estoy feliz.** (Pronounced yoh es-TOY feh-LEES) - I am happy.

- **Tú estás cansado.** (Pronounced too es-TAHS kahn-SAH-doh) - You are tired.

- **Él está en la escuela.** (Pronounced el es-TAH en lah es-KWEH-lah) - He is at school.

- **Nosotros estamos en casa.** (Pronounced noh-SOH-trohs es-TAH-mohs en KAH-sah) - We are at home.

- **Ellas están tristes.** (Pronounced EH-yahs es-TAHN TREES-tess) - They are sad.

Use "estar" to talk about how someone feels, where they are, or how something is temporarily. For example, if you're describing someone's mood, their physical state, or where they are at the moment, you'll use "estar."

Comparing Ser and Estar

One of the trickiest parts of learning Spanish is knowing when to use "ser" and when to use "estar." The key difference is that "ser" is used for things that are more permanent, while "estar" is used for things that are temporary. Let's look at a few examples to see how this works:

- **Ella es inteligente.** (Pronounced EH-yah ess een-teh-lee-HEN-teh) - She is intelligent. (This is a characteristic of her personality, so it's more permanent.)

- **Ella está cansada.** (Pronounced EH-yah es-TAH kahn-SAH-dah) - She is tired. (This is how she feels right now, so it's temporary.)

- **Él es mi hermano.** (Pronounced el ess mee ehr-MAH-noh) - He is my brother. (This is a relationship, which is permanent.)

- **Él está en casa.** (Pronounced el es-TAH en KAH-sah) - He is at home. (This is a location, which can change, so it's temporary.)

When deciding whether to use "ser" or "estar," think about whether you're talking about something that's a permanent part of who someone is, like their profession or nationality, or if you're talking about something that can change, like their mood or location.

Tener: The Verb "To Have"

The verb "tener" means "to have" in Spanish. You use "tener" to talk about things that people possess, such as objects, feelings, or characteristics. Here's how you conjugate "tener" for different subjects:

- **Yo tengo** (Pronounced yoh TEN-goh) - I have

- **Tú tienes** (Pronounced too tee-EH-ness) - You have (informal)

- **Él/Ella/Usted tiene** (Pronounced el/EH-yah/oo-STEHD tee-EH-neh) - He/She/You (formal) has

- **Nosotros/Nosotras tenemos** (Pronounced noh-SOH-trohs/noh-SOH-trahs teh-NEH-moh s) - We have

- **Vosotros/Vosotras tenéis** (Pronounced voh-SOH-trohs/voh-SOH-trahs teh-NAYS) - You all have (informal, used in Spain)

- **Ellos/Ellas/Ustedes tienen** (Pronounced EH-yohs/EH-yahs/oo-STEH-dehs tee-EH-nen) - They/You all have

Here are some examples of how to use "tener" in a sentence:

- **Yo tengo un perro.** (Pronounced yoh TEN-goh oon PEH-rroh) - I have a dog.

- **Tú tienes un libro.** (Pronounced too tee-EH-ness oon LEE-broh) - You have a book.

- **Ella tiene una hermana.** (Pronounced EH-yah tee-EH-neh OO-nah ehr-MAH-nah) - She has a sister.

- **Nosotros tenemos una casa grande.** (Pronounced noh-SOH-trohs teh-NEH-mohs OO-nah KAH-sah GRAHN-deh) - We have a big house.

- **Ellos tienen mucha tarea.** (Pronounced EH-yohs tee-EH-nen MOO-chah tah-REH-ah) - They have a lot of homework.

You'll use "tener" whenever you want to talk about what someone has. This could be anything from physical possessions like a car or a pet to more abstract things like time or responsibilities.

Special Uses of Tener

In addition to talking about possessions, "tener" is also used in some expressions to talk about how people feel. For example, in Spanish, you don't say "I am hungry" like you do in English. Instead, you say "I have hunger," which is "Tengo hambre" (Pronounced TEN-goh AHm-bray). Here are some other examples:

- **Tengo frío.** (Pronounced TEN-goh FREE-oh) - I am cold. (Literally, "I have cold.")

- **Tienes calor.** (Pronounced tee-EH-ness kah-LOR) - You are hot. (Literally, "You have heat.")

- **Él tiene miedo.** (Pronounced el tee-EH-neh MYEH-doh) - He is scared. (Literally, "He has fear.")

- **Tenemos prisa.** (Pronounced teh-NEH-mohs PREE-sah) - We are in a hurry. (Literally, "We have hurry.")

These expressions are important to learn because they're used a lot in everyday conversations. Remember that when you're talking about being hungry, cold, hot, or scared in Spanish, you'll use "tener" instead of "ser" or "estar."

Putting It All Together

Now that you know how to use "ser," "estar," and "tener," you can start using them in your sentences. Here are some examples that combine these verbs:

- **Yo soy estudiante y estoy en la escuela.** (Pronounced yoh soy ehs-too-dee-AHN-teh ee es-TOY en lah es-KWEH-lah) - I am a student, and I am at school.

- **Tú eres mi amigo y tienes un perro.** (Pronounced too EH-rehs mee ah-MEE-goh ee tee-EH-ness oon PEH-rroh) - You are my friend, and you have a dog.

- **Ella es doctora, pero está cansada hoy.** (Pronounced EH-yah ess dok-TOH-rah, PEH-roh es-TAH kahn-SAH-dah oy) - She is a doctor, but she is tired today.

- **Nosotros tenemos una casa grande y estamos muy contentos.** (Pronounced noh-SOH-trohs teh-NEH-mohs OO-nah KAH-sah GRAHN-deh ee es-TAH-mohs MOO-ee kohn-TEN-tohs) - We have a big house, and we are very happy.

- **Ellos son de México y tienen muchos amigos allí.** (Pronounced EH-yohs sohn deh MEH-hee-koh ee tee-EH-nen MOO-chohs ah-MEE-gohs ah-YEE) - They are from Mexico, and they have many friends there.

By practicing these sentences and understanding when to use each verb, you'll be able to describe yourself, others, and your surroundings more accurately in Spanish.

Key Points to Remember

1. **Ser: The Verb "To Be" (Permanent)**
   Use "ser" to describe permanent traits like identity, profession, or origin. For example, "Yo soy estudiante" means "I am a student."

2. **Estar: The Verb "To Be" (Temporary)**
   Use "estar" to describe temporary conditions or locations, such as emotions or physical states. For instance, "Ella está cansada" means "She is tired.

3. **Tener: The Verb "To Have"**

   "Tener" is used to indicate possession or describe certain physical sensations and conditions. For example, "Tengo un perro" means "I have a dog."

4. **Comparing Ser and Estar**

   Remember, "ser" is for permanent traits (e.g., "Es mi amigo") while "estar" is for temporary states (e.g., "Está en casa").

5. **Special Uses of Tener**

   "Tener" is also used in expressions to describe feelings, like "Tengo hambre" (I am hungry) or "Tienes frío" (You are cold).

Chapter 16

Common Nouns and Articles

Nouns are words that name people, places, things, or ideas. In Spanish, just like in English, nouns are very important because they help us talk about the world around us. Along with nouns, we also use articles, which are little words like "the" and "a" that come before nouns. In this chapter, you'll learn about common nouns in Spanish and how to use articles with them. By the end of this chapter, you'll be able to talk about people, places, and things using the correct nouns and articles.

What Are Nouns?

First, let's talk about what nouns are. A noun is a word that names something. For example, in English, "dog," "school," and "friend" are all nouns. In Spanish, nouns work the same way, but there are some differences in how they are used. One big difference is that Spanish nouns have gender—they are either masculine or feminine. This means that you need to know whether a noun is masculine or feminine so that you can use the right article with it.

Masculine and Feminine Nouns

In Spanish, nouns are divided into two groups: masculine and feminine. Masculine nouns usually end in the letter "-o," while feminine nouns usually end in "-a." Here are some examples:

- **El libro** (Pronounced el LEE-broh) - The book (masculine)

- **La casa** (Pronounced lah KAH-sah) - The house (feminine)

- **El gato** (Pronounced el GAH-toh) - The cat (masculine)

- **La mesa** (Pronounced lah MEH-sah) - The table (feminine)

Sometimes, there are exceptions to these rules, and not all nouns that end in "-o" are masculine or that end in "-a" are feminine. However, these endings are a good guide to help you get started. It's important to remember that when you learn a new noun in Spanish, you should also learn its gender.

Articles: "The" and "A"

Now that you know about nouns, let's talk about articles. Articles are little words that come before nouns. In English, we use "the" for specific things and "a" or "an" for things that are not specific. Spanish has articles too, but they change depending on whether the noun is masculine or feminine and whether it's singular or plural.

Here are the definite articles in Spanish, which are used when you're talking about something specific:

- **El** (Pronounced el) - The (masculine singular)
- **La** (Pronounced lah) - The (feminine singular)
- **Los** (Pronounced lohs) - The (masculine plural)
- **Las** (Pronounced lahs) - The (feminine plural)

Here are the indefinite articles in Spanish, which are used when you're talking about something that is not specific:

- **Un** (Pronounced oon) - A/An (masculine singular)
- **Una** (Pronounced OO-nah) - A/An (feminine singular)
- **Unos** (Pronounced OO-nohs) - Some (masculine plural)
- **Unas** (Pronounced OO-nahs) - Some (feminine plural)

Let's look at some examples of how to use these articles with nouns:

- **El perro** (Pronounced el PEH-rroh) - The dog
- **La silla** (Pronounced lah SEE-yah) - The chair
- **Un coche** (Pronounced oon KOH-chay) - A car
- **Una ventana** (Pronounced OO-nah ven-TAH-nah) - A window

Notice how the article changes depending on whether the noun is masculine or feminine, and whether it's singular or plural. In Spanish, you always need to match the article with the noun in both gender and number.

Using Articles with Plural Nouns

When you're talking about more than one thing, you use plural nouns. In Spanish, making a noun plural usually involves adding "-s" or "-es" to the end of the word. Here are some examples:

- **El libro** becomes **Los libros** (Pronounced los LEE-brohs) - The books

- **La casa** becomes **Las casas** (Pronounced las KAH-sahs) - The houses

- **Un perro** becomes **Unos perros** (Pronounced OO-nohs PEH-rrohs) - Some dogs

- **Una silla** becomes **Unas sillas** (Pronounced OO-nahs SEE-yahs) - Some chairs

When you make a noun plural, you also need to make the article plural. That's why "el" becomes "los" and "la" becomes "las" when talking about more than one thing.

Common Nouns in Spanish

Now that you know how to use articles, let's look at some common nouns in Spanish that you'll use often. Here are some nouns for people, places, and things:

People:

- **El niño/La niña** (Pronounced el NEEN-yoh/lah NEEN-yah) - The boy/The girl

- **El amigo/La amiga** (Pronounced el ah-MEE-goh/lah ah-MEE-gah) - The friend (masculine/feminine)

- **El profesor/La profesora** (Pronounced el proh-feh-SOR/lah proh-feh-SOH-rah) - The teacher (masculine/feminine)

- **El padre/La madre** (Pronounced el PAH-dray/lah MAH-dray) - The father/The mother

Places:

- **La escuela** (Pronounced lah es-KWEH-lah) - The school

- **El parque** (Pronounced el PAR-kay) - The park

- **El hospital** (Pronounced el ohs-pee-TAL) - The hospital

- **La tienda** (Pronounced lah TYEHN-dah) - The store

Things:

- **El coche** (Pronounced el KOH-chay) - The car

- **La mesa** (Pronounced lah MEH-sah) - The table

- **El teléfono** (Pronounced el teh-LEH-foh-noh) - The phone

- **La puerta** (Pronounced lah PWER-tah) - The door

These are just a few examples of common nouns that you'll use in everyday conversations. As you learn more Spanish, you'll start to recognize these nouns and use them in your sentences.

Combining Nouns and Articles in Sentences

Once you know some nouns and how to use articles, you can start putting them together in sentences. Here are some examples:

- **La niña está en la escuela.** (Pronounced lah NEEN-yah es-TAH en lah es-KWEH-lah) - The girl is at school.

- **El coche es rojo.** (Pronounced el KOH-chay ess ROH-hoh) - The car is red.

- **Un amigo me llamó por teléfono.** (Pronounced oon ah-MEE-goh meh yah-MOH por teh-LEH-foh-noh) - A friend called me on the phone.

- **Las puertas están abiertas.** (Pronounced las PWER-tahs es-TAHN ah-byehr-tahs) - The doors are open.

By combining nouns and articles, you can start to form complete thoughts and communicate more effectively in Spanish.

Practice with Nouns and Articles

The best way to get comfortable with using nouns and articles in Spanish is to practice. You can start by practicing with the nouns and articles you've learned in this chapter. Try making sentences about things around you or people you know. For example:

- **El perro está en el parque.** (Pronounced el PEH-rroh es-TAH en el PAR-kay) - The dog is in the park.

- **Una amiga viene a mi casa.** (Pronounced OO-nah ah-MEE-gah VYEH-neh ah mee KAH-sah) - A friend is coming to my house.

- **Los niños juegan en la escuela.** (Pronounced lohs NEEN-yohs HWEH-gahn en lah es-KWEH-lah) - The children play at school.

- **Un coche está en la calle.** (Pronounced oon KOH-chay es-TAH en lah KAH-yay) - A car is on the street.

Key Points to Remember

1. **Nouns Define People, Places, and Things:** Nouns in Spanish name people, places, things, or ideas. They are essential for describing the world around us and must be paired with the correct articles.

2. **Gender in Nouns:** Spanish nouns have gender—they are either masculine or feminine. Masculine nouns typically end in "-o," and feminine nouns usually end in "-a." It's important to learn the gender of each noun to use the correct article.

3. **Articles in Spanish:** Articles are words like "the" and "a" that come before nouns. In Spanish, articles change based on the gender and number of the noun. For example, "el" is used for masculine singular nouns, and "la" is used for feminine singular nouns.

4. **Plural Nouns and Articles:** To make nouns plural in Spanish, add "-s" or "-es" to the noun, and match it with a plural article like "los" (masculine) or "las" (feminine).

5. **Combining Nouns and Articles:** To create meaningful sentences in Spanish, combine nouns with the correct articles. For example, "La niña está en la escuela" means "The girl is at school." Practice is key to mastering the use of nouns and articles.

Chapter 17

Food and Drink Vocabulary

One of the most fun and useful parts of learning a new language is learning how to talk about food and drinks! Whether you're ordering at a restaurant, talking about your favorite meals, or just having a snack, knowing the right words for food and drinks in Spanish will help you a lot. In this chapter, you'll learn the names of common foods and drinks, as well as some useful phrases you can use when talking about them.

Basic Food Vocabulary

Let's start with some basic words for different types of food. These are words you'll use often when talking about meals, snacks, and ingredients.

Fruits (Frutas)

- **La manzana** (Pronounced lah mahn-SAH-nah) - The apple

- **La banana** (Pronounced lah bah-NAH-nah) - The banana

- **La naranja** (Pronounced lah nah-RAHN-hah) - The orange

- **La fresa** (Pronounced lah FREH-sah) - The strawberry

- **Las uvas** (Pronounced lahs OO-vahs) - The grapes

Vegetables (Verduras)

- **El tomate** (Pronounced el toh-MAH-teh) - The tomato

- **La zanahoria** (Pronounced lah sah-nah-OH-ree-ah) - The carrot

- **El pepino** (Pronounced el peh-PEE-noh) - The cucumber

- **La lechuga** (Pronounced lah leh-CHOO-gah) - The lettuce

- **El brócoli** (Pronounced el BROH-koh-lee) - The broccoli

Grains and Carbs (Cereales y Carbohidratos)

- **El pan** (Pronounced el pahn) - The bread
- **El arroz** (Pronounced el ah-ROHS) - The rice
- **La pasta** (Pronounced lah PAHS-tah) - The pasta
- **Las papas** (Pronounced lahs PAH-pahs) - The potatoes
- **La tortilla** (Pronounced lah tor-TEE-yah) - The tortilla

Proteins (Proteínas)

- **El pollo** (Pronounced el POY-yoh) - The chicken
- **El pescado** (Pronounced el pehs-KAH-doh) - The fish
- **La carne** (Pronounced lah KAR-neh) - The meat
- **El huevo** (Pronounced el WEH-voh) - The egg
- **Los frijoles** (Pronounced lohs free-HOH-less) - The beans

Dairy (Lácteos)

- **La leche** (Pronounced lah LEH-cheh) - The milk
- **El queso** (Pronounced el KEH-soh) - The cheese
- **El yogur** (Pronounced el yoh-GOOR) - The yogurt
- **La mantequilla** (Pronounced lah mahn-teh-KEE-yah) - The butter
- **El helado** (Pronounced el eh-LAH-doh) - The ice cream

These are some of the most common foods you'll talk about when discussing meals and snacks. Learning these words will help you describe what you like to eat and ask for food when you're at a restaurant or a friend's house.

Basic Drink Vocabulary

Now let's move on to drinks. Here are some common words for different types of drinks in Spanish.

- **El agua** (Pronounced el AH-gwah) - The water

- **El jugo** (Pronounced el HOO-goh) - The juice

- **La leche** (Pronounced lah LEH-cheh) - The milk

- **El refresco** (Pronounced el reh-FRES-koh) - The soda

- **El té** (Pronounced el teh) - The tea

- **El café** (Pronounced el kah-FEH) - The coffee

These words will help you talk about what you like to drink and order drinks when you're out. For example, you might say:

- **Quiero agua, por favor.** (Pronounced kee-EH-roh AH-gwah, pohr fah-VOR) - I want water, please.

- **¿Tienes jugo de naranja?** (Pronounced tee-EH-ness HOO-goh deh nah-RAHN-hah) - Do you have orange juice?

Talking About Meals

Now that you know some basic food and drink vocabulary, let's talk about how to use these words to describe meals. Here are the names for the three main meals of the day in Spanish:

- **El desayuno** (Pronounced el deh-sah-YOO-noh) - The breakfast

- **El almuerzo** (Pronounced el al-MWEHR-soh) - The lunch

- **La cena** (Pronounced lah SEH-nah) - The dinner

Here's how you might use these words in a sentence:

- **Desayuno cereal y leche.** (Pronounced deh-sah-YOO-noh seh-REH-al ee LEH-cheh) - I have cereal and milk for breakfast.

- **Almuerzo un sándwich de jamón.** (Pronounced al-MWEHR-soh oon SAHN-dweech deh hah-MOHN) - I have a ham sandwich for lunch.

- **Ceno pollo con arroz.** (Pronounced SEH-noh POY-yoh kohn ah-ROHS) - I have chicken with rice for dinner.

These sentences show how you can talk about what you eat during different meals of the day. Whether you're describing your favorite breakfast or what you had for dinner, these words will help you communicate about your meals.

Describing Food and Drink Preferences

It's also important to know how to talk about what foods and drinks you like or don't like. Here are some phrases that can help you express your preferences:

- **Me gusta el helado.** (Pronounced meh GOOS-tah el eh-LAH-doh) - I like ice cream.

- **No me gusta la leche.** (Pronounced noh meh GOOS-tah lah LEH-cheh) - I don't like milk.

- **Prefiero el jugo de manzana.** (Pronounced preh-FYEH-roh el HOO-goh deh mahn-SAH-nah) - I prefer apple juice.

- **No me gusta mucho el brócoli.** (Pronounced noh meh GOOS-tah MOO-choh el BROH-koh-lee) - I don't like broccoli very much.

These phrases help you share your likes and dislikes with others. For example, if you're at a restaurant and someone asks if you want dessert, you could say, "Me gusta el helado" to let them know you like ice cream.

Asking for Food and Drinks

Knowing how to ask for food and drinks is very useful, especially when you're at a restaurant or someone's house. Here are some common phrases you can use:

- **¿Puedo tener...?** (Pronounced PWEH-doh teh-NER) - Can I have...?

- **Quisiera...** (Pronounced kee-SYEH-rah) - I would like...

- **¿Qué quieres comer?** (Pronounced keh kee-EH-rehs koh-MEHR) - What do you want to eat?

- **¿Qué te gustaría beber?** (Pronounced keh teh goos-tah-REE-ah beh-BEHR) - What would you like to drink?

Here's how you might use these phrases in a conversation:

- **¿Puedo tener un sándwich de queso?** (Pronounced PWEH-doh teh-NER oon SAHN-dweech deh KEH-soh) - Can I have a cheese sandwich?

- **Quisiera un vaso de agua, por favor.** (Pronounced kee-SYEH-rah oon VAH-soh deh AH-gwah, pohr fah-VOR) - I would like a glass of water, please.

These phrases will help you ask for what you want politely and clearly, whether you're at a friend's house, a restaurant, or a café.

Talking About Eating Habits

You might also want to talk about your eating habits, like what you usually eat or drink during the day. Here are some phrases that can help you do that:

- **Siempre desayuno cereal.** (Pronounced SYEM-preh deh-sah-YOO-noh seh-REH-al) - I always have cereal for breakfast.

- **Nunca como carne.** (Pronounced NOON-kah KOH-moh KAR-neh) - I never eat meat.

- **A veces bebo jugo en la mañana.** (Pronounced ah VEH-sehs BEH-boh HOO-goh en lah mah-NYAH-nah) - Sometimes I drink juice in the morning.

- **No tomo refrescos.** (Pronounced noh TOH-moh reh-FRES-kohs) - I don't drink sodas.

These phrases help you talk about your daily routines when it comes to food and drinks. Whether you always have a certain food for breakfast or never drink a certain drink, these sentences will help you explain your eating habits.

Key Points to Remember

1. **Basic Food Vocabulary:** Learn the names of common foods in Spanish, such as fruits, vegetables, grains, proteins, and dairy products. Examples include la manzana (apple), el pan (bread), and el pollo (chicken).

2. **Basic Drink Vocabulary:** Familiarize yourself with common drinks, including el agua (water), el café (coffee), and el jugo (juice). This will help you order and talk about your favorite beverages.

3. **Talking About Meals:** Use the correct terms for meals in Spanish: el desayuno (breakfast), el almuerzo (lunch), and la cena (dinner). Practice forming sentences like "Ceno pollo con arroz" (I have chicken with rice for dinner).

4. **Expressing Food and Drink Preferences:** Use phrases like "Me gusta" (I like) and "No me gusta" (I don't like) to share your preferences. For example, "Prefiero el jugo de manzana" (I prefer apple juice).

5. **Asking for Food and Drinks:** Learn useful phrases for requesting food and drinks, such as "¿Puedo tener...?" (Can I have...?) and "Quisiera..." (I would like...). These are essential for polite interactions at restaurants and cafés.

Chapter 18

Shopping Vocabulary

Shopping is something we all do, whether we're buying clothes, food, or gifts. Knowing how to talk about shopping in Spanish is important, especially if you're visiting a Spanish-speaking country or want to practice your Spanish in real-life situations. In this chapter, you'll learn key shopping vocabulary, phrases for asking prices, and how to talk about different stores and items. By the end of this chapter, you'll be ready to go shopping in Spanish!

Basic Shopping Vocabulary

Let's start with some basic words you'll need to know when talking about shopping. These are words for different types of stores, common items you might buy, and important shopping-related terms.

Types of Stores (Tipos de Tiendas)

- **La tienda** (Pronounced lah TYEHN-dah) - The store

- **El supermercado** (Pronounced el soo-pehr-mehr-KAH-doh) - The supermarket

- **La panadería** (Pronounced lah pah-nah-deh-REE-ah) - The bakery

- **La zapatería** (Pronounced lah sah-pah-teh-REE-ah) - The shoe store

- **La farmacia** (Pronounced lah fahr-MAH-syah) - The pharmacy

- **La librería** (Pronounced lah lee-breh-REE-ah) - The bookstore

- **El centro comercial** (Pronounced el SEN-troh koh-mehr-SYAHL) - The shopping mall

These are some of the most common types of stores where you might go shopping. Knowing the names of different stores will help you when you're looking for something specific, like bread at the bakery or shoes at the shoe store.

Common Shopping Items (Artículos Comunes)

Here are some common items that you might buy while shopping. These words will help you talk about the things you're looking for or want to buy.

- **La ropa** (Pronounced lah ROH-pah) - The clothes

- **Los zapatos** (Pronounced lohs sah-PAH-tohs) - The shoes

- **El libro** (Pronounced el LEE-broh) - The book

- **El pan** (Pronounced el pahn) - The bread

- **La medicina** (Pronounced lah meh-dee-SEE-nah) - The medicine

- **El regalo** (Pronounced el reh-GAH-loh) - The gift

These words will help you describe what you're buying, whether it's a new pair of shoes, a book for school, or a gift for a friend.

Important Shopping Terms (Términos Importantes)

Here are some important shopping-related terms that will help you during your shopping trips:

- **El precio** (Pronounced el PREH-syoh) - The price

- **El dinero** (Pronounced el dee-NEH-roh) - The money

- **La tarjeta de crédito** (Pronounced lah tar-HEH-tah deh KREH-dee-toh) - The credit card

- **El efectivo** (Pronounced el eh-fek-TEE-voh) - The cash

- **La bolsa** (Pronounced lah BOHL-sah) - The bag

- **La oferta** (Pronounced lah oh-FEHR-tah) - The sale

- **El recibo** (Pronounced el reh-SEE-boh) - The receipt

These terms are important because they'll help you talk about how much something costs, how you'll pay for it, and what you need to complete your purchase.

Asking About Prices

When you're shopping, it's important to know how to ask about prices. Here are some useful phrases for asking how much something costs:

- **¿Cuánto cuesta?** (Pronounced KWAN-toh KWEH-stah) - How much does it cost?

- **¿Cuánto vale?** (Pronounced KWAN-toh VAH-leh) - How much is it worth?

- **¿Cuál es el precio?** (Pronounced KWAL ess el PREH-syoh) - What is the price?

Here's how you might use these phrases in a conversation:

- **¿Cuánto cuesta esta camisa?** (Pronounced KWAN-toh KWEH-stah ESS-tah kah-MEE-sah) - How much does this shirt cost?

- **¿Cuánto vale el libro?** (Pronounced KWAN-toh VAH-leh el LEE-broh) - How much is the book worth?

- **¿Cuál es el precio de estos zapatos?** (Pronounced KWAL ess el PREH-syoh deh ESS-tohs sah-PAH-tohs) - What is the price of these shoes?

Knowing how to ask about prices will help you when you're deciding whether to buy something or when you're comparing the costs of different items.

Talking About Paying

Once you've decided what to buy, you'll need to know how to talk about paying. Here are some phrases that can help you during the checkout process:

- **Voy a pagar con tarjeta.** (Pronounced boy ah pah-GAHR kohn tar-HEH-tah) - I'm going to pay with a card.

- **¿Puedo pagar en efectivo?** (Pronounced PWEH-doh pah-GAHR en eh-fek-TEE-voh) - Can I pay in cash?

- **¿Aceptan tarjetas de crédito?** (Pronounced ah-SEP-tahn tar-HEH-tahs deh KREH-dee-toh) - Do you accept credit cards?

- **¿Tiene cambio?** (Pronounced tee-EH-neh KAHM-byoh) - Do you have change?

Here's how you might use these phrases when you're at the checkout:

- **Voy a pagar con efectivo.** (Pronounced boy ah pah-GAHR kohn eh-fek-TEE-voh) - I'm going to pay with cash.

- **¿Aceptan tarjetas de débito?** (Pronounced ah-SEP-tahn tar-HEH-tahs deh DEH-bee-toh) - Do you accept debit cards?

- **¿Puede darme un recibo, por favor?** (Pronounced PWEH-deh DAR-meh oon reh-SEE-boh, pohr fah-VOR) - Can you give me a receipt, please?

These phrases will help you navigate the payment process smoothly, whether you're using cash, a credit card, or a debit card.

Shopping for Specific Items

Sometimes, you're shopping for something specific, like a new pair of shoes or a gift for a friend. Here are some phrases that can help you find exactly what you're looking for:

- **Estoy buscando...** (Pronounced es-TOY boos-KAHN-doh) - I'm looking for...

- **Necesito...** (Pronounced neh-seh-SEE-toh) - I need...

- **¿Tienen...?** (Pronounced tee-EH-nen) - Do you have...?

Here's how you might use these phrases while shopping:

- **Estoy buscando una chaqueta.** (Pronounced es-TOY boos-KAHN-doh OO-nah chah-KEH-tah) - I'm looking for a jacket.

- **Necesito un regalo para mi amigo.** (Pronounced neh-seh-SEE-toh oon reh-GAH-loh PAH-rah mee ah-MEE-goh) - I need a gift for my friend.

- **¿Tienen este libro en otro idioma?** (Pronounced tee-EH-nen ESS-teh LEE-broh en OH-troh ee-dee-OH-mah) - Do you have this book in another language?

These phrases will help you communicate clearly with store employees and find the items you need more quickly.

Shopping in a Market

If you're shopping at a market, you might need some different phrases. Markets are usually places where you can buy fresh food, handmade items, or unique products. Here are some phrases that might come in handy:

- **¿Cuánto cuesta el kilo de manzanas?** (Pronounced KWAN-toh KWEH-stah el KEE-loh deh mahn-SAH-nahs) - How much does a kilo of apples cost?

- **Quiero medio kilo de tomates.** (Pronounced kee-EH-roh MEH-dyoh KEE-loh deh toh-MAH-tess) - I want half a kilo of tomatoes.

- **¿Puedo probar?** (Pronounced PWEH-doh proh-BAHR) - Can I try it?

These phrases will help you when you're buying fresh produce or other items at a market. It's common to ask about prices, quantities, and sometimes even try a sample before you buy something.

Describing What You're Looking For

When shopping, you might need to describe the item you're looking for. Here are some phrases that can help you do that:

- **Estoy buscando una camisa roja.** (Pronounced es-TOY boos-KAHN-doh OO-nah kah-MEE-sah ROH-hah) - I'm looking for a red shirt.

- **Necesito unos zapatos negros.** (Pronounced neh-seh-SEE-toh OO-nohs sah-PAH-tohs NEH-grohs) - I need some black shoes.

- **Quiero un libro sobre animales.** (Pronounced kee-EH-roh oon LEE-broh SOH-breh ah-nee-MAH-less) - I want a book about animals.

These sentences will help you explain exactly what you're looking for, whether it's a specific color, size, or type of item.

Key Points to Remember

1. **Basic Shopping Vocabulary:** Learn essential words for shopping, including types of stores like la tienda (store) and el supermercado (supermarket), as well as common shopping items like la ropa (clothes) and el pan (bread).

2. **Asking About Prices:** Use phrases such as "¿Cuánto cuesta?" (How much does it cost?) and "¿Cuál es el precio?" (What is the price?) to inquire about the cost of items while shopping.

3. **Talking About Paying:** Familiarize yourself with phrases for the payment process, like "Voy a pagar con tarjeta" (I'm going to pay with a card) and "¿Aceptan tarjetas de crédito?" (Do you accept credit cards?).

4. **Shopping for Specific Items:** Use phrases like "Estoy buscando..." (I'm looking for...) and "Necesito..." (I need...) to ask for specific products in stores, making it easier to find what you need.

5. **Shopping in a Market:** Learn useful phrases for market shopping, such as "¿Cuánto cuesta el kilo de manzanas?" (How much does a kilo of apples cost?) and "Quiero medio

kilo de tomates" (I want half a kilo of tomatoes) to navigate market transactions.

Chapter 19

Navigating Directions and Places

One of the most useful skills you can have when learning a new language is knowing how to ask for and understand directions. Whether you're exploring a new city, finding your way to a friend's house, or just trying to get to a nearby store, being able to navigate directions and places in Spanish will help you a lot. In this chapter, you'll learn key vocabulary and phrases to help you ask for directions, understand what someone tells you, and describe places in Spanish.

Basic Direction Words

Let's start with some basic direction words. These are words you'll need to know when asking for or giving directions.

- **Izquierda** (Pronounced ees-KYEHR-dah) - Left

- **Derecha** (Pronounced deh-REH-chah) - Right

- **Recto** (Pronounced REK-toh) - Straight

- **Arriba** (Pronounced ah-REE-bah) - Up

- **Abajo** (Pronounced ah-BAH-hoh) - Down

- **Cerca** (Pronounced SEHR-kah) - Near

- **Lejos** (Pronounced LEH-hohs) - Far

These words will help you understand the general directions someone might give you. For example, if someone tells you to go "izquierda" (left) or "derecha" (right), you'll know which way to turn.

Common Phrases for Asking Directions

When you're in a new place and need to find your way, it's important to know how to ask for directions. Here are some common phrases you can use:

- **¿Dónde está...?** (Pronounced DOHN-deh ess-TAH) - Where is...?

- **¿Cómo llego a...?** (Pronounced KOH-moh YEH-goh ah) - How do I get to...?

- **¿Está cerca?** (Pronounced ess-TAH SEHR-kah) - Is it near?

- **¿Qué tan lejos está?** (Pronounced KEH tahn LEH-hohs ess-TAH) - How far is it?

Here's how you might use these phrases in a conversation:

- **¿Dónde está la estación de tren?** (Pronounced DOHN-deh ess-TAH lah eh-stah-SYOHN deh TREHN) - Where is the train station?

- **¿Cómo llego a la plaza?** (Pronounced KOH-moh YEH-goh ah lah PLAH-sah) - How do I get to the plaza?

- **¿Está cerca el supermercado?** (Pronounced ess-TAH SEHR-kah el soo-pehr-mehr-KAH-doh) - Is the supermarket near?

- **¿Qué tan lejos está el parque?** (Pronounced KEH tahn LEH-hohs ess-TAH el PAR-kay) - How far is the park?

These questions will help you get the information you need to find your way around. You can ask where something is, how to get there, and if it's close by or far away.

Understanding Directions

Once you've asked for directions, it's important to understand what the person tells you. Here are some common phrases you might hear when someone is giving you directions:

- **Gira a la izquierda.** (Pronounced HEE-rah ah lah ees-KYEHR-dah) - Turn left.

- **Gira a la derecha.** (Pronounced HEE-rah ah lah deh-REH-chah) - Turn right.

- **Sigue recto.** (Pronounced SEE-geh REK-toh) - Go straight.

- **Sube por la calle.** (Pronounced SOO-beh pohr lah KAH-yay) - Go up the street.

- **Baja por la avenida.** (Pronounced BAH-hah pohr lah ah-veh-NEE-dah) - Go down the avenue.

- **Está cerca.** (Pronounced ess-TAH SEHR-kah) - It's near.
- **Está lejos.** (Pronounced ess-TAH LEH-hohs) - It's far.

Here's how you might hear these phrases used:

- **Gira a la derecha y sigue recto.** (Pronounced HEE-rah ah lah deh-REH-chah ee SEE-geh REK-toh) - Turn right and go straight.
- **Sube por la calle y luego gira a la izquierda.** (Pronounced SOO-beh pohr lah KAH-yay ee LWEH-goh HEE-rah ah lah ees-KYEHR-dah) - Go up the street and then turn left.
- **El parque está cerca, solo sigue recto.** (Pronounced el PAR-kay ess-TAH SEHR-kah, SOH-loh SEE-geh REK-toh) - The park is near, just go straight.

These directions will help you understand how to get where you're going. Pay attention to the words for left ("izquierda"), right ("derecha"), and straight ("recto") so you can follow the instructions correctly.

Describing Places

Knowing how to describe places is also important when navigating in Spanish. Here are some phrases that can help you describe where something is located:

- **Está al lado de...** (Pronounced ess-TAH ahl LAH-doh deh) - It's next to...
- **Está enfrente de...** (Pronounced ess-TAH ehn-FREHN-teh deh) - It's in front of...
- **Está detrás de...** (Pronounced ess-TAH deh-TRAHS deh) - It's behind...
- **Está cerca de...** (Pronounced ess-TAH SEHR-kah deh) - It's near...
- **Está lejos de...** (Pronounced ess-TAH LEH-hohs deh) - It's far from...

Here's how you might use these phrases:

- **La escuela está al lado del parque.** (Pronounced lah es-KWEH-lah ess-TAH ahl LAH-doh del PAR-kay) - The school is next to the park.
- **El supermercado está enfrente de la plaza.** (Pronounced el soo-pehr-mehr-KAH-doh ess-TAH ehn-FREHN-teh deh lah PLAH-sah) - The supermarket is in front of the plaza.
- **La farmacia está detrás de la tienda.** (Pronounced lah fahr-MAH-syah ess-TAH deh-TRAHS deh lah TYEHN-dah) - The pharmacy is behind the store.

These phrases will help you describe the location of a place in relation to another place. Whether something is next to, in front of, or behind something else, these phrases will help you explain where it is.

Important Places in Town

It's also helpful to know the names of common places you might visit in a town or city. Here are some important places you might need to ask about or visit:

- **El banco** (Pronounced el BAHN-koh) - The bank

- **La estación de tren** (Pronounced lah eh-stah-SYOHN deh TREHN) - The train station

- **La parada de autobús** (Pronounced lah pah-RAH-dah deh ow-toh-BOOS) - The bus stop

- **El hospital** (Pronounced el ohs-pee-TAL) - The hospital

- **El supermercado** (Pronounced el soo-pehr-mehr-KAH-doh) - The supermarket

- **La plaza** (Pronounced lah PLAH-sah) - The plaza or town square

- **La iglesia** (Pronounced lah ee-GLEH-syah) - The church

Here's how you might ask about these places:

- **¿Dónde está el banco?** (Pronounced DOHN-deh ess-TAH el BAHN-koh) - Where is the bank?

- **¿Cómo llego a la estación de tren?** (Pronounced KOH-moh YEH-goh ah lah eh-stah-SYOHN deh TREHN) - How do I get to the train station?

- **¿Está cerca la parada de autobús?** (Pronounced ess-TAH SEHR-kah lah pah-RAH-dah deh ow-toh-BOOS) - Is the bus stop near?

Knowing these place names will help you ask for directions and understand where to go when you're in a new town or city.

Landmarks and Reference Points

When giving or following directions, people often use landmarks or reference points to make it easier to find a place. Here are some common landmarks and reference points you might hear:

- **El edificio** (Pronounced el eh-dee-FEE-syoh) - The building

- **La esquina** (Pronounced lah es-KEE-nah) - The corner

- **El puente** (Pronounced el PWEHN-teh) - The bridge

- **El parque** (Pronounced el PAR-kay) - The park

- **El semáforo** (Pronounced el seh-MAH-foh-roh) - The traffic light

Here's how you might use these words in a sentence:

- **El restaurante está en la esquina.** (Pronounced el reh-stow-RAHN-teh ess-TAH en lah es-KEE-nah) - The restaurant is on the corner.

- **Cruza el puente y sigue recto.** (Pronounced KROO-sah el PWEHN-teh ee SEE-geh REK-toh) - Cross the bridge and go straight.

- **El banco está al lado del edificio grande.** (Pronounced el BAHN-koh ess-TAH ahl LAH-doh del eh-dee-FEE-syoh GRAHN-deh) - The bank is next to the big building.

Using landmarks and reference points can make it easier to understand and follow directions, especially if you're in an unfamiliar area.

Getting Directions in Different Situations

Here are some common situations where you might need to ask for or give directions:

- **Finding a specific place:** "¿Cómo llego al cine?" (Pronounced KOH-moh YEH-goh ahl SEE-neh) - How do I get to the movie theater?

- **Asking for help in a store:** "¿Dónde está la sección de ropa?" (Pronounced DOHN-deh ess-TAH lah sehk-SYOHN deh ROH-pah) - Where is the clothing section?

- **Locating a landmark:** "¿Dónde está el monumento?" (Pronounced DOHN-deh ess-TAH el moh-noo-MEN-toh) - Where is the monument?

In these situations, it's important to be clear and specific about what you're looking for. Using the vocabulary and phrases you've learned in this chapter, you'll be able to ask for directions and understand how to get to where you need to go.

Key Points to Remember

1. **Basic Direction Words:** Learn essential direction words like izquierda (left), derecha (right), and recto (straight) to understand and give directions effectively.

2. **Common Phrases for Asking Directions:** Use phrases such as "¿Dónde está...?"

(Where is...?) and "¿Cómo llego a...?" (How do I get to...?) to ask for directions in Spanish.

3. **Understanding Directions:** Be familiar with phrases like "Gira a la izquierda" (Turn left) and "Sigue recto" (Go straight) to follow directions accurately.

4. **Describing Places:** Use expressions like "Está al lado de..." (It's next to...) and "Está enfrente de..." (It's in front of...) to describe the location of places in relation to others.

5. **Important Places and Landmarks:** Know the names of common places and landmarks, such as el banco (the bank) and la esquina (the corner), to help navigate and understand directions better.

Chapter 20

Around the House: Rooms and Objects

Knowing how to talk about different rooms and objects around the house is important when learning a new language. Whether you're describing your home, asking where something is, or helping out with chores, understanding the vocabulary for rooms and objects in Spanish will help you communicate more effectively. In this chapter, you'll learn the names of different rooms in a house, common household objects, and how to describe where things are located.

Rooms in the House

Let's start by learning the names of different rooms in a house. These words will help you describe where things are and talk about different parts of your home.

- **La cocina** (Pronounced lah koh-SEE-nah) - The kitchen

- **El baño** (Pronounced el BAH-nyoh) - The bathroom

- **El dormitorio** (Pronounced el dohr-mee-TOH-ryoh) - The bedroom

- **La sala** (Pronounced lah SAH-lah) - The living room

- **El comedor** (Pronounced el koh-meh-DOR) - The dining room

- **El garaje** (Pronounced el gah-RAH-heh) - The garage

- **El jardín** (Pronounced el har-DEEN) - The garden or yard

These are some of the most common rooms you'll find in a house. Knowing these words will help you describe your home or ask someone about theirs.

Common Objects Around the House

Now that you know the names of the rooms, let's learn some common objects you might find in each room. These words will help you talk about the things you use every day.

In the Kitchen (En la Cocina)

- **El refrigerador** (Pronounced el reh-free-heh-rah-DOR) - The refrigerator
- **La estufa** (Pronounced lah eh-STOO-fah) - The stove
- **El horno** (Pronounced el OR-noh) - The oven
- **El microondas** (Pronounced el mee-kroh-OHN-dahs) - The microwave
- **El fregadero** (Pronounced el freh-gah-DEH-roh) - The sink
- **El lavaplatos** (Pronounced el lah-vah-PLAH-tohs) - The dishwasher
- **La mesa** (Pronounced lah MEH-sah) - The table
- **La silla** (Pronounced lah SEE-yah) - The chair

In the Bathroom (En el Baño)

- **La ducha** (Pronounced lah DOO-chah) - The shower
- **La bañera** (Pronounced lah bah-NYEH-rah) - The bathtub
- **El inodoro** (Pronounced el ee-noh-DOH-roh) - The toilet
- **El lavabo** (Pronounced el lah-BAH-boh) - The sink
- **El espejo** (Pronounced el eh-SPEH-hoh) - The mirror
- **La toalla** (Pronounced lah toh-AH-yah) - The towel

In the Bedroom (En el Dormitorio)

- **La cama** (Pronounced lah KAH-mah) - The bed
- **La almohada** (Pronounced lah ahl-moh-AH-dah) - The pillow
- **La sábana** (Pronounced lah SAH-bah-nah) - The sheet
- **El armario** (Pronounced el ahr-MAH-ryoh) - The closet

- **La lámpara** (Pronounced lah LAHM-pah-rah) - The lamp

- **El escritorio** (Pronounced el ehs-kree-TOH-ryoh) - The desk

In the Living Room (En la Sala)

- **El sofá** (Pronounced el soh-FAH) - The sofa

- **El televisor** (Pronounced el teh-leh-vee-SOR) - The television

- **La alfombra** (Pronounced lah al-FOHM-brah) - The rug

- **La mesa de centro** (Pronounced lah MEH-sah deh SEHN-troh) - The coffee table

- **El cuadro** (Pronounced el KWAH-droh) - The painting or picture

In the Dining Room (En el Comedor)

- **La mesa del comedor** (Pronounced lah MEH-sah del koh-meh-DOR) - The dining table

- **Las sillas del comedor** (Pronounced lahs SEE-yahs del koh-meh-DOR) - The dining chairs

- **El mantel** (Pronounced el mahn-TEL) - The tablecloth

- **Los cubiertos** (Pronounced lohs koo-BYEHR-tohs) - The cutlery (forks, knives, spoons)

- **Los platos** (Pronounced lohs PLAH-tohs) - The plates

- **Los vasos** (Pronounced lohs VAH-sohs) - The glasses

In the Garage (En el Garaje)

- **El coche** (Pronounced el KOH-cheh) - The car

- **La bicicleta** (Pronounced lah bee-see-KLEH-tah) - The bicycle

- **Las herramientas** (Pronounced lahs eh-rrah-mee-EHN-tahs) - The tools

- **La caja de herramientas** (Pronounced lah KAH-hah deh eh-rrah-mee-EHN-tahs) - The toolbox

- **El estante** (Pronounced el eh-STAHN-teh) - The shelf

In the Garden (En el Jardín)

- **Las flores** (Pronounced lahs FLOH-rehs) - The flowers
- **Las plantas** (Pronounced lahs PLAHN-tahs) - The plants
- **La hierba** (Pronounced lah YER-bah) - The grass
- **El árbol** (Pronounced el AHR-bohl) - The tree
- **El césped** (Pronounced el SES-pehd) - The lawn

These are just some of the common objects you might find in different rooms of the house. Knowing these words will help you describe your home, ask where something is, or even help out with chores.

Talking About Where Things Are

When talking about objects around the house, it's useful to know how to describe where things are located. Here are some phrases that can help you do that:

- **Está en...** (Pronounced ess-TAH en) - It's in/on...
- **Está encima de...** (Pronounced ess-TAH en-SEE-mah deh) - It's on top of...
- **Está debajo de...** (Pronounced ess-TAH deh-BAH-hoh deh) - It's under...
- **Está al lado de...** (Pronounced ess-TAH ahl LAH-doh deh) - It's next to...
- **Está dentro de...** (Pronounced ess-TAH DEHN-troh deh) - It's inside...
- **Está fuera de...** (Pronounced ess-TAH FWEH-rah deh) - It's outside of...

Here's how you might use these phrases in a conversation:

- **El libro está en la mesa.** (Pronounced el LEE-broh ess-TAH en lah MEH-sah) - The book is on the table.
- **La pelota está debajo de la cama.** (Pronounced lah peh-LOH-tah ess-TAH deh-BAH-hoh deh lah KAH-mah) - The ball is under the bed.
- **La lámpara está al lado del sofá.** (Pronounced lah LAHM-pah-rah ess-TAH ahl LAH-doh del soh-FAH) - The lamp is next to the sofa.
- **Las herramientas están dentro de la caja.** (Pronounced lahs eh-rrah-mee-EHN-tahs

ess-TAHN DEHN-troh deh lah KAH-hah) - The tools are inside the box.

These phrases will help you explain where things are in your home or ask someone else where to find something. It's a useful way to describe the location of objects in a clear and precise way.

Describing Your Home

Now that you know the vocabulary for different rooms and objects, you can start describing your home in Spanish. Here's an example of how you might do that:

Mi casa tiene una cocina grande y moderna. En la cocina, hay un refrigerador, una estufa, y un microondas. La sala es cómoda, con un sofá y un televisor. En mi dormitorio, tengo una cama grande, un armario, y un escritorio para hacer mi tarea. También, tenemos un jardín con muchas flores y un árbol grande. (Pronounced mee KAH-sah tee-EH-neh OO-nah koh-SEE-nah GRAHN-deh ee moh-DEHR-nah. En lah koh-SEE-nah, ay oon reh-free-heh-rah-DOR, OO-nah eh-STOO-fah, ee oon mee-kroh-OHN-dahs. Lah SAH-lah ess KOH-moh-dah, kohn oon soh-FAH ee oon teh-leh-vee-SOR. En mee dohr-mee-TOH-ryoh, TEHN-goh OO-nah KAH-mah GRAHN-deh, oon ahr-MAH-ryoh, ee oon ehs-kree-TOH-ryoh PAH-rah ah-SEHR mee TAH-reh-ah. Tahm-BYEHN, teh-NEH-mohs oon har-DEEN kohn MOO-chahs FLOH-rehs ee oon AHR-bohl GRAHN-deh) - My house has a big, modern kitchen. In the kitchen, there is a refrigerator, a stove, and a microwave. The living room is cozy, with a sofa and a television. In my bedroom, I have a big bed, a closet, and a desk for doing my homework. We also have a garden with lots of flowers and a big tree.

This example shows how you can use the vocabulary you've learned to talk about different rooms and objects in your home. It's a great way to practice describing your surroundings and talking about your daily life in Spanish.

Key Points to Remember

1. **Rooms in the House:** Learn the names of common rooms like la cocina (kitchen), el baño (bathroom), and el dormitorio (bedroom) to describe different parts of your home.

2. **Common Household Objects:** Familiarize yourself with everyday objects found in various rooms, such as el refrigerador (refrigerator) in the kitchen and la cama (bed) in the bedroom.

3. **Talking About Location:** Use phrases like "Está en..." (It's in/on) and "Está al lado de..." (It's next to) to describe where objects are located around the house.

4. **Describing Your Home:** Practice combining room and object vocabulary to describe your home in detail, like mentioning una cocina grande (a big kitchen) or un jardín con flores (a garden with flowers).

5. **Using Location Phrases:** Improve your ability to give and understand directions within the house by using phrases such as "Está debajo de..." (It's under) and "Está dentro de..." (It's inside).

Chapter 21

Basic Adjectives and Their Agreement

Adjectives are words that describe nouns. They can tell you what something looks like, how it feels, or even what kind of personality someone has. In Spanish, just like in English, adjectives are very important because they help you give more detail and color to your sentences. However, in Spanish, adjectives have to agree with the nouns they describe in both gender and number. This means that the form of the adjective can change depending on whether the noun is masculine or feminine, singular or plural. In this chapter, you'll learn how to use basic adjectives in Spanish and how to make sure they agree with the nouns they describe.

Understanding Adjective Agreement

In Spanish, every noun has a gender: it's either masculine or feminine. Masculine nouns generally end in "-o," while feminine nouns usually end in "-a." Adjectives that describe these nouns must match the gender of the noun. For example, if you're describing a "libro" (book), which is masculine, you would use a masculine form of the adjective. If you're describing a "mesa" (table), which is feminine, you would use the feminine form of the adjective.

Let's start with a simple adjective: "grande" (big). The good thing about "grande" is that it doesn't change whether the noun is masculine or feminine. So you would say:

El libro grande (Pronounced el LEE-broh GRAHN-deh) - The big book

La mesa grande (Pronounced lah MEH-sah GRAHN-deh) - The big table

However, not all adjectives are this simple. Many adjectives in Spanish do change depending on the gender of the noun. Let's look at an adjective that does change: "bonito" (pretty).

El libro bonito (Pronounced el LEE-broh boh-NEE-toh) - The pretty book

La mesa bonita (Pronounced lah MEH-sah boh-NEE-tah) - The pretty table

As you can see, "bonito" changes to "bonita" when describing a feminine noun. This is something you'll need to remember when using adjectives in Spanish.

Making Adjectives Plural

Just like nouns, adjectives in Spanish also have a plural form. To make an adjective plural, you generally add "-s" if the adjective ends in a vowel, or "-es" if it ends in a consonant. Let's look at some examples using the adjective "grande" again, as well as "bonito":

Los libros grandes (Pronounced lohs LEE-brohs GRAHN-dehs) - The big books

Las mesas grandes (Pronounced lah MEH-sahs GRAHN-dehs) - The big tables

Los libros bonitos (Pronounced lohs LEE-brohs boh-NEE-tohs) - The pretty books

Las mesas bonitas (Pronounced lah MEH-sahs boh-NEE-tahs) - The pretty tables

Notice how the ending "-s" is added to "grande" and "bonito" to make them plural, and how "bonito" changes to "bonitos" or "bonitas" to match the gender of the noun. Remember that the adjective must always agree with the noun in both gender and number.

Common Adjectives and Their Forms

Now that you understand how adjective agreement works, let's look at some common adjectives you might use in everyday conversations. Here are some basic adjectives and how they change depending on the gender and number of the noun they describe:

Alto/Alta (Pronounced AHL-toh/AHL-tah) - Tall

El chico alto (Pronounced el CHEE-koh AHL-toh) - The tall boy

La chica alta (Pronounced lah CHEE-kah AHL-tah) - The tall girl

Los chicos altos (Pronounced lohs CHEE-kohs AHL-tohs) - The tall boys

Las chicas altas (Pronounced lah CHEE-kahs AHL-tahs) - The tall girls

Bajo/Baja (Pronounced BAH-hoh/BAH-hah) - Short

El chico bajo (Pronounced el CHEE-koh BAH-hoh) - The short boy

La chica baja (Pronounced lah CHEE-kah BAH-hah) - The short girl

Los chicos bajos (Pronounced lohs CHEE-kohs BAH-hohs) - The short boys

Las chicas bajas (Pronounced lah CHEE-kahs BAH-hahs) - The short girls

Nuevo/Nueva (Pronounced NWEH-voh/NWEH-vah) - New

El coche nuevo (Pronounced el KOH-cheh NWEH-voh) - The new car

La casa nueva (Pronounced lah KAH-sah NWEH-vah) - The new house

Los coches nuevos (Pronounced lohs KOH-chehs NWEH-vohs) - The new cars

Las casas nuevas (Pronounced lah KAH-sahs NWEH-vahs) - The new houses

Viejo/Vieja (Pronounced VYEH-hoh/VYEH-hah) - Old

El libro viejo (Pronounced el LEE-broh VYEH-hoh) - The old book

La mesa vieja (Pronounced lah MEH-sah VYEH-hah) - The old table

Los libros viejos (Pronounced lohs LEE-brohs VYEH-hohs) - The old books

Las mesas viejas (Pronounced lah MEH-sahs VYEH-hahs) - The old tables

These adjectives are very common and will help you describe people, places, and things in more detail. As you can see, each adjective has four forms: masculine singular, feminine singular, masculine plural, and feminine plural. It's important to use the correct form depending on the noun you're describing.

Adjectives That Don't Change

Not all adjectives in Spanish change according to gender. Some adjectives stay the same whether they're describing a masculine or feminine noun. These adjectives often end in "-e" or a consonant. Let's look at some examples:

Grande (Pronounced GRAHN-deh) - Big

El perro grande (Pronounced el PEH-rroh GRAHN-deh) - The big dog

La casa grande (Pronounced lah KAH-sah GRAHN-deh) - The big house

Los perros grandes (Pronounced lohs PEH-rrohs GRAHN-dehs) - The big dogs

Las casas grandes (Pronounced lah KAH-sahs GRAHN-dehs) - The big houses

Feliz (Pronounced feh-LEES) - Happy

El niño feliz (Pronounced el NEEN-yoh feh-LEES) - The happy boy

La niña feliz (Pronounced lah NEEN-yah feh-LEES) - The happy girl

Los niños felices (Pronounced lohs NEEN-yohs feh-LEE-sehs) - The happy boys

Las niñas felices (Pronounced lah NEEN-yahs feh-LEE-sehs) - The happy girls

Notice that "grande" and "feliz" stay the same whether they are describing masculine or feminine nouns, but they do change to "grandes" and "felices" in the plural form. This is a pattern you'll see with many adjectives that end in "-e" or a consonant.

Using Adjectives in Sentences

Now that you've learned some common adjectives and how they agree with nouns, let's practice using them in sentences. Here are a few examples:

El gato negro (Pronounced el GAH-toh NEH-groh) - The black cat

La casa blanca (Pronounced lah KAH-sah BLAHN-kah) - The white house

Los niños contentos (Pronounced lohs NEEN-yohs kohn-TEN-tohs) - The happy boys

Las chicas inteligentes (Pronounced lah CHEE-kahs een-teh-lee-HEN-tehs) - The smart girls

In each of these sentences, the adjective matches the gender and number of the noun it describes. This is how you create clear, grammatically correct sentences in Spanish.

Key Points to Remember

1. **Adjective Agreement:** Adjectives in Spanish must agree with the gender and number of the nouns they describe. For example, bonito changes to bonita when describing a feminine noun.

2. **Making Adjectives Plural:** To make adjectives plural, add "-s" if they end in a vowel, or "-es" if they end in a consonant. Ensure the adjective agrees in both gender and number with the noun.

3. **Common Adjectives:** Learn the four forms of common adjectives like alto/alta (tall) and nuevo/nueva (new) to describe people, places, and things accurately.

4. **Adjectives That Don't Change:** Some adjectives, like grande (big) and feliz (happy), remain the same for both masculine and feminine nouns but change in the plural form.

5. **Using Adjectives in Sentences:** Practice using adjectives in sentences, ensuring they match the gender and number of the nouns they describe, like el gato negro (the black cat) and las casas grandes (the big houses).

Chapter 22

School and Education Vocabulary

School is a big part of your life, and knowing how to talk about it in Spanish is really useful. Whether you're talking about your classes, your teachers, or the things you do at school, having the right vocabulary will help you communicate better. In this chapter, you'll learn the basic words and phrases you need to talk about school and education in Spanish.

Basic Vocabulary for School

Let's start with some of the basic words you'll need to know when talking about school:

La escuela (Pronounced lah ehs-KWEH-lah) - The school

El estudiante/La estudiante (Pronounced el ehs-too-DYAHN-teh/lah ehs-too-DYAHN-teh) - The student

El profesor/La profesora (Pronounced el proh-feh-SOR/lah proh-feh-SOR-ah) - The teacher

La clase (Pronounced lah KLAH-seh) - The class

El aula (Pronounced el OW-lah) - The classroom

El libro (Pronounced el LEE-broh) - The book

El cuaderno (Pronounced el kwah-DEHR-noh) - The notebook

El lápiz (Pronounced el LAH-pees) - The pencil

La pluma (Pronounced lah PLOO-mah) - The pen

El pupitre (Pronounced el poo-PEE-treh) - The desk

These are some of the most common words you'll use when talking about school. Knowing these words will help you describe your day at school and the things you use every day.

Subjects and Classes

Now that you know some basic school vocabulary, let's learn the names of different subjects and classes you might take:

Las matemáticas (Pronounced lahss mah-teh-MAH-tee-kahs) - Mathematics/Math

La ciencia (Pronounced lah SYEN-see-ah) - Science

La historia (Pronounced lah ees-TOH-ryah) - History

El inglés (Pronounced el een-GLEHS) - English

El español (Pronounced el ehs-pah-NYOHL) - Spanish

El arte (Pronounced el AHR-teh) - Art

La música (Pronounced lah MOO-see-kah) - Music

La educación física (Pronounced lah eh-doo-kah-SYOHN FEE-see-kah) - Physical Education (P.E.)

These are the subjects you might study at school. Each one has its own vocabulary, but for now, these basic words will help you talk about your classes and what you're learning.

Talking About Your Schedule

At school, you follow a schedule that tells you which classes you have each day. Here's how you can talk about your schedule in Spanish:

Mi horario (Pronounced mee oh-RAH-ryoh) - My schedule

Tengo matemáticas a las ocho. (Pronounced TEHN-goh mah-teh-MAH-tee-kahs ah lahss OH-choh) - I have math at eight o'clock.

La clase de ciencias empieza a las nueve. (Pronounced lah KLAH-seh deh SYEN-see-ahs ehm-PYEH-sah ah lahss NWEH-veh) - Science class starts at nine o'clock.

Termino la escuela a las tres. (Pronounced tehr-MEE-noh lah ehs-KWEH-lah ah lahss TREHS) - I finish school at three o'clock.

These sentences help you talk about when your classes are and when your school day ends.

Describing Your School Day

Now that you have the vocabulary for different subjects and your schedule, let's put it all together to describe your school day:

Por la mañana, tengo clase de matemáticas y luego clase de ciencias. Después del recreo, voy a la clase de inglés. Por la tarde, tengo arte y música. Termino el día con educación física. (Pronounced pohr lah mah-NYAH-nah, TEHN-goh KLAH-seh deh mah-teh-MAH-tee-kahs ee LWEH-goh KLAH-seh deh SYEN-see-ahs. dehsp-WEHS del reh-KREH-oh, voy ah lah KLAH-seh deh een-GLEHS. pohr lah TAR-deh, TEHN-goh AHR-teh ee MOO-see-kah. tehr-MEE-noh el dee-AH kohn eh-doo-kah-SYOHN FEE-see-kah) - In the morning, I have math class and then science class. After recess, I go to English class. In the afternoon, I have art and music. I finish the day with P.E.

This description gives a basic overview of your school day, including the classes you take and when they happen.

Talking About Your Favorite Classes

Everyone has a favorite class or subject. Here's how you can talk about your favorite parts of school:

Mi clase favorita es el arte. (Pronounced mee KLAH-seh fah-boh-REE-tah ess el AHR-teh) - My favorite class is art.

Me gusta la clase de matemáticas porque es interesante. (Pronounced meh GOOS-tah lah KLAH-seh deh mah-teh-MAH-tee-kahs por-KEH ess een-teh-reh-SAHN-teh) - I like math class because it's interesting.

Prefiero la clase de música. (Pronounced preh-FYEH-roh lah KLAH-seh deh MOO-see-kah) - I prefer music class.

These sentences help you express your preferences and what you enjoy most about school.

Talking About School Supplies

Every student needs certain supplies for school. Here are some common school supplies and how to talk about them in Spanish:

Los útiles escolares (Pronounced lohs OO-tee-lehs ehs-koh-LAHR-ehs) - School supplies

La mochila (Pronounced lah moh-CHEE-lah) - The backpack

El libro de texto (Pronounced el LEE-broh deh TEHKS-toh) - The textbook

El bolígrafo (Pronounced el boh-LEE-grah-foh) - The pen

La regla (Pronounced lah REH-glah) - The ruler

Las tijeras (Pronounced lahss tee-HEH-rahs) - The scissors

El pegamento (Pronounced el peh-gah-MEN-toh) - The glue

These are some of the supplies you might need to bring to school each day. Knowing these words will help you talk about what you need for class.

Talking About Homework

Homework is an important part of school. Here's how to talk about your homework in Spanish:

La tarea (Pronounced lah tah-REH-ah) - The homework

Tengo mucha tarea. (Pronounced TEHN-goh MOO-chah tah-REH-ah) - I have a lot of homework.

Necesito hacer mi tarea de ciencias. (Pronounced neh-seh-SEE-toh ah-SEHR mee tah-REH-ah deh SYEN-see-ahs) - I need to do my science homework.

Terminé mi tarea de matemáticas. (Pronounced tehr-mee-NEH mee tah-REH-ah deh mah-teh-MAH-tee-kahs) - I finished my math homework.

These sentences help you talk about the homework you have to do and whether you've finished it or not.

Talking About Your Teachers

Teachers play a big role in your education. Here's how you can talk about your teachers in Spanish:

Mi profesor es muy amable. (Pronounced mee proh-feh-SOR ess MOO-ee ah-MAH-bleh) - My teacher is very kind.

La profesora de inglés es muy divertida. (Pronounced lah proh-feh-SOR-ah deh een-GLEHS ess MOO-ee dee-ver-TEE-dah) - The English teacher is very fun.

Me gusta la manera en que el profesor de ciencias explica las cosas. (Pronounced meh GOOS-tah lah mah-NEH-rah en keh el proh-feh-SOR deh SYEN-see-ahs ehks-PLEE-kah lahss KOH-sahs) - I like the way the science teacher explains things.

These sentences help you describe your teachers and what you think about them.

Talking About School Activities

Besides classes, there are many other activities at school. Here are some common activities and how to talk about them:

El recreo (Pronounced el reh-KREH-oh) - Recess

El almuerzo (Pronounced el al-MWEHR-soh) - Lunch

El club (Pronounced el kloom) - The club

El equipo (Pronounced el eh-KEE-poh) - The team

Here are some sentences using these words:

En el recreo, juego con mis amigos. (Pronounced en el reh-KREH-oh, HWEH-goh kohn mees ah-MEE-gohs) - At recess, I play with my friends.

Almuerzo con mis compañeros de clase. (Pronounced al-MWEHR-soh kohn mees kohm-pah-NYER-ohs deh KLAH-seh) - I have lunch with my classmates.

Estoy en el club de arte. (Pronounced eh-STOY en el kloom deh AHR-teh) - I'm in the art club.

Juego en el equipo de fútbol. (Pronounced HWEH-goh en el eh-KEE-poh deh FOOT-bol) - I play on the soccer team.

These sentences help you talk about what you do during breaks, lunchtime, and after school.

Key Points to Remember

1. **Basic Vocabulary for School:** Learn essential school-related words in Spanish, such as la escuela (school), el estudiante (student), el profesor/la profesora (teacher), and la clase (class).

2. **Subjects and Classes:** Familiarize yourself with the names of common subjects, including las matemáticas (math), la ciencia (science), el inglés (English), and el arte (art).

3. **Talking About Your Schedule:** Use phrases like Mi horario (My schedule) and Tengo matemáticas a las ocho (I have math at eight o'clock) to discuss your daily school routine.

4. **Describing Your School Day:** Combine vocabulary and phrases to describe your typical school day, such as Por la mañana, tengo clase de matemáticas (In the morning, I have math class).

5. **Talking About Your Favorite Classes:** Express your preferences with sentences like Mi clase favorita es el arte (My favorite class is art) or Me gusta la clase de matemáticas porque es interesante (I like math class because it's interesting).

Chapter 23

Work and Professions

As you grow up, you might start thinking about what you want to be when you're older. Whether you want to be a teacher, a doctor, or something else, it's important to know how to talk about different jobs and professions in Spanish. In this chapter, you'll learn some basic vocabulary related to work and professions, how to describe what people do for a living, and how to talk about your own future job aspirations.

Basic Vocabulary for Jobs and Professions

Let's start by learning some of the most common words for different jobs and professions. These words will help you describe what people do for work:

El médico/La médica (Pronounced el MEH-dee-koh/lah MEH-dee-kah) - The doctor

El maestro/La maestra (Pronounced el mah-EHS-troh/lah mah-EHS-trah) - The teacher

El policía/La policía (Pronounced el poh-lee-SEE-ah/lah poh-lee-SEE-ah) - The police officer

El bombero/La bombera (Pronounced el bohm-BEH-roh/lah bohmb-EH-rah) - The firefighter

El abogado/La abogada (Pronounced el ah-boh-GAH-doh/lah ah-boh-GAH-dah) - The lawyer

El ingeniero/La ingeniera (Pronounced el een-hehn-YEH-roh/lah een-hehn-YEH-rah) - The engineer

El enfermero/La enfermera (Pronounced el ehn-fehr-MEH-roh/lah ehn-fehr-MEH-rah) - The nurse

El escritor/La escritora (Pronounced el ehs-kree-TOR/lah ehs-kree-TOR-ah) - The writer

El arquitecto/La arquitecta (Pronounced el ahr-kee-TEK-toh/lah ahr-kee-TEK-tah) - The architect

El músico/La música (Pronounced el MOO-see-koh/lah MOO-see-kah) - The musician

These are just a few examples of common jobs and professions. Knowing these words will help you talk about what people do for work and ask others about their jobs.

Describing What People Do

Now that you know some job titles, let's learn how to describe what people do. Here are some useful phrases to help you talk about different professions:

Él es médico. (Pronounced el ess MEH-dee-koh) - He is a doctor.

Ella es maestra. (Pronounced EH-yah ess mah-EHS-trah) - She is a teacher.

Mi papá es ingeniero. (Pronounced mee pah-PAH ess een-hehn-YEH-roh) - My dad is an engineer.

Mi mamá es abogada. (Pronounced mee mah-MAH ess ah-boh-GAH-dah) - My mom is a lawyer.

These sentences show how you can use the job titles you've learned to describe what someone does for a living.

Asking About Jobs and Professions

When you're talking with others, you might want to ask them about their jobs. Here are some phrases to help you ask about someone's profession:

¿Qué haces? (Pronounced keh AH-sehs) - What do you do?

¿En qué trabajas? (Pronounced en keh trah-BAH-hahs) - What do you work as?

¿Dónde trabaja tu papá? (Pronounced DOHN-deh trah-BAH-hah too pah-PAH) - Where does your dad work?

¿Qué quiere ser cuando seas grande? (Pronounced keh KYEH-reh sehr kwahn-doh SEH-ahs GRAHN-deh) - What do you want to be when you grow up?

These questions are great for finding out more about what someone does for work and what they might want to do in the future.

Talking About Workplaces

Every job takes place in a certain environment, whether it's an office, a hospital, or a school. Here are some words to help you describe where people work:

El hospital (Pronounced el ohs-pee-TAHL) - The hospital

La oficina (Pronounced lah oh-fee-SEE-nah) - The office

La escuela (Pronounced lah ehs-KWEH-lah) - The school

La estación de policía (Pronounced lah ehs-tah-SYOHN deh poh-lee-SEE-ah) - The police station

El parque de bomberos (Pronounced el PAR-keh deh bohmb-EH-rohs) - The fire station

Here's how you can use these words in sentences:

Mi mamá trabaja en un hospital. (Pronounced mee mah-MAH trah-BAH-hah en oon ohs-pee-TAHL) - My mom works in a hospital.

El arquitecto trabaja en una oficina. (Pronounced el ahr-kee-TEK-toh trah-BAH-hah en OO-nah oh-fee-SEE-nah) - The architect works in an office.

Mi papá es policía y trabaja en la estación de policía. (Pronounced mee pah-PAH ess poh-lee-SEE-ah ee trah-BAH-hah en lah ehs-tah-SYOHN deh poh-lee-SEE-ah) - My dad is a police officer and works at the police station.

These sentences help you describe where people do their jobs, giving more context to what they do.

Talking About What You Want to Be

It's common to think about what you might want to be when you grow up. Here's how to talk about your future career plans in Spanish:

Quiero ser médico. (Pronounced kee-EH-roh sehr MEH-dee-koh) - I want to be a doctor.

Me gustaría ser ingeniero. (Pronounced meh goos-tah-REE-ah sehr een-hehn-YEH-roh) - I would like to be an engineer.

Prefiero ser maestro. (Pronounced preh-FYEH-roh sehr mah-EHS-troh) - I prefer to be a teacher.

These sentences help you express your goals and what you're interested in doing in the future.

Talking About Different Kinds of Work

Not all work is the same. Some jobs are creative, some involve helping others, and some require working with technology. Here are some words to help you talk about different types of work:

El trabajo creativo (Pronounced el trah-BAH-hoh kreh-ah-TEE-voh) - Creative work

El trabajo técnico (Pronounced el trah-BAH-hoh TEHK-nee-koh) - Technical work

El trabajo social (Pronounced el trah-BAH-hoh soh-SYAL) - Social work

Here are some examples of how you can use these words in sentences:

Me gusta el trabajo creativo, como escribir y dibujar. (Pronounced meh GOOS-tah el trah-BAH-hoh kreh-ah-TEE-voh, KOH-moh ehs-kree-BEER ee dee-boo-HAR) - I like creative work, like writing and drawing.

Mi papá hace trabajo técnico con computadoras. (Pronounced mee pah-PAH AH-seh trah-BAH-hoh TEHK-nee-koh kohn kohm-poo-tah-DOH-rahs) - My dad does technical work with computers.

Quiero hacer trabajo social porque me gusta ayudar a las personas. (Pronounced kee-EH-roh ah-SEHR trah-BAH-hoh soh-SYAL por-KEH meh GOOS-tah ah-yoo-DAHR ah lahss pehr-SOH-nahs) - I want to do social work because I like helping people.

These sentences help you describe what kind of work you're interested in and what you enjoy doing.

Key Points to Remember

1. **Basic Vocabulary for Jobs and Professions:** Learn common job titles in Spanish, such as el médico/la médica (doctor), el maestro/la maestra (teacher), and el ingeniero/la ingeniera (engineer). This vocabulary will help you describe what people do for a living.

2. **Describing What People Do:** Use phrases like Él es médico (He is a doctor) or Ella es maestra (She is a teacher) to describe professions. This is useful for talking about what someone does for work.

3. **Asking About Jobs and Professions:** Learn to ask about someone's job with questions like ¿Qué haces? (What do you do?) or ¿En qué trabajas? (What do you work as?). These questions help you learn more about others' professions.

4. **Talking About Workplaces:** Describe where people work with phrases like Mi mamá trabaja en un hospital (My mom works in a hospital) or El arquitecto trabaja en una oficina (The architect works in an office).

5. **Talking About Future Career Plans:** Express your aspirations with sentences like Quiero ser médico (I want to be a doctor) or Me gustaría ser ingeniero (I would like to be an engineer). This helps you talk about your goals and future plans.

Chapter 24

Animals in Spanish

Learning the names of animals in Spanish is both fun and useful. Whether you're talking about your favorite pet, animals at the zoo, or creatures you see in the wild, knowing how to name them in Spanish helps you describe the world around you. In this chapter, you'll learn the basic vocabulary for different types of animals, how to describe them, and some fun facts about animals in Spanish-speaking countries.

Basic Vocabulary for Animals

Let's start with some of the most common animals you might see every day or hear about often:

El perro (Pronounced el PEH-rroh) - The dog

El gato (Pronounced el GAH-toh) - The cat

El pájaro (Pronounced el PAH-hah-roh) - The bird

El pez (Pronounced el PEHS) - The fish

El conejo (Pronounced el koh-NEH-hoh) - The rabbit

El caballo (Pronounced el kah-BAH-yoh) - The horse

La vaca (Pronounced lah VAH-kah) - The cow

El cerdo (Pronounced el SEHR-doh) - The pig

El elefante (Pronounced el eh-leh-FAHN-teh) - The elephant

El león (Pronounced el leh-OWN) - The lion

These are some of the animals you might talk about most often. Knowing these words will help you describe your pets, animals you see at the zoo, and more.

Talking About Pets

If you have pets, you'll want to know how to talk about them in Spanish. Here are some useful phrases:

Tengo un perro. (Pronounced TEHN-goh oon PEH-rroh) - I have a dog.

Mi gato se llama Luna. (Pronounced mee GAH-toh seh YAH-mah LOO-nah) - My cat's name is Luna.

Mi pez es muy colorido. (Pronounced mee PEHS ess MOO-ee koh-loh-REE-doh) - My fish is very colorful.

These sentences help you describe your pets and tell others about them.

Farm Animals

On a farm, you'll find many different animals. Here are some common farm animals in Spanish:

La oveja (Pronounced lah oh-VEH-hah) - The sheep

La cabra (Pronounced lah KAH-brah) - The goat

El gallo (Pronounced el GAH-yoh) - The rooster

La gallina (Pronounced lah gah-YEE-nah) - The hen

El pato (Pronounced el PAH-toh) - The duck

El burro (Pronounced el BOO-rroh) - The donkey

Here's how you can use these words in sentences:

La vaca da leche. (Pronounced lah VAH-kah dah LEH-cheh) - The cow gives milk.

El gallo canta en la mañana. (Pronounced el GAH-yoh KAHN-tah en lah mah-NYAH-nah) - The rooster crows in the morning.

Tenemos ovejas en la granja. (Pronounced teh-NEH-mohs oh-VEH-hahs en lah GRAHN-hah) - We have sheep on the farm.

These sentences will help you talk about what farm animals do and what they are known for.

Wild Animals

In the wild, you'll find many different types of animals. Here are some common wild animals in Spanish:

El tigre (Pronounced el TEE-greh) - The tiger

El oso (Pronounced el OH-soh) - The bear

El lobo (Pronounced el LOH-boh) - The wolf

El zorro (Pronounced el SOH-rroh) - The fox

El ciervo (Pronounced el SYEHR-voh) - The deer

El cocodrilo (Pronounced el koh-koh-DREE-loh) - The crocodile

Here are some sentences using these words:

El tigre es muy fuerte. (Pronounced el TEE-greh ess MOO-ee FWEHR-teh) - The tiger is very strong.

Los osos viven en el bosque. (Pronounced lohs OH-sohs VEE-vehn en el BOHS-keh) - Bears live in the forest.

El lobo aúlla por la noche. (Pronounced el LOH-boh ow-YAH por lah NOH-cheh) - The wolf howls at night.

These sentences help you describe wild animals and their behaviors.

Animals in Spanish-Speaking Countries

Different Spanish-speaking countries have unique animals. Here are a few examples:

La llama (Pronounced lah YAH-mah) - The llama (found in the Andes mountains)

El jaguar (Pronounced el hah-GWAR) - The jaguar (found in the rainforests of Central and South America)

El quetzal (Pronounced el keht-SAHL) - The quetzal (a brightly colored bird found in Central America)

El armadillo (Pronounced el ahr-mah-DEE-yoh) - The armadillo (found in the Americas, especially in Central and South America)

Here are some examples of how to talk about these animals:

Las llamas viven en las montañas de los Andes. (Pronounced lahs YAH-mahs VEE-vehn en lahs mohn-TAHN-yahs deh lohs AHN-dehs) - Llamas live in the Andes mountains.

El jaguar es un animal fuerte y rápido. (Pronounced el hah-GWAR ess oon ah-nee-MAHL FWEHR-teh ee RAH-pee-doh) - The jaguar is a strong and fast animal.

El quetzal tiene plumas de muchos colores. (Pronounced el keht-SAHL TYEH-neh PLOO-mahs deh MOO-chohs koh-LOH-rehs) - The quetzal has feathers of many colors.

These examples show how you can describe animals that are native to Spanish-speaking countries.

Describing Animals

To talk about animals in more detail, you can describe their size, color, and what they do. Here are some useful words and phrases for describing animals:

Grande (Pronounced GRAHN-deh) - Big

Pequeño (Pronounced peh-KEH-nyoh) - Small

Rápido (Pronounced RAH-pee-doh) - Fast

Lento (Pronounced LEHN-toh) - Slow

Fuerte (Pronounced FWEHR-teh) - Strong

Peligroso (Pronounced peh-lee-GROH-soh) - Dangerous

Here's how you can use these words in sentences:

El elefante es muy grande. (Pronounced el eh-leh-FAHN-teh ess MOO-ee GRAHN-deh) - The elephant is very big.

El ratón es pequeño y rápido. (Pronounced el rah-TOHN ess peh-KEH-nyoh ee RAH-pee-doh) - The mouse is small and fast.

El león es fuerte y peligroso. (Pronounced el leh-OWN ess FWEHR-teh ee peh-lee-GROH-soh) - The lion is strong and dangerous.

These descriptions help you talk about the characteristics of different animals.

Animal Sounds in Spanish

Just like in English, animals make different sounds in Spanish. Here are a few examples:

El perro hace "guau guau". (Pronounced el PEH-rroh AH-seh GWAU GWAU) - The dog goes "woof woof".

El gato hace "miau". (Pronounced el GAH-toh AH-seh MYAU) - The cat goes "meow".

El gallo hace "quiquiriquí". (Pronounced el GAH-yoh AH-seh kee-kee-ree-KEE) - The rooster goes "cock-a-doodle-doo".

These sounds are fun to learn and use when talking about animals.

Key Points to Remember

1. **Basic Vocabulary for Animals:** Learn the names of common animals in Spanish, such as el perro (dog), el gato (cat), and el elefante (elephant). This vocabulary helps you talk about pets, zoo animals, and more.

2. **Talking About Pets:** Use phrases like Tengo un perro (I have a dog) or Mi gato se llama Luna (My cat's name is Luna) to describe and talk about your pets.

3. **Farm and Wild Animals:** Familiarize yourself with words for farm animals like la vaca (cow) and el gallo (rooster), as well as wild animals like el tigre (tiger) and el oso (bear), to describe animals in different environments.

4. **Describing Animals:** Use descriptive words like grande (big), pequeño (small), and rápido (fast) to talk about the size, speed, and other characteristics of animals.

5. **Animal Sounds in Spanish:** Learn how animal sounds are expressed in Spanish, such as el perro hace "guau guau" (the dog goes "woof woof") and el gallo hace "quiquiriquí" (the rooster goes "cock-a-doodle-doo"). These are fun and practical when talking about animals.

Chapter 25

Basic Sentence Structure

When you start learning Spanish, one of the most important things to understand is how to put together sentences. A sentence is a group of words that express a complete thought. In Spanish, just like in English, sentences have a basic structure that you need to follow. This structure usually includes a subject, a verb, and sometimes an object. In this chapter, we'll learn about the basic sentence structure in Spanish and how you can start building sentences on your own.

The Basic Structure: Subject + Verb + Object

The most common sentence structure in Spanish is similar to English: Subject + Verb + Object. Let's break down what each part means:

Subject (Sujeto): The subject is the person, place, or thing that is doing the action. For example, in the sentence "The cat sleeps," the subject is "the cat."

Verb (Verbo): The verb is the action word in the sentence. It tells us what the subject is doing. In the sentence "The cat sleeps," the verb is "sleeps."

Object (Objeto): The object is the person, place, or thing that receives the action of the verb. Not all sentences have an object, but when they do, it usually comes after the verb. For example, in the sentence "The cat eats the food," the object is "the food."

Here's how this looks in a simple Spanish sentence:

El gato come. (Pronounced el GAH-toh KOH-meh) - The cat eats.

In this sentence, "El gato" (the cat) is the subject, and "come" (eats) is the verb. There's no object in this sentence, so it's just Subject + Verb.

If we add an object, the sentence becomes:

El gato come la comida. (Pronounced el GAH-toh KOH-meh lah koh-MEE-dah) - The cat eats the food.

Now, "la comida" (the food) is the object of the sentence, so we have Subject + Verb + Object.

Word Order in Spanish

In Spanish, the word order is generally similar to English, but there are some important differences to keep in mind. For example, in English, adjectives (words that describe nouns) usually come before the noun, like in "a big house." But in Spanish, adjectives usually come after the noun:

Una casa grande. (Pronounced OO-nah KAH-sah GRAHN-deh) - A big house.

So, the order is Noun + Adjective in Spanish, which is the opposite of English. Let's look at another example:

El perro pequeño. (Pronounced el PEH-rroh peh-KEH-nyoh) - The small dog.

Here, "perro" (dog) is the noun, and "pequeño" (small) is the adjective, so the adjective comes after the noun.

Making Sentences Negative

To make a sentence negative in Spanish, you simply add "no" before the verb. This is like adding "not" in English:

El gato no come. (Pronounced el GAH-toh noh KOH-meh) - The cat does not eat.

In this sentence, "no" comes before the verb "come" to make it negative. Let's try another example:

No tengo dinero. (Pronounced noh TEHN-goh dee-NEH-roh) - I don't have money.

Here, "no" is added before "tengo" (I have) to say that you don't have money.

Asking Questions in Spanish

In Spanish, you can turn a statement into a question by simply changing your intonation (the way your voice rises at the end of a sentence). You can also use question words like "¿Qué?" (What?), "¿Cómo?" (How?), and "¿Dónde?" (Where?). Let's see how this works:

El gato come. (Pronounced el GAH-toh KOH-meh) - The cat eats. (Statement)

¿El gato come? (Pronounced el GAH-toh KOH-meh) - Does the cat eat? (Question)

Notice that the word order doesn't change, but the sentence becomes a question because of the rising intonation. If you use a question word, the sentence might look like this:

¿Qué come el gato? (Pronounced keh KOH-meh el GAH-toh) - What does the cat eat?

Here, "¿Qué?" (What?) is added at the beginning of the sentence to ask a specific question about what the cat eats.

Subject Pronouns in Spanish

In Spanish, the subject of a sentence can often be left out because the verb endings usually indicate who the subject is. For example:

Como pan. (Pronounced KOH-moh pahn) - I eat bread.

Here, the verb "como" already tells us that the subject is "I" (yo), so you don't need to say "yo como pan" unless you want to emphasize that you are the one eating.

However, you can include the subject pronoun if you want to make it clear who is doing the action. Here are some subject pronouns in Spanish:

Yo (Pronounced yoh) - I

Tú (Pronounced too) - You (informal)

Él (Pronounced el) - He

Ella (Pronounced EH-yah) - She

Nosotros/Nosotras (Pronounced noh-SOH-trohs/noh-SOH-trahs) - We (masculine/feminine)

Ellos/Ellas (Pronounced EH-yohs/EH-yahs) - They (masculine/feminine)

Here's how you might use these in a sentence:

Yo como pizza. (Pronounced yoh KOH-moh PEET-sah) - I eat pizza.

Ella estudia mucho. (Pronounced EH-yah ehs-TOO-dyah MOO-choh) - She studies a lot.

Nosotros jugamos al fútbol. (Pronounced noh-SOH-trohs hoo-GAH-mohs ahl FOOT-bol) - We play soccer.

Key Points to Remember

1. **Basic Sentence Structure:** The most common sentence structure in Spanish is Subject + Verb + Object, similar to English. Example: El gato come la comida (The cat eats the food).

2. **Word Order in Spanish:** Adjectives typically follow nouns in Spanish, unlike English. Example: Una casa grande (A big house).

3. **Making Sentences Negative:** To make a sentence negative in Spanish, add "no"

before the verb. Example: El gato no come (The cat does not eat).

4. **Asking Questions:** You can ask questions by changing intonation or adding question words. Example: ¿Qué come el gato? (What does the cat eat?).

5. **Subject Pronouns:** Subject pronouns in Spanish are often optional since verb endings indicate the subject. Example: Como pan (I eat bread) without needing to say "Yo."

Chapter 26

The Present Tense: Regular Verbs

In Spanish, verbs are words that describe actions, like "to eat" (comer), "to run" (correr), or "to live" (vivir). When you want to talk about actions happening right now, you use the present tense. In this chapter, you'll learn how to use regular verbs in the present tense, which are verbs that follow a predictable pattern when they change from their base form to match the subject of the sentence.

Understanding Regular Verbs

Regular verbs in Spanish are divided into three categories based on their endings: "-ar," "-er," and "-ir." Each category has its own set of rules for how to change the verb to match the subject in the present tense.

Let's start by looking at a few examples of regular verbs:

Hablar (Pronounced ah-BLAR) - To speak (an "-ar" verb)

Comer (Pronounced koh-MEHR) - To eat (an "-er" verb)

Vivir (Pronounced vee-VEER) - To live (an "-ir" verb)

These verbs are called regular because they follow the same pattern when you conjugate them (change their form) in the present tense.

Conjugating "-ar" Verbs in the Present Tense

To conjugate a regular "-ar" verb in the present tense, you start with the base form of the verb (called the stem) and then add the correct ending based on the subject. Here's how it works using the verb "hablar" (to speak):

- **Yo hablo** (Pronounced yoh AH-bloh) - I speak

- **Tú hablas** (Pronounced too AH-blahs) - You speak

- **Él/Ella/Usted habla** (Pronounced el/eh-yah/oo-STEHD AH-blah) - He/She/You (formal) speaks

- **Nosotros/Nosotras hablamos** (Pronounced noh-SOH-trohs/noh-SOH-trahs ah-BLAH-mohs) - We speak

- **Vosotros/Vosotras habláis** (Pronounced boh-SOH-trohs/boh-SOH-trahs ah-BLAYS) - You all speak (used mainly in Spain)

- **Ellos/Ellas/Ustedes hablan** (Pronounced EH-yohs/EH-yahs/oo-STEH-dehs AH-blahn) - They/You all speak

Notice how the ending of the verb changes depending on who is doing the action. Here are the endings you add to the stem for regular "-ar" verbs:

- Yo: -o

- Tú: -as

- Él/Ella/Usted: -a

- Nosotros/Nosotras: -amos

- Vosotros/Vosotras: -áis

- Ellos/Ellas/Ustedes: -an

For example, if you want to say "We speak," you would take the stem "habl-" and add "-amos" to get "hablamos."

Conjugating "-er" Verbs in the Present Tense

Now let's look at how to conjugate regular "-er" verbs. The process is very similar, but the endings are different. Here's how it works using the verb "comer" (to eat):

- **Yo como** (Pronounced yoh KOH-moh) - I eat

- **Tú comes** (Pronounced too KOH-mehs) - You eat

- **Él/Ella/Usted come** (Pronounced el/eh-yah/oo-STEHD KOH-meh) - He/She/You (formal) eats

- **Nosotros/Nosotras comemos** (Pronounced noh-SOH-trohs/noh-SOH-trahs koh-MEH-mohs) - We eat

- **Vosotros/Vosotras coméis** (Pronounced boh-SOH-trohs/boh-SOH-trahs koh-MAYS) -

You all eat (used mainly in Spain)

- **Ellos/Ellas/Ustedes comen** (Pronounced EH-yohs/EH-yahs/oo-STEH-dehs KOH-mehn) - They/You all eat

Here are the endings you add to the stem for regular "-er" verbs:

- Yo: -o
- Tú: -es
- Él/Ella/Usted: -e
- Nosotros/Nosotras: -emos
- Vosotros/Vosotras: -éis
- Ellos/Ellas/Ustedes: -en

For example, if you want to say "They eat," you would take the stem "com-" and add "-en" to get "comen."

Conjugating "-ir" Verbs in the Present Tense

Finally, let's look at how to conjugate regular "-ir" verbs. The process is again similar, but with slightly different endings. Here's how it works using the verb "vivir" (to live):

- **Yo vivo** (Pronounced yoh VEE-voh) - I live

- **Tú vives** (Pronounced too VEE-vehs) - You live

- **Él/Ella/Usted vive** (Pronounced el/eh-yah/oo-STEHD VEE-veh) - He/She/You (formal) lives

- **Nosotros/Nosotras vivimos** (Pronounced noh-SOH-trohs/noh-SOH-trahs vee-VEE-mohs) - We live

- **Vosotros/Vosotras vivís** (Pronounced boh-SOH-trohs/boh-SOH-trahs vee-VEES) - You all live (used mainly in Spain)

- **Ellos/Ellas/Ustedes viven** (Pronounced EH-yohs/EH-yahs/oo-STEH-dehs VEE-vehn) - They/You all live

Here are the endings you add to the stem for regular "-ir" verbs:

- Yo: -o
- Tú: -es
- Él/Ella/Usted: -e
- Nosotros/Nosotras: -imos
- Vosotros/Vosotras: -ís
- Ellos/Ellas/Ustedes: -en

For example, if you want to say "We live," you would take the stem "viv-" and add "-imos" to get "vivimos."

Using Regular Verbs in Sentences

Now that you know how to conjugate regular verbs in the present tense, you can start using them in sentences. Here are some examples:

Yo hablo español. (Pronounced yoh AH-bloh ehs-pah-NYOHL) - I speak Spanish.

Nosotros comemos pizza. (Pronounced noh-SOH-trohs koh-MEH-mohs PEET-sah) - We eat pizza.

Ellos viven en una casa grande. (Pronounced EH-yohs VEE-vehn en OO-nah KAH-sah GRAHN-deh) - They live in a big house.

These sentences show how you can use regular verbs to talk about what you or others are doing right now.

Common Regular Verbs to Know

Here are some other common regular verbs that you might find useful as you start speaking and writing in Spanish:

Aprender (Pronounced ah-prehn-DEHR) - To learn

Escribir (Pronounced ehs-kree-BEER) - To write

Escuchar (Pronounced ehs-koo-CHAR) - To listen

Leer (Pronounced leh-EHR) - To read

Caminar (Pronounced kah-mee-NAR) - To walk

You can practice conjugating these verbs in the same way we've practiced with "hablar," "comer," and "vivir."

Key Points to Remember

1. **Understanding Regular Verbs:** Regular verbs in Spanish fall into three categories based on their endings: "-ar," "-er," and "-ir." These verbs follow predictable patterns when conjugated in the present tense.

2. **Conjugating "-ar" Verbs:** For "-ar" verbs like "hablar," the present tense endings are: -o, -as, -a, -amos, -áis, -an. Example: Yo hablo (I speak).

3. **Conjugating "-er" Verbs:** For "-er" verbs like "comer," the present tense endings are: -o, -es, -e, -emos, -éis, -en. Example: Tú comes (You eat).

4. **Conjugating "-ir" Verbs:** For "-ir" verbs like "vivir," the present tense endings are: -o, -es, -e, -imos, -ís, -en. Example: Nosotros vivimos (We live).

5. **Using Regular Verbs in Sentences:** Conjugated regular verbs can be used to describe present actions. Example: Ellos viven en una casa grande (They live in a big house).

Chapter 27

The Present Tense: Irregular Verbs

In the last chapter, you learned about regular verbs in Spanish and how to conjugate them in the present tense. However, not all verbs follow the regular patterns. Some verbs are irregular, meaning they change in different ways when you conjugate them. In this chapter, you'll learn about some common irregular verbs in the present tense and how to use them correctly.

What Makes a Verb Irregular?

Irregular verbs don't follow the normal conjugation patterns that you learned with regular verbs. This means that you can't simply take the stem of the verb and add the usual endings. Instead, you have to learn how each irregular verb changes on its own.

Let's start with one of the most important irregular verbs in Spanish: **ser** (to be).

Conjugating "Ser" in the Present Tense

The verb "ser" is used to talk about who someone is or what something is like. It's an essential verb in Spanish, but it's also irregular, which means its conjugation is different from the regular "-er" verbs. Here's how "ser" is conjugated in the present tense:

- **Yo soy** (Pronounced yoh SOY) - I am

- **Tú eres** (Pronounced too EH-rehs) - You are

- **Él/Ella/Usted es** (Pronounced el/EH-yah/oo-STEHD ess) - He/She/You (formal) is/are

- **Nosotros/Nosotras somos** (Pronounced noh-SOH-trohs/noh-SOH-trahs SOH-mohs) - We are

- **Vosotros/Vosotras sois** (Pronounced boh-SOH-trohs/boh-SOH-trahs SOYS) - You all are (used mainly in Spain)

- **Ellos/Ellas/Ustedes son** (Pronounced EH-yohs/EH-yahs/oo-STEH-dehs SOHN) -

They/You all are

For example, you might say:

Yo soy estudiante. (Pronounced yoh SOY ehs-too-DYAHN-teh) - I am a student.

Ella es mi amiga. (Pronounced EH-yah ess mee ah-MEE-gah) - She is my friend.

Notice how "ser" changes completely in the present tense depending on the subject. This is what makes it an irregular verb.

Conjugating "Estar" in the Present Tense

Another important irregular verb is "estar," which also means "to be." However, "estar" is used to talk about temporary states or locations. Here's how "estar" is conjugated in the present tense:

- **Yo estoy** (Pronounced yoh ehs-TOY) - I am

- **Tú estás** (Pronounced too ehs-TAHS) - You are

- **Él/Ella/Usted está** (Pronounced el/EH-yah/oo-STEHD ehs-TAH) - He/She/You (formal) is/are

- **Nosotros/Nosotras estamos** (Pronounced noh-SOH-trohs/noh-SOH-trahs ehs-TAH-mohs) - We are

- **Vosotros/Vosotras estáis** (Pronounced boh-SOH-trohs/boh-SOH-trahs ehs-TAH-ees) - You all are (used mainly in Spain)

- **Ellos/Ellas/Ustedes están** (Pronounced EH-yohs/EH-yahs/oo-STEH-dehs ehs-TAHN) - They/You all are

For example, you might say:

Yo estoy en la escuela. (Pronounced yoh ehs-TOY en lah ehs-KWEH-lah) - I am at school.

Nosotros estamos cansados. (Pronounced noh-SOH-trohs ehs-TAH-mohs kahn-SAH-dohs) - We are tired.

Like "ser," the verb "estar" changes its form depending on the subject, making it an irregular verb.

Conjugating "Ir" in the Present Tense

The verb "ir" means "to go," and it's another irregular verb that you'll use often. Here's how "ir" is conjugated in the present tense:

- **Yo voy** (Pronounced yoh BOY) - I go

- **Tú vas** (Pronounced too VAHS) - You go

- **Él/Ella/Usted va** (Pronounced el/EH-yah/oo-STEHD VAH) - He/She/You (formal) goes/go

- **Nosotros/Nosotras vamos** (Pronounced noh-SOH-trohs/noh-SOH-trahs VAH-mohs) - We go

- **Vosotros/Vosotras vais** (Pronounced boh-SOH-trohs/boh-SOH-trahs VAH-ees) - You all go (used mainly in Spain)

- **Ellos/Ellas/Ustedes van** (Pronounced EH-yohs/EH-yahs/oo-STEH-dehs VAHN) - They/You all go

For example, you might say:

Yo voy al parque. (Pronounced yoh BOY ahl PAR-keh) - I go to the park.

Ellos van a la tienda. (Pronounced EH-yohs VAHN ah lah TYEHN-dah) - They go to the store.

Since "ir" doesn't follow the regular patterns, it's important to memorize how it changes in the present tense.

Conjugating "Tener" in the Present Tense

The verb "tener" means "to have" and is another common irregular verb. Here's how "tener" is conjugated in the present tense:

- **Yo tengo** (Pronounced yoh TEHN-goh) - I have

- **Tú tienes** (Pronounced too TYEH-nehs) - You have

- **Él/Ella/Usted tiene** (Pronounced el/EH-yah/oo-STEHD TYEH-neh) - He/She/You (formal) has/have

- **Nosotros/Nosotras tenemos** (Pronounced noh-SOH-trohs/noh-SOH-trahs teh-NEH-mohs) - We have

- **Vosotros/Vosotras tenéis** (Pronounced boh-SOH-trohs/boh-SOH-trahs teh-NEH-ees) - You all have (used mainly in Spain)

- **Ellos/Ellas/Ustedes tienen** (Pronounced EH-yohs/EH-yahs/oo-STEH-dehs TYEH-nehn) - They/You all have

For example, you might say:

Yo tengo un perro. (Pronounced yoh TEHN-goh oon PEH-rroh) - I have a dog.

Ella tiene dos hermanos. (Pronounced EH-yah TYEH-neh dohs ehr-MAH-nohs) - She has two brothers.

The verb "tener" is irregular because it changes more than just the ending when conjugated.

Other Common Irregular Verbs

Here are a few more common irregular verbs that you should be familiar with:

Hacer (Pronounced ah-SEHR) - To do/make

- **Yo hago** (Pronounced yoh AH-goh) - I do/make

- **Tú haces** (Pronounced too AH-sehs) - You do/make

- **Él/Ella/Usted hace** (Pronounced el/EH-yah/oo-STEHD AH-seh) - He /She/You (formal) does/do/makes/make

- **Nosotros/Nosotras hacemos** (Pronounced noh-SOH-trohs/noh-SOH-trahs ah-SEH-mohs) - We do/make

- **Vosotros/Vosotras hacéis** (Pronounced boh-SOH-trohs/boh-SOH-trahs ah-SEH-ees) - You all do/make (used mainly in Spain)

- **Ellos/Ellas/Ustedes hacen** (Pronounced EH-yohs/EH-yahs/oo-STEH-dehs AH-sehn) - They/You all do/make

Decir (Pronounced deh-SEER) - To say/tell

- **Yo digo** (Pronounced yoh DEE-goh) - I say/tell

- **Tú dices** (Pronounced too DEE-sehs) - You say/tell

- **Él/Ella/Usted dice** (Pronounced el/EH-yah/oo-STEHD DEE-seh) - He/She/You (formal) says/say/tells/tell

- **Nosotros/Nosotras decimos** (Pronounced noh-SOH-trohs/noh-SOH-trahs deh-SEE-mohs) - We say/tell

- **Vosotros/Vosotras decís** (Pronounced boh-SOH-trohs/boh-SOH-trahs deh-SEES) - You all say/tell (used mainly in Spain)

- **Ellos/Ellas/Ustedes dicen** (Pronounced EH-yohs/EH-yahs/oo-STEH-dehs DEE-sehn) - They/You all say/tell

These verbs are irregular because they change in unique ways that don't follow the regular patterns.

Key Points to Remember

1. **Understanding Irregular Verbs:** Irregular verbs in Spanish do not follow the regular conjugation patterns, requiring you to learn their unique forms individually.

2. **Conjugating "Ser":** The verb "ser" (to be) is highly irregular and essential for describing identity and characteristics. Example: Yo soy (I am), Ellos son (They are).

3. **Conjugating "Estar":** "Estar" (to be) is another irregular verb used for temporary states and locations. Example: Yo estoy (I am), Nosotros estamos (We are).

4. **Conjugating "Ir" and "Tener":** The verbs "ir" (to go) and "tener" (to have) are frequently used irregular verbs with distinct conjugations. Example: Yo voy (I go), Él tiene (He has).

5. **Other Common Irregular Verbs:** Verbs like "hacer" (to do/make) and "decir" (to say/tell) are also irregular and change significantly in the present tense. Example: Yo hago (I do/make), Tú dices (You say/tell).

Chapter 28

Reflexive Verbs

In Spanish, some verbs are reflexive, meaning that the action of the verb reflects back on the person doing it. In other words, the person doing the action is also the person receiving the action. Reflexive verbs are an important part of Spanish and are used frequently in everyday conversation. In this chapter, we'll learn what reflexive verbs are, how to conjugate them, and how to use them in sentences.

What Are Reflexive Verbs?

A reflexive verb is a verb that is used when the subject of the sentence is both performing and receiving the action. In English, this idea is often expressed by using words like "myself," "yourself," or "themselves." In Spanish, reflexive verbs have a special pronoun that is added to show that the action is being done to oneself.

For example, the verb "lavar" means "to wash," but "lavarse" means "to wash oneself." The reflexive pronoun "se" at the end of the verb indicates that the action is reflexive.

Here are some common reflexive verbs:

Levantarse (Pronounced leh-vahn-TAR-seh) - To get up

Ducharse (Pronounced doo-CHAR-seh) - To take a shower

Vestirse (Pronounced behs-TEER-seh) - To get dressed

Peinarse (Pronounced pay-NAR-seh) - To comb one's hair

Acostarse (Pronounced ah-kohs-TAR-seh) - To go to bed

These verbs are reflexive because the person doing the action is also receiving the action.

Reflexive Pronouns

To use reflexive verbs correctly, you need to use reflexive pronouns. These pronouns come before the verb and match the subject of the sentence. Here are the reflexive pronouns in Spanish:

- **Me** (Pronounced meh) - Myself

- **Te** (Pronounced teh) - Yourself (informal)

- **Se** (Pronounced seh) - Himself, Herself, Yourself (formal), Themselves

- **Nos** (Pronounced nohs) - Ourselves

- **Os** (Pronounced ohs) - Yourselves (used mainly in Spain)

- **Se** (Pronounced seh) - Themselves, Yourselves (formal)

These pronouns are used with reflexive verbs to indicate who is performing and receiving the action.

Conjugating Reflexive Verbs

When you conjugate reflexive verbs in the present tense, you follow the same steps as with regular verbs, but you also add the correct reflexive pronoun before the verb. Let's look at how to conjugate the reflexive verb "levantarse" (to get up):

- **Yo me levanto** (Pronounced yoh meh leh-VAHN-toh) - I get up

- **Tú te levantas** (Pronounced too teh leh-VAHN-tahs) - You get up

- **Él/Ella/Usted se levanta** (Pronounced el/EH-yah/oo-STEHD seh leh-VAHN-tah) - He/She/You (formal) gets up

- **Nosotros/Nosotras nos levantamos** (Pronounced noh-SOH-trohs/noh-SOH-trahs nohs leh-vahn-TAH-mohs) - We get up

- **Vosotros/Vosotras os levantáis** (Pronounced boh-SOH-trohs/boh-SOH-trahs ohs leh-vahn-TAYS) - You all get up (used mainly in Spain)

- **Ellos/Ellas/Ustedes se levantan** (Pronounced EH-yohs/EH-yahs/oo-STEH-dehs seh leh-VAHN-tahn) - They/You all get up

As you can see, the verb "levantarse" is conjugated just like any regular "-ar" verb, but the reflexive pronoun is added before the verb to show that the action is being done to oneself.

Let's look at another example with the verb "ducharse" (to take a shower):

- **Yo me ducho** (Pronounced yoh meh DOO-choh) - I take a shower

- **Tú te duchas** (Pronounced too teh DOO-chahs) - You take a shower

- **Él/Ella/Usted se ducha** (Pronounced el/EH-yah/oo-STEHD seh DOO-chah) - He/She/You (formal) takes a shower

- **Nosotros/Nosotras nos duchamos** (Pronounced noh-SOH-trohs/noh-SOH-trahs nohs doo-CHAH-mohs) - We take a shower

- **Vosotros/Vosotras os ducháis** (Pronounced boh-SOH-trohs/boh-SOH-trahs ohs doo-CHAYS) - You all take a shower (used mainly in Spain)

- **Ellos/Ellas/Ustedes se duchan** (Pronounced EH-yohs/EH-yahs/oo-STEH-dehs seh DOO-chahn) - They/You all take a shower

Again, the verb is conjugated like a regular "-ar" verb, but the reflexive pronoun shows that the action is done to the subject.

Using Reflexive Verbs in Sentences

Now that you know how to conjugate reflexive verbs, let's see how to use them in sentences:

Yo me levanto a las siete. (Pronounced yoh meh leh-VAHN-toh ah lahss SYEH-teh) - I get up at seven.

Ella se viste rápidamente. (Pronounced EH-yah seh VEES-teh RAH-pee-dah-men-teh) - She gets dressed quickly.

Nosotros nos acostamos temprano. (Pronounced noh-SOH-trohs nohs ah-kohs-TAH-mohs tehm-PRAH-noh) - We go to bed early.

In these sentences, the reflexive pronoun matches the subject, and the verb is conjugated to show that the action is being done by and to the subject.

Some Common Reflexive Verbs

Here are a few more common reflexive verbs that you might find useful:

Afeitarse (Pronounced ah-fay-TAR-seh) - To shave

Maquillarse (Pronounced mah-kee-YAR-seh) - To put on makeup

Sentarse (Pronounced sehn-TAR-seh) - To sit down

Despertarse (Pronounced dehs-pehr-TAR-seh) - To wake up

Bañarse (Pronounced bah-NYAR-seh) - To take a bath

You can conjugate these verbs using the same pattern you learned, adding the correct reflexive pronoun to match the subject.

When to Use Reflexive Verbs

Reflexive verbs are used in many different situations. Here are a few examples of when you might use them:

- **Daily routines:** Reflexive verbs are often used to describe daily activities that you do to yourself, like getting up, brushing your teeth, and getting dressed.

- **Personal care:** Many reflexive verbs describe actions related to taking care of yourself, such as showering, shaving, or putting on makeup.

- **Emotions and feelings:** Reflexive verbs can also be used to describe changes in emotion or state of mind, like getting angry (enojarse) or feeling happy (alegrarse).

Understanding when to use reflexive verbs will help you talk about your own actions.

Key Points to Remember

1. **Definition of Reflexive Verbs:** Reflexive verbs indicate actions where the subject is both performing and receiving the action. They are marked by the reflexive pronoun "se" attached to the verb, such as in "lavarse" (to wash oneself).

2. **Reflexive Pronouns:** Reflexive verbs require specific pronouns that match the subject. These pronouns are: me (myself), te (yourself), se (himself, herself, themselves), nos (ourselves), os (yourselves in Spain).

3. **Conjugating Reflexive Verbs:** To conjugate reflexive verbs in the present tense, you use the appropriate reflexive pronoun and then conjugate the verb according to regular verb rules, like "me levanto" (I get up) or "nos duchamos" (we shower).

4. **Usage in Sentences:** Reflexive verbs are commonly used to describe daily routines, personal care, and emotional states. For example, "Ella se viste" (She gets dressed) or "Nosotros nos acostamos" (We go to bed).

5. **Common Reflexive Verbs:** Key reflexive verbs include levantarse (to get up), ducharse (to shower), afeitarse (to shave), and despertarse (to wake up), which are essential for describing personal routines and actions.

Chapter 29

Expressing Likes and Dislikes

Being able to talk about what you like and dislike is an important part of learning any language. In Spanish, there are special ways to express your preferences, whether you're talking about your favorite food, hobbies, or activities. In this chapter, you'll learn how to say what you like and don't like in Spanish, as well as how to ask others about their preferences.

Using "Gustar" to Express Likes

In Spanish, the verb "gustar" is commonly used to express likes and preferences. However, "gustar" works a little differently than most verbs you've learned so far. Instead of saying "I like" something directly, you're actually saying that something "is pleasing to me." Because of this, the structure of the sentence is different from English.

Let's start with a simple example:

Me gusta el helado. (Pronounced meh GOOS-tah el eh-LAH-doh) - I like ice cream.

In this sentence, "me" is the pronoun that means "to me," and "gusta" is the form of the verb "gustar." The subject of the sentence is "el helado" (ice cream), so the sentence literally means "Ice cream is pleasing to me."

If you want to say that you like something plural, like "books," you need to change "gusta" to "gustan":

Me gustan los libros. (Pronounced meh GOOS-tahn lohs LEE-brohs) - I like books.

Here, "libros" (books) is plural, so "gusta" changes to "gustan" to agree with the plural noun. The pronoun "me" stays the same because you're still talking about something that is pleasing to you.

Changing the Pronoun

To talk about what someone else likes, you change the pronoun. Here are the pronouns you'll use with "gustar":

- **Me** (Pronounced meh) - To me

- **Te** (Pronounced teh) - To you (informal)

- **Le** (Pronounced leh) - To him/her/you (formal)

- **Nos** (Pronounced nohs) - To us

- **Os** (Pronounced ohs) - To you all (informal, used mainly in Spain)

- **Les** (Pronounced lehs) - To them/you all

Here's how you can use these pronouns with "gustar":

Te gusta la música. (Pronounced teh GOOS-tah lah MOO-see-kah) - You like music.

Le gustan las películas. (Pronounced leh GOOS-tahn lahss peh-LEE-kool-ahs) - He/She/You (formal) likes movies.

Nos gusta el fútbol. (Pronounced nohs GOOS-tah el FOOT-bol) - We like soccer.

As you can see, the verb "gustar" changes depending on whether the thing you like is singular or plural, but the pronoun changes depending on who likes it.

Expressing Dislikes

To say that you don't like something, you simply add "no" before the pronoun. This makes the sentence negative:

No me gusta el brócoli. (Pronounced noh meh GOOS-tah el BROH-koh-lee) - I don't like broccoli.

No les gustan los gatos. (Pronounced noh lehs GOOS-tahn lohs GAH-tohs) - They don't like cats.

Adding "no" before "me," "te," "le," etc., changes the meaning of the sentence to express a dislike.

Talking About What You Love

In addition to "gustar," you can use the verb "encantar" to talk about things you love. "Encantar" works just like "gustar" but is stronger, meaning "to love" or "to really like."

Here's how you use "encantar":

Me encanta el chocolate. (Pronounced meh ehn-KAHN-tah el choh-koh-LAH-teh) - I love chocolate.

Nos encantan los animales. (Pronounced nohs ehn-KAHN-tahn lohs ah-nee-MAH-lehs) - We love animals.

Just like with "gustar," you change the form of "encantar" to agree with the thing you love, and the pronoun changes to show who loves it.

Asking About Preferences

To ask someone what they like or dislike, you can use the same structure but turn it into a question:

¿Te gusta la pizza? (Pronounced teh GOOS-tah lah PEET-sah) - Do you like pizza?

¿Les gustan los deportes? (Pronounced lehs GOOS-tahn lohs deh-POR-tehs) - Do they/you all like sports?

You can also ask someone what they love using "encantar":

¿Te encanta leer? (Pronounced teh ehn-KAHN-tah leh-EHR) - Do you love to read?

These questions help you learn about someone's preferences and start conversations about things you both like.

Talking About Multiple Likes

If you like more than one thing, you can list them in the same sentence. Here's how you can do that:

Me gustan los perros y los gatos. (Pronounced meh GOOS-tahn lohs PEH-rrohs ee lohs GAH-tohs) - I like dogs and cats.

Nos gusta bailar y cantar. (Pronounced nohs GOOS-tah by-LAHR ee kahn-TAR) - We like to dance and sing.

When listing multiple likes, make sure the verb agrees with the first noun in the list.

Expressing Preferences

Sometimes you might want to say that you like something more than something else. Here's how you can express preferences in Spanish:

Prefiero el helado de chocolate. (Pronounced preh-FYEH-roh el eh-LAH-doh deh choh-koh-LAH-teh) - I prefer chocolate ice cream.

Nos gusta más el verano que el invierno. (Pronounced nohs GOOS-tah mahs el veh-RAH-noh keh el eem-VYEHR-noh) - We like summer more than winter.

The word "prefiero" comes from the verb "preferir," which means "to prefer." You can use it to say what you like better, and "más...que" means "more...than" to compare two things.

Giving Reasons for Your Likes and Dislikes

When talking about your preferences, it's often interesting to explain why you like or dislike something. Here are some phrases that can help you do that:

Porque es divertido. (Pronounced por-KEH ess dee-ver-TEE-doh) - Because it's fun.

Porque no me gusta el sabor. (Pronounced por-KEH noh meh GOOS-tah el sah-BOR) - Because I don't like the taste.

Porque me hace sentir bien. (Pronounced por-KEH meh AH-seh sehn-TEER byen) - Because it makes me feel good.

These reasons can be added after you express your likes or dislikes to give more information and start deeper conversations.

Key Points to Remember

1. **Using "Gustar" to Express Likes:** In Spanish, "gustar" is used to express likes, where the structure translates to "something is pleasing to me." For example, "Me gusta el helado" means "I like ice cream."

2. **Changing the Pronoun:** The pronoun before "gustar" changes based on who likes something, such as me (to me), te (to you), and le (to him/her). The verb "gustar" itself changes to agree with the number of the thing liked, like "gusta" (singular) or "gustan" (plural).

3. **Expressing Dislikes:** To say you don't like something, add "no" before the pronoun, as in "No me gusta el brócoli," meaning "I don't like broccoli."

4. **Talking About What You Love with "Encantar":** Use "encantar" to express love or strong likes, following the same structure as "gustar." For example, "Me encanta el chocolate" means "I love chocolate."

5. **Asking About Preferences:** To ask others about their likes or dislikes, use the structure with "gustar" or "encantar" in a question form, like "¿Te gusta la pizza?" (Do you like pizza?) or "¿Te encanta leer?" (Do you love to read?).

Chapter 30

Talking About the Past: Preterite Tense

When you want to talk about things that happened in the past in Spanish, you use the preterite tense. The preterite tense is used to describe actions that were completed at a specific point in time. In this chapter, you'll learn how to form the preterite tense, how to use it in sentences, and how to talk about past events clearly and effectively.

What Is the Preterite Tense?

The preterite tense is one of the past tenses in Spanish. It's used to talk about actions that are seen as completed, meaning they started and finished at a specific time in the past. For example, if you want to say "I ate pizza yesterday," you would use the preterite tense because eating pizza is an action that was completed in the past.

Let's start by learning how to form the preterite tense for regular verbs.

Conjugating Regular "-ar" Verbs in the Preterite Tense

To conjugate regular "-ar" verbs in the preterite tense, you take the stem of the verb (the part of the verb that stays the same) and add the correct ending for the subject. Here's how it works with the verb "hablar" (to speak):

- **Yo hablé** (Pronounced yoh ah-BLEH) - I spoke

- **Tú hablaste** (Pronounced too ah-BLAHS-teh) - You spoke

- **Él/Ella/Usted habló** (Pronounced el/EH-yah/oo-STEHD ah-BLOH) - He/She/You (formal) spoke

- **Nosotros/Nosotras hablamos** (Pronounced noh-SOH-trohs/noh-SOH-trahs ah-BLAH-mohs) - We spoke

- **Vosotros/Vosotras hablasteis** (Pronounced boh-SOH-trohs/boh-SOH-trahs ah-BLAHS-teys) - You all spoke (used mainly in Spain)

- **Ellos/Ellas/Ustedes hablaron** (Pronounced EH-yohs/EH-yahs/oo-STEH-dehs ah-BLAH-rohn) - They/You all spoke

Here are the endings you add to the stem of regular "-ar" verbs:

- Yo: -é

- Tú: -aste

- Él/Ella/Usted: -ó

- Nosotros/Nosotras: -amos

- Vosotros/Vosotras: -asteis

- Ellos/Ellas/Ustedes: -aron

For example, if you want to say "I spoke with my friend," you would say:

Yo hablé con mi amigo. (Pronounced yoh ah-BLEH kohn mee ah-MEE-goh) - I spoke with my friend.

Conjugating Regular "-er" and "-ir" Verbs in the Preterite Tense

Regular "-er" and "-ir" verbs share the same endings in the preterite tense. Let's look at how to conjugate the verb "comer" (to eat) and "vivir" (to live):

- **Yo comí** (Pronounced yoh koh-MEE) - I ate

- **Tú comiste** (Pronounced too koh-MEES-teh) - You ate

- **Él/Ella/Usted comió** (Pronounced el/EH-yah/oo-STEHD koh-MYOH) - He/She/You (formal) ate

- **Nosotros/Nosotras comimos** (Pronounced noh-SOH-trohs/noh-SOH-trahs koh-MEE-mohs) - We ate

- **Vosotros/Vosotras comisteis** (Pronounced boh-SOH-trohs/boh-SOH-trahs koh-MEES-teys) - You all ate (used mainly in Spain)

- **Ellos/Ellas/Ustedes comieron** (Pronounced EH-yohs/EH-yahs/oo-STEH-dehs koh-MYEH-rohn) - They/You all ate

And here's how you would conjugate "vivir" (to live):

- **Yo viví** (Pronounced yoh vee-VEE) - I lived

- **Tú viviste** (Pronounced too vee-VEES-teh) - You lived

- **Él/Ella/Usted vivió** (Pronounced el/EH-yah/oo-STEHD vee-VYOH) - He/She/You (formal) lived

- **Nosotros/Nosotras vivimos** (Pronounced noh-SOH-trohs/noh-SOH-trahs vee-VEE-mohs) - We lived

- **Vosotros/Vosotras vivisteis** (Pronounced boh-SOH-trohs/boh-SOH-trahs vee-VEES-teys) - You all lived (used mainly in Spain)

- **Ellos/Ellas/Ustedes vivieron** (Pronounced EH-yohs/EH-yahs/oo-STEH-dehs vee-VYEH-rohn) - They/You all lived

Notice that the endings for "-er" and "-ir" verbs are the same. Let's see an example sentence:

Yo comí pizza ayer. (Pronounced yoh koh-MEE PEET-sah ah-YEHR) - I ate pizza yesterday.

Nosotros vivimos en esa casa el año pasado. (Pronounced noh-SOH-trohs vee-VEE-mohs en EH-sah KAH-sah el AH-nyoh pah-SAH-doh) - We lived in that house last year.

Irregular Verbs in the Preterite Tense

Just like in the present tense, some verbs are irregular in the preterite tense, meaning they don't follow the regular conjugation patterns. Here are a few common irregular verbs and their conjugations:

Ser/Ir (to be/to go)

- **Yo fui** (Pronounced yoh FWEE) - I was/I went

- **Tú fuiste** (Pronounced too FWEE-steh) - You were/You went

- **Él/Ella/Usted fue** (Pronounced el/EH-yah/oo-STEHD FWEH) - He/She/You (formal) was/went

- **Nosotros/Nosotras fuimos** (Pronounced noh-SOH-trohs/noh-SOH-trahs FWEE-mohs) - We were/Went

- **Vosotros/Vosotras fuisteis** (Pronounced boh-SOH-trohs/boh-SOH-trahs FWEE-stehys) - You all were/Went (used mainly in Spain)

- **Ellos/Ellas/Ustedes fueron** (Pronounced EH-yohs/EH-yahs/oo-STEH-dehs FWEH-rohn) - They/You all were/Went

For example:

Yo fui al parque. (Pronounced yoh FWEE ahl PAR-keh) - I went to the park.

Él fue mi profesor. (Pronounced el FWEH mee proh-feh-SOR) - He was my teacher.

Hacer (to do/make)

- **Yo hice** (Pronounced yoh EE-seh) - I did/I made

- **Tú hiciste** (Pronounced too ee-SEES-teh) - You did/You made

- **Él/Ella/Usted hizo** (Pronounced el/EH-yah/oo-STEHD EE-soh) - He/She/You (formal) did/made

- **Nosotros/Nosotras hicimos** (Pronounced noh-SOH-trohs/noh-SOH-trahs ee-SEE-mohs) - We did/We made

- **Vosotros/Vosotras hicisteis** (Pronounced boh-SOH-trohs/boh-SOH-trahs ee-SEES-teys) - You all did/made (used mainly in Spain)

- **Ellos/Ellas/Ustedes hicieron** (Pronounced EH-yohs/EH-yahs/oo-STEH-dehs ee-SYEH-rohn) - They/You all did/made

For example:

Yo hice mi tarea. (Pronounced yoh EE-seh mee tah-REH-ah) - I did my homework.

Nosotros hicimos una fiesta. (Pronounced noh-SOH-trohs ee-SEE-mohs OO-nah FYEH-stah) - We had a party.

Using the Preterite Tense in Sentences

Now that you know how to conjugate regular and irregular verbs in the preterite tense, you can start using them in sentences to talk about past events. Here are some examples:

Ayer, yo comí una hamburguesa. (Pronounced ah-YEHR yoh koh-MEE OO-nah ahm-boor-GEH-sah) - Yesterday, I ate a hamburger.

Ellos fueron al cine la semana pasada. (Pronounced EH-yohs FWEH-rohn ahl SEE-neh lah seh-MAH-nah pah-SAH-dah) - They went to the movies last week.

El año pasado, nosotros viajamos a México. (Pronounced el AH-nyoh pah-SAH-doh noh-SOH-trohs vyah-HAH-mohs ah MEH-hee-koh) - Last year, we traveled to Mexico.

These sentences show how you can talk about things that happened at specific times in the past using the preterite tense.

Key Points to Remember

1. **Understanding the Preterite Tense:** The preterite tense in Spanish is used to describe actions that were completed at a specific point in the past. It's essential for talking about events that have a clear beginning and end.

2. **Conjugating Regular "-ar" Verbs:** For regular "-ar" verbs in the preterite tense, endings change as follows: -é (yo), -aste (tú), -ó (él/ella/usted), -amos (nosotros/nosotras), -asteis (vosotros/vosotras), -aron (ellos/ellas/ustedes).

3. **Conjugating Regular "-er" and "-ir" Verbs:** Regular "-er" and "-ir" verbs share the same preterite endings: -í (yo), -iste (tú), -ió (él/ella/usted), -imos (nosotros/nosotras), -isteis (vosotros/vosotras), -ieron (ellos/ellas/ustedes).

4. **Irregular Verbs in the Preterite:** Some verbs, like ser/ir (to be/to go) and hacer (to do/make), are irregular in the preterite and have unique conjugations, which must be memorized.

5. **Using the Preterite in Sentences:** The preterite tense allows you to describe completed actions in the past, such as "Ayer, yo comí una hamburguesa" (Yesterday, I ate a hamburger) or "Ellos fueron al cine la semana pasada" (They went to the movies last week).

Chapter 31

Talking About the Past: Imperfect Tense

When you want to talk about things that happened in the past but were not completed or were ongoing, you use the imperfect tense in Spanish. The imperfect tense is used to describe actions that happened repeatedly or over a period of time in the past. In this chapter, you'll learn how to form the imperfect tense, how to use it in sentences, and how to talk about past events that are not seen as finished.

What Is the Imperfect Tense?

The imperfect tense is another past tense in Spanish. Unlike the preterite tense, which is used to talk about actions that were completed, the imperfect tense is used to describe actions that were ongoing, habitual, or not seen as having a definite end. For example, if you want to say "I used to play soccer," you would use the imperfect tense because playing soccer was something you did regularly in the past, not just once.

Let's start by learning how to form the imperfect tense for regular verbs.

Conjugating Regular "-ar" Verbs in the Imperfect Tense

To conjugate regular "-ar" verbs in the imperfect tense, you take the stem of the verb and add the correct ending for the subject. Here's how it works with the verb "hablar" (to speak):

- **Yo hablaba** (Pronounced yoh ah-BLAH-bah) - I used to speak/I was speaking

- **Tú hablabas** (Pronounced too ah-BLAH-bahs) - You used to speak/You were speaking

- **Él/Ella/Usted hablaba** (Pronounced el/EH-yah/oo-STEHD ah-BLAH-bah) - He/She/You (formal) used to speak/was speaking

- **Nosotros/Nosotras hablábamos** (Pronounced noh-SOH-trohs/noh-SOH-trahs ah-BLAH-bah-mohs) - We used to speak/We were speaking

- **Vosotros/Vosotras hablabais** (Pronounced boh-SOH-trohs/boh-SOH-trahs ah-BLAH-bah-ees) - You all used to speak/You all were speaking (used mainly in Spain)

- **Ellos/Ellas/Ustedes hablaban** (Pronounced EH-yohs/EH-yahs/oo-STEH-dehs ah-BLAH-bahn) - They/You all used to speak/were speaking

Here are the endings you add to the stem of regular "-ar" verbs:

- Yo: -aba
- Tú: -abas
- Él/Ella/Usted: -aba
- Nosotros/Nosotras: -ábamos
- Vosotros/Vosotras: -abais
- Ellos/Ellas/Ustedes: -aban

For example, if you want to say "I used to speak with my friend," you would say:

Yo hablaba con mi amigo. (Pronounced yoh ah-BLAH-bah kohn mee ah-MEE-goh) - I used to speak with my friend.

Conjugating Regular "-er" and "-ir" Verbs in the Imperfect Tense

Regular "-er" and "-ir" verbs share the same endings in the imperfect tense. Let's look at how to conjugate the verbs "comer" (to eat) and "vivir" (to live):

- **Yo comía** (Pronounced yoh koh-MEE-ah) - I used to eat/I was eating

- **Tú comías** (Pronounced too koh-MEE-ahs) - You used to eat/You were eating

- **Él/Ella/Usted comía** (Pronounced el/EH-yah/oo-STEHD koh-MEE-ah) - He/She/You (formal) used to eat/was eating

- **Nosotros/Nosotras comíamos** (Pronounced noh-SOH-trohs/noh-SOH-trahs koh-MEE-ah-mohs) - We used to eat/We were eating

- **Vosotros/Vosotras comíais** (Pronounced boh-SOH-trohs/boh-SOH-trahs koh-MEE-ah-ees) - You all used to eat/You all were eating (used mainly in Spain)

- **Ellos/Ellas/Ustedes comían** (Pronounced EH-yohs/EH-yahs/oo-STEH-dehs koh-MEE-ahn) - They/You all used to eat/were eating

And here's how you would conjugate "vivir" (to live):

- **Yo vivía** (Pronounced yoh vee-VEE-ah) - I used to live/I was living
- **Tú vivías** (Pronounced too vee-VEE-ahs) - You used to live/You were living
- **Él/Ella/Usted vivía** (Pronounced el/EH-yah/oo-STEHD vee-VEE-ah) - He/She/You (formal) used to live/was living
- **Nosotros/Nosotras vivíamos** (Pronounced noh-SOH-trohs/noh-SOH-trahs vee-VEE-ah-mohs) - We used to live/We were living
- **Vosotros/Vosotras vivíais** (Pronounced boh-SOH-trohs/boh-SOH-trahs vee-VEE-ah-ees) - You all used to live/You all were living (used mainly in Spain)
- **Ellos/Ellas/Ustedes vivían** (Pronounced EH-yohs/EH-yahs/oo-STEH-dehs vee-VEE-ahn) - They/You all used to live/were living

Notice that the endings for "-er" and "-ir" verbs are the same. Let's see an example sentence:

Yo comía pizza todos los días. (Pronounced yoh koh-MEE-ah PEET-sah TOH-dohs lohs DEE-ahs) - I used to eat pizza every day.

Nosotros vivíamos en esa casa. (Pronounced noh-SOH-trohs vee-VEE-ah-mohs en EH-sah KAH-sah) - We used to live in that house.

Irregular Verbs in the Imperfect Tense

Just like in other tenses, some verbs are irregular in the imperfect tense. Fortunately, there are only three irregular verbs in the imperfect tense: "ser" (to be), "ir" (to go), and "ver" (to see).

Ser (to be)

- **Yo era** (Pronounced yoh EH-rah) - I used to be
- **Tú eras** (Pronounced too EH-rahs) - You used to be
- **Él/Ella/Usted era** (Pronounced el/EH-yah/oo-STEHD EH-rah) - He/She/You (formal) used to be
- **Nosotros/Nosotras éramos** (Pronounced noh-SOH-trohs/noh-SOH-trahs EH-rah-mohs) - We used to be
- **Vosotros/Vosotras erais** (Pronounced boh-SOH-trohs/boh-SOH-trahs EH-rah-ees) -

You all used to be (used mainly in Spain)

- **Ellos/Ellas/Ustedes eran** (Pronounced EH-yohs/EH-yahs/oo-STEH-dehs EH-rahn) - They/You all used to be

For example:

Yo era muy tímido. (Pronounced yoh EH-rah MOO-ee TEE-mee-doh) - I used to be very shy.

Ir (to go)

- **Yo iba** (Pronounced yoh EE-bah) - I used to go

- **Tú ibas** (Pronounced too EE-bahs) - You used to go

- **Él/Ella/Usted iba** (Pronounced el/EH-yah/oo-STEHD EE-bah) - He/She/You (formal) used to go

- **Nosotros/Nosotras íbamos** (Pronounced noh-SOH-trohs/noh-SOH-trahs EE-bah-mohs) - We used to go

- **Vosotros/Vosotras ibais** (Pronounced boh-SOH-trohs/boh-SOH-trahs EE-bah-ees) - You all used to go (used mainly in Spain)

- **Ellos/Ellas/Ustedes iban** (Pronounced EH-yohs/EH-yahs/oo-STEH-dehs EE-bahn) - They/You all used to go

For example:

Nosotros íbamos al parque todos los sábados. (Pronounced noh-SOH-trohs EE-bah-mohs ahl PAR-keh TOH-dohs lohs SAH-bah-dohs) - We used to go to the park every Saturday.

Ver (to see)

- **Yo veía** (Pronounced yoh veh-EE-ah) - I used to see

- **Tú veías** (Pronounced too veh-EE-ahs) - You used to see

- **Él/Ella/Usted veía** (Pronounced el/EH-yah/oo-STEHD veh-EE-ah) - He/She/You (formal) used to see

- **Nosotros/Nosotras veíamos** (Pronounced noh-SOH-trohs/noh-SOH-trahs veh-EE-ah-mohs) - We used to see

- **Vosotros/Vosotras veíais** (Pronounced boh-SOH-trohs/boh-SOH-trahs veh-EE-ah-ees) - You all used to see (used mainly in Spain)

- **Ellos/Ellas/Ustedes veían** (Pronounced EH-yohs/EH-yahs/oo-STEH-dehs veh-EE-ahn) - They/You all used to see

For example:

Yo veía muchas películas. (Pronounced yoh veh-EE-ah MOO-chahs peh-LEE-koo-lahs) - I used to watch a lot of movies.

Using the Imperfect Tense in Sentences

Now that you know how to conjugate regular and irregular verbs in the imperfect tense, you can start using them in sentences to talk about past habits, routines, and ongoing actions. Here are some examples:

Cuando era niño, yo jugaba con mis amigos todos los días. (Pronounced KWAHN-doh EH-rah NEE-nyoh, yoh hoo-GAH-bah kohn mees ah-MEE-gohs TOH-dohs lohs DEE-ahs) - When I was a child, I used to play with my friends every day.

Nosotros vivíamos cerca de la escuela. (Pronounced noh-SOH-trohs vee-VEE-ah-mohs SEHR-kah deh lah ehs-KWEH-lah) - We used to live near the school.

Siempre íbamos a la playa en verano. (Pronounced SYEM-preh EE-bah-mohs ah lah PLAH-yah en veh-RAH-noh) - We always used to go to the beach in the summer.

These sentences show how you can use the imperfect tense to describe things that were ongoing, habitual, or repeated in the past.

Key Points to Remember

1. **Understanding the Imperfect Tense:** The imperfect tense in Spanish is used to describe ongoing, habitual, or repeated actions in the past. Unlike the preterite tense, it focuses on actions that don't have a definite end.

2. **Conjugating Regular "-ar" Verbs:** Regular "-ar" verbs in the imperfect tense use these endings: -aba (yo), -abas (tú), -aba (él/ella/usted), -ábamos (nosotros/nosotras), -abais (vosotros/vosotras), -aban (ellos/ellas/ustedes).

3. **Conjugating Regular "-er" and "-ir" Verbs:** Regular "-er" and "-Ir" verbs share the same imperfect endings: -ía (yo), -ías (tú), -ía (él/ella/usted), -íamos (nosotros/nosotras), -íais (vosotros/vosotras), -ían (ellos/ellas/ustedes).

4. **Irregular Verbs in the Imperfect Tense:** There are only three irregular verbs in the

imperfect tense: ser (yo era, tú eras, etc.), ir (yo iba, tú ibas, etc.), and ver (yo veía, tú veías, etc.).

5. **Using the Imperfect Tense:** The imperfect tense is ideal for talking about past habits, routines, and actions that were ongoing. Example: "Cuando era niño, yo jugaba con mis amigos todos los días" (When I was a child, I used to play with my friends every day).

Chapter 32

The Future Tense

When you want to talk about things that will happen in the future, you use the future tense in Spanish. The future tense is used to describe actions that are going to happen, plans you have, or predictions about what might occur. In this chapter, you'll learn how to form the future tense, how to use it in sentences, and how to talk about your future plans and dreams.

What Is the Future Tense?

The future tense is used when you want to talk about something that will happen later on. It's like saying "I will" or "I am going to" in English. For example, if you want to say "I will study tomorrow," you use the future tense in Spanish. The future tense can be used for all kinds of actions, whether you're talking about something definite or something you think might happen.

Let's start by learning how to form the future tense for regular verbs.

Forming the Future Tense

One of the easiest things about the future tense in Spanish is that it's the same for all regular verbs, whether they end in "-ar," "-er," or "-ir." You don't need to remove the ending of the verb; instead, you add the future tense endings directly to the infinitive (the base form of the verb).

Here's how it works with the verb "hablar" (to speak):

- **Yo hablaré** (Pronounced yoh ah-blah-REH) - I will speak

- **Tú hablarás** (Pronounced too ah-blah-RAHS) - You will speak

- **Él/Ella/Usted hablará** (Pronounced el/EH-yah/oo-STEHD ah-blah-RAH) - He/She/You (formal) will speak

- **Nosotros/Nosotras hablaremos** (Pronounced noh-SOH-trohs/noh-SOH-trahs ah-blah-REH-mohs) - We will speak

- **Vosotros/Vosotras hablaréis** (Pronounced boh-SOH-trohs/boh-SOH-trahs ah-blah-RAYS) - You all will speak (used mainly in Spain)

- **Ellos/Ellas/Ustedes hablarán** (Pronounced EH-yohs/EH-yahs/oo-STEH-dehs ah-blah-RAHN) - They/You all will speak

As you can see, you simply add the future tense endings to the infinitive form of the verb. Here are the endings you add to all regular verbs:

- Yo: -é

- Tú: -ás

- Él/Ella/Usted: -á

- Nosotros/Nosotras: -emos

- Vosotros/Vosotras: -éis

- Ellos/Ellas/Ustedes: -án

For example, if you want to say "We will eat pizza," you would say:

Nosotros comeremos pizza. (Pronounced noh-SOH-trohs koh-meh-REH-mohs PEET-sah) - We will eat pizza.

Using the Future Tense in Sentences

Now that you know how to form the future tense, you can start using it in sentences to talk about what you or others will do. Here are some examples:

Yo estudiaré para el examen mañana. (Pronounced yoh ehs-too-dee-ah-REH pah-rah el ehs-SAH-mehn mah-NYAH-nah) - I will study for the exam tomorrow.

Ellos viajarán a España el próximo año. (Pronounced EH-yohs vyah-hah-RAHN ah ehs-PAH-nyah el PROHK-see-moh AH-nyoh) - They will travel to Spain next year.

Tú aprenderás mucho en esta clase. (Pronounced too ah-prehn-deh-RAHS MOO-choh en EHS-tah KLAH-seh) - You will learn a lot in this class.

The future tense is very useful for talking about plans, goals, and predictions. It helps you express what you intend to do or what you think will happen.

Irregular Verbs in the Future Tense

Just like in other tenses, there are some irregular verbs in the future tense. These verbs don't follow the regular pattern, so their stems change before you add the future tense endings. Here are some common irregular verbs in the future tense:

Decir (to say/tell) - Future stem: dir-

- **Yo diré** (Pronounced yoh dee-REH) - I will say

- **Tú dirás** (Pronounced too dee-RAHS) - You will say

- **Él/Ella/Usted dirá** (Pronounced el/EH-yah/oo-STEHD dee-RAH) - He/She/You (formal) will say

- **Nosotros/Nosotras diremos** (Pronounced noh-SOH-trohs/noh-SOH-trahs dee-REH-mohs) - We will say

- **Vosotros/Vosotras diréis** (Pronounced boh-SOH-trohs/boh-SOH-trahs dee-RAYS) - You all will say (used mainly in Spain)

- **Ellos/Ellas/Ustedes dirán** (Pronounced EH-yohs/EH-yahs/oo-STEH-dehs dee-RAHN) - They/You all will say

Tener (to have) - Future stem: tendr-

- **Yo tendré** (Pronounced yoh tehn-DREH) - I will have

- **Tú tendrás** (Pronounced too tehn-DRAHS) - You will have

- **Él/Ella/Usted tendrá** (Pronounced el/EH-yah/oo-STEHD tehn-DRAH) - He/She/You (formal) will have

- **Nosotros/Nosotras tendremos** (Pronounced noh-SOH-trohs/noh-SOH-trahs tehn-DREH-mohs) - We will have

- **Vosotros/Vosotras tendréis** (Pronounced boh-SOH-trohs/boh-SOH-trahs tehn-DREYS) - You all will have (used mainly in Spain)

- **Ellos/Ellas/Ustedes tendrán** (Pronounced EH-yohs/EH-yahs/oo-STEH-dehs tehn-DRAHN) - They/You all will have

Hacer (to do/make) - Future stem: har-

- **Yo haré** (Pronounced yoh ah-REH) - I will do/make

- **Tú harás** (Pronounced too ah-RAHS) - You will do/make

- **Él/Ella/Usted hará** (Pronounced el/EH-yah/oo-STEHD ah-RAH) - He/She/You (formal) will do/make

- **Nosotros/Nosotras haremos** (Pronounced noh-SOH-trohs/noh-SOH-trahs ah-REH-mohs) - We will do/make

- **Vosotros/Vosotras haréis** (Pronounced boh-SOH-trohs/boh-SOH-trahs ah-RAYS) - You all will do/make (used mainly in Spain)

- **Ellos/Ellas/Ustedes harán** (Pronounced EH-yohs/EH-yahs/oo-STEH-dehs ah-RAHN) - They/You all will do/make

Even though these verbs are irregular, the future tense endings are still the same as for regular verbs. The only difference is the change in the stem.

Talking About Plans and Intentions

The future tense is great for discussing your plans and intentions. You can use it to talk about what you're going to do later today, next week, or even years from now. Here are some examples:

Mañana, visitaré a mis abuelos. (Pronounced mah-NYAH-nah vee-see-tah-REH ah mees ah-BWEH-lohs) - Tomorrow, I will visit my grandparents.

Estudiaré en la universidad después de la escuela. (Pronounced ehs-too-dee-ah-REH en lah oo-nee-vehr-see-DAHD dehs-PWEHS deh lah ehs-KWEH-lah) - I will study at university after school.

Ellos trabajarán en un proyecto importante. (Pronounced EH-yohs trah-bah-hah-RAHN en oon proh-YEK-toh eem-por-TAHN-teh) - They will work on an important project.

Using the future tense allows you to express your intentions and what you plan to achieve.

Making Predictions

The future tense is also used to make predictions about what might happen. Whether you're making a guess or thinking about possibilities, the future tense helps you express what you think will occur:

El clima será cálido mañana. (Pronounced el KLEE-mah seh-RAH KAH-lee-doh mah-NYAH-nah) - The weather will be warm tomorrow.

Pienso que ellos ganarán el partido. (Pronounced PYEHN-soh keh EH-yohs gah-nah-RAHN el par-TEE-doh) - I think they will win the game.

Este año, habrá muchas sorpresas. (Pronounced EHS-teh AH-nyoh ah-BRAH MOO-chahs sor-PREH-sahs) - This year, there will be many surprises.

Making predictions in the future tense is a fun way to talk about what you think might happen in the days or years ahead.

Key Points to Remember

1. **Understanding the Future Tense:** The future tense in Spanish is used to talk about actions that will happen, plans you have, or predictions about what might occur. It's similar to saying "I will" in English.

2. **Forming the Future Tense:** To form the future tense for regular verbs, simply add the future endings (-é, -ás, -á, -emos, -éis, -án) directly to the infinitive form of the verb. This applies to all regular "-ar," "-er," and "-ir" verbs.

3. **Using the Future Tense in Sentences:** The future tense is useful for expressing plans, goals, and predictions. Example: "Yo estudiaré para el examen mañana" (I will study for the exam tomorrow).

4. **Irregular Verbs in the Future Tense:** Some verbs have irregular stems in the future tense, but the endings remain the same. Common irregular verbs include decir (dir-), tener (tendr-), and hacer (har-).

5. **Talking About Plans and Predictions:** The future tense is used to discuss your plans, intentions, and predictions. Example: "Mañana, visitaré a mis abuelos" (Tomorrow, I will visit my grandparents).

Chapter 33

Expressing Obligations: Tener que, Deber, and More

When you need to talk about things that you have to do or should do, Spanish has specific ways to express these obligations. In this chapter, you'll learn how to use phrases like "tener que," "deber," and others to talk about responsibilities, duties, and things you're required to do. These phrases are very useful in everyday conversation, especially when you want to explain what needs to be done.

Using "Tener que" to Express Obligations

The phrase "tener que" is one of the most common ways to express obligations in Spanish. It's similar to saying "have to" or "must" in English. The verb "tener" means "to have," and when you add "que," it changes the meaning to "have to" do something.

Here's how "tener que" works:

Yo tengo que hacer la tarea. (Pronounced yoh TEHN-goh keh ah-SEHR lah tah-REH-ah) - I have to do the homework.

In this sentence, "tener que" is used to express that doing the homework is something you are required to do. Let's break it down:

- **Tengo** (Pronounced TEHN-goh) - This is the form of "tener" that matches the subject "yo" (I).

- **Que** (Pronounced keh) - This word is added after "tener" to indicate obligation.

- **Hacer** (Pronounced ah-SEHR) - This is the infinitive form of the verb "to do," showing what you have to do.

The structure for "tener que" is always the same: "tener" + "que" + infinitive verb. Here are some more examples:

Tú tienes que estudiar para el examen. (Pronounced too TYEH-nehs keh ehs-too-dee-AHR pah-rah el ehs-SAH-mehn) - You have to study for the exam.

Nosotros tenemos que ir a la escuela. (Pronounced noh-SOH-trohs teh-NEH-mohs keh eer ah lah ehs-KWEH-lah) - We have to go to school.

Ellos tienen que limpiar la casa. (Pronounced EH-yohs TYEH-nehn keh leem-PYAR lah KAH-sah) - They have to clean the house.

Using "tener que" is a straightforward way to talk about what you or others must do.

Using "Deber" to Express Obligations or Duties

The verb "deber" is another way to express obligations in Spanish, but it's a little different from "tener que." "Deber" is often translated as "should" or "must," and it carries a sense of moral obligation or duty. It's used when you want to suggest that something is the right thing to do or is necessary.

Here's how "deber" works:

Yo debo ayudar a mi mamá. (Pronounced yoh DEH-boh ah-yoo-DAR ah mee mah-MAH) - I should help my mom.

In this sentence, "deber" expresses a moral obligation to help your mom. Here are some more examples:

Tú debes comer verduras. (Pronounced too DEH-behs koh-MEHR vehr-DOO-rahs) - You should eat vegetables.

Nosotros debemos respetar a los demás. (Pronounced noh-SOH-trohs DEH-beh-mohs rehs-peh-TAR ah lohs deh-MAHS) - We must respect others.

Ellas deben llegar a tiempo. (Pronounced EH-yahs DEH-behn yeh-GAR ah TYEM-poh) - They should arrive on time.

Notice that "deber" is followed directly by an infinitive verb (like "comer" or "respetar"). This structure is used to suggest that something is necessary or the right thing to do.

Other Ways to Express Obligation

Besides "tener que" and "deber," there are a few other phrases and verbs that you can use to talk about obligations in Spanish:

- **Hay que** (Pronounced eye keh) - This phrase means "one must" or "it's necessary to." It's used when you want to say that something needs to be done, but you're not specifying who has to do it. For example, **Hay que estudiar para el examen.** (Pronounced eye keh ehs-too-dee-AHR pah-rah el ehs-SAH-mehn) - One must study for the exam.

- **Tener la obligación de** (Pronounced TEHN-ehr lah oh-blee-gah-SYOHN deh) - This phrase is a more formal way to express obligation, meaning "to have the obligation to." For example, **Tengo la obligación de cuidar a mi hermano.** (Pronounced TEHN-goh lah oh-blee-gah-SYOHN deh kwee-DAR ah mee ehr-MAH-noh) - I have the obligation to take care of my brother.

- **Necesitar** (Pronounced neh-seh-see-TAR) - This verb means "to need" and can also be used to express a need or obligation. For example, **Necesito terminar mi proyecto.** (Pronounced neh-seh-SEE-toh tehr-mee-NAR mee proh-YEK-toh) - I need to finish my project.

These phrases give you different ways to talk about what needs to be done, depending on the situation and the level of formality.

Using Obligation Phrases in Conversations

Now that you know how to express obligations in Spanish, let's see how you can use these phrases in everyday conversations. Here are some scenarios:

Talking about Schoolwork:

Tengo que leer un libro para la clase de inglés. (Pronounced TEHN-goh keh leh-EHR oon LEE-broh pah-rah lah KLAH-seh deh een-GLEHS) - I have to read a book for English class.

Deberías hacer la tarea antes de ver la televisión. (Pronounced deh-beh-REE-ahs ah-SEHR lah tah-REH-ah AHN-tehs deh vehr lah teh-leh-bee-SYOHN) - You should do your homework before watching TV.

Talking about Chores:

Nosotros tenemos que lavar los platos después de la cena. (Pronounced noh-SOH-trohs teh-NEH-mohs keh lah-BAHR lohs PLAH-tohs dehs-PWEHS deh lah SEH-nah) - We have to wash the dishes after dinner.

Hay que sacar la basura todos los días. (Pronounced eye keh sah-KAR lah bah-SOO-rah TOH-dohs lohs DEE-ahs) - The trash must be taken out every day.

Talking about Responsibilities:

Debo estudiar más para mejorar mis notas. (Pronounced DEH-boh ehs-too-dee-AHR mahs pah-rah meh-hoh-RAHR mees NOH-tahs) - I should study more to improve my grades.

Necesito hablar con mi profesor sobre el proyecto. (Pronounced neh-seh-SEE-toh ah-BLAR kohn mee proh-feh-SOR SOH-breh el proh-YEK-toh) - I need to talk to my teacher about the project.

These examples show how you can use different phrases to talk about obligations and responsibilities in different contexts.

Key Points to Remember

1. **Using "Tener que" for Obligations:** "Tener que" is a common phrase in Spanish to express obligations, similar to "have to" in English. It's formed by "tener" + "que" + infinitive verb. Example: Yo tengo que estudiar (I have to study).

2. **Using "Deber" to Express Duties:** "Deber" conveys a sense of moral obligation or duty, similar to "should" or "must" in English. It's used with an infinitive verb to suggest something necessary or right. Example: Tú debes comer verduras (You should eat vegetables).

3. **Other Ways to Express Obligation:** Spanish offers additional phrases like "hay que" (one must), "tener la obligación de" (to have the obligation to), and "necesitar" (to need) to express obligations in various contexts. Example: Hay que estudiar para el examen (One must study for the exam).

4. **Applying Obligation Phrases in Conversations:** These phrases are versatile and can be used in different scenarios, such as discussing schoolwork, chores, or responsibilities. Example: Nosotros tenemos que lavar los platos (We have to wash the dishes).

5. **Choosing the Right Expression:** Depending on the situation, you can choose between "tener que," "deber," "hay que," or other phrases to accurately convey the level of obligation or necessity.

Chapter 34

Making Comparisons

In everyday conversations, we often compare things, people, and situations. Whether you're talking about who is taller, which movie is better, or which food is tastier, knowing how to make comparisons is an important skill in any language. In this chapter, you'll learn how to make comparisons in Spanish using different structures and phrases. By the end, you'll be able to compare things like a pro!

Comparing Two Things: More... Than

The most common way to compare two things in Spanish is by using "más... que," which means "more... than" in English. This structure is used when you want to say that one thing has more of a quality than another. For example:

Mi hermano es más alto que yo. (Pronounced mee ehr-MAH-noh ehs mahs AHL-toh keh yoh) - My brother is taller than me.

In this sentence, "más" means "more," "alto" means "tall," and "que" is used to compare "mi hermano" (my brother) with "yo" (me).

Here are some more examples:

Este libro es más interesante que ese. (Pronounced EHS-teh LEE-broh ehs mahs een-teh-reh-SAHN-teh keh EHS-eh) - This book is more interesting than that one.

El perro es más grande que el gato. (Pronounced el PEH-rroh ehs mahs GRAHN-deh keh el GAH-toh) - The dog is bigger than the cat.

Comparing Two Things: Less... Than

When you want to say that one thing has less of a quality than another, you use "menos... que," which means "less... than" in English. Here's how it works:

Este coche es menos caro que aquel. (Pronounced EHS-teh KOH-cheh ehs MEH-nohs KAH-roh keh ah-KEL) - This car is less expensive than that one.

In this sentence, "menos" means "less," "caro" means "expensive," and "que" is used to compare "este coche" (this car) with "aquel" (that one).

Here are some more examples:

Mi casa es menos grande que la tuya. (Pronounced mee KAH-sah ehs MEH-nohs GRAHN-deh keh lah TOO-yah) - My house is less big than yours.

Él es menos inteligente que su hermana. (Pronounced el ehs MEH-nohs een-teh-lee-HEN-teh keh soo ehr-MAH-nah) - He is less intelligent than his sister.

Comparing Equals: As… As

When you want to say that two things are equal in some way, you use "tan… como," which means "as… as" in English. This structure is used to compare two things that have the same level of a quality. For example:

Ella es tan alta como su madre. (Pronounced EH-yah ehs tahn AHL-tah KOH-moh soo MAH-dreh) - She is as tall as her mother.

In this sentence, "tan" means "as," "alta" means "tall," and "como" is used to compare "ella" (she) with "su madre" (her mother).

Here are some more examples:

Esta clase es tan difícil como la otra. (Pronounced EHS-tah KLAH-seh ehs tahn dee-FEE-seel KOH-moh lah OH-trah) - This class is as difficult as the other one.

Mi hermano es tan rápido como yo. (Pronounced mee ehr-MAH-noh ehs tahn RAH-pee-doh KOH-moh yoh) - My brother is as fast as me.

Comparing Quantities: More/Fewer… Than

When you want to compare quantities, like saying one person has more or fewer of something than another person, you use "más… que" for more and "menos… que" for fewer. Here's how it works:

Tengo más libros que tú. (Pronounced TEHN-goh mahs LEE-brohs keh too) - I have more books than you.

In this sentence, "más" means "more," "libros" means "books," and "que" is used to compare the quantity "más libros" (more books) between "yo" (I) and "tú" (you).

Here are some more examples:

Hay menos estudiantes en esta clase que en la otra. (Pronounced eye MEH-nohs ehs-too-dee-AHN-tehs en EHS-tah KLAH-seh keh en lah OH-trah) - There are fewer students in this class than in the other one.

Él tiene más dinero que su amigo. (Pronounced el TYEH-neh mahs dee-NEH-roh keh soo ah-MEE-goh) - He has more money than his friend.

Superlatives: The Most/The Least

Sometimes you want to say that something or someone is the most or least of a group. In Spanish, you can use "el/la/los/las más..." or "el/la/los/las menos..." to express this. Here's how it works:

Él es el más alto de la clase. (Pronounced el ehs el mahs AHL-toh deh lah KLAH-seh) - He is the tallest in the class.

In this sentence, "el más alto" means "the tallest," and "de la clase" indicates that he is the tallest among everyone in the class.

Here are some more examples:

Ella es la menos habladora de todas. (Pronounced EH-yah ehs lah MEH-nohs ah-blah-DOH-rah deh TOH-dahs) - She is the least talkative of all.

Este es el mejor libro que he leído. (Pronounced EHS-teh ehs el meh-HOR LEE-broh keh eh LEH-ee-doh) - This is the best book I have read.

Notice how "el más," "la más," "el menos," or "la menos" are used before the adjective to express "the most" or "the least."

Using "Que" vs. "De" in Comparisons

When making comparisons in Spanish, you generally use "que" to compare two things, but there are some cases where you use "de" instead. Here's a simple rule to remember:

- Use "que" when you're comparing two people, places, things, or ideas directly. For example: **Más grande que** (more big than).

- Use "de" when you're comparing numbers or quantities, like saying "more than 5" or "less than 10." For example: **Más de cinco personas** (more than five people).

Here's an example to illustrate this:

Hay más de veinte estudiantes en la clase. (Pronounced eye mahs deh BYEN-teh ehs-too-dee-AHN-tehs en lah KLAH-seh) - There are more than twenty students in the class.

Ella es más alta que su hermana. (Pronounced EH-yah ehs mahs AHL-tah keh soo ehr-MAH-nah) - She is taller than her sister.

Remembering when to use "que" and "de" will help you make comparisons correctly.

Key Points to Remember

1. **Comparing with "Más... que" and "Menos... que":** Use "más... que" to express that something has more of a quality (e.g., Mi hermano es más alto que yo), and "menos... que" to express less of a quality (e.g., Este coche es menos caro que aquel).

2. **Expressing Equality with "Tan... como":** Use "tan... como" to say that two things are equal in some way (e.g., Ella es tan alta como su madre).

3. **Comparing Quantities with "Más... que" and "Menos... que":** Use "más... que" for more of something (e.g., Tengo más libros que tú) and "menos... que" for fewer of something (e.g., Hay menos estudiantes en esta clase que en la otra).

4. **Using Superlatives with "El/La más" or "El/La menos":** Use these structures to describe something as the most or least in a group (e.g., Él es el más alto de la clase).

5. **When to Use "Que" vs. "De":** Use "que" for direct comparisons and "de" when comparing numbers or quantities (e.g., Hay más de veinte estudiantes en la clase).

Chapter 35

The Subjunctive Mood: Introduction

The subjunctive mood is a unique and important part of the Spanish language. Unlike the indicative mood, which is used to talk about facts and reality, the subjunctive is used to express doubts, wishes, hopes, emotions, and things that are not certain or real. Learning the subjunctive can seem tricky at first, but once you understand when and how to use it, you'll find it very useful in everyday conversations.

What Is the Subjunctive Mood?

The subjunctive mood is a way of using verbs to express things that are not certain, like wishes, doubts, possibilities, or hypothetical situations. While the indicative mood is used to talk about things that are real and concrete, the subjunctive is used when there is some uncertainty or subjectivity involved.

For example, if you want to say "I hope that it rains tomorrow," you're expressing a wish or hope, not a fact. Since there's uncertainty about whether it will actually rain, you would use the subjunctive mood in Spanish.

Let's start by looking at how the subjunctive is formed for regular verbs.

Forming the Present Subjunctive

The present subjunctive is formed by starting with the yo (I) form of the verb in the present tense, removing the -o ending, and then adding the opposite vowel endings. For -ar verbs, you add -e, and for -er and -ir verbs, you add -a. Here's how it works with the verb "hablar" (to speak):

- **Yo hable** (Pronounced yoh AH-bleh) - I speak

- **Tú hables** (Pronounced too AH-blehs) - You speak

THE SUBJUNCTIVE MOOD: INTRODUCTION

- **Él/Ella/Usted hable** (Pronounced el/EH-yah/oo-STEHD AH-bleh) - He/She/You (formal) speaks

- **Nosotros/Nosotras hablemos** (Pronounced noh-SOH-trohs/noh-SOH-trahs ah-BLEH-mohs) - We speak

- **Vosotros/Vosotras habléis** (Pronounced boh-SOH-trohs/boh-SOH-trahs ah-BLEH-ees) - You all speak (used mainly in Spain)

- **Ellos/Ellas/Ustedes hablen** (Pronounced EH-yohs/EH-yahs/oo-STEH-dehs AH-blen) - They/You all speak

Notice how the endings are different from the regular present tense. The -ar verbs use endings that typically belong to -er and -ir verbs, and vice versa.

Now let's see how this works with an -er verb, like "comer" (to eat):

- **Yo coma** (Pronounced yoh KOH-mah) - I eat

- **Tú comas** (Pronounced too KOH-mahs) - You eat

- **Él/Ella/Usted coma** (Pronounced el/EH-yah/oo-STEHD KOH-mah) - He/She/You (formal) eats

- **Nosotros/Nosotras comamos** (Pronounced noh-SOH-trohs/noh-SOH-trahs koh-MAH-mohs) - We eat

- **Vosotros/Vosotras comáis** (Pronounced boh-SOH-trohs/boh-SOH-trahs koh-MAH-ees) - You all eat (used mainly in Spain)

- **Ellos/Ellas/Ustedes coman** (Pronounced EH-yohs/EH-yahs/oo-STEH-dehs KOH-mahn) - They/You all eat

For -er and -ir verbs, the endings you add are typically used for -ar verbs. This swapping of endings is one of the key features of the subjunctive mood.

When to Use the Subjunctive Mood

The subjunctive mood is used in several different situations in Spanish. Here are some of the most common cases:

- **Wishes and Desires:** When you want to express a wish, hope, or desire for something that is not certain, you use the subjunctive. For example: **Quiero que tú vengas a la fiesta.** (Pronounced kee-EH-roh keh too BEHN-gahs ah lah FYEHS-tah) - I want you to come to the party.

- **Doubts and Uncertainty:** If you're not sure about something or doubt that something is true, the subjunctive is used. For example: **Dudo que él tenga razón.** (Pronounced DOO-doh keh el TEHN-gah rah-SOHN) - I doubt that he is right.

- **Emotions:** When expressing emotions like happiness, sadness, fear, or surprise about something that is not certain, you use the subjunctive. For example: **Me alegra que estés aquí.** (Pronounced meh ah-LEH-grah keh ehs-TEHS ah-KEE) - I'm glad that you are here.

- **Impersonal Expressions:** Certain impersonal expressions that express necessity, possibility, or importance are followed by the subjunctive. For example: **Es importante que estudies.** (Pronounced ehs eem-por-TAHN-teh keh ehs-TOO-dee-ehs) - It's important that you study.

These are just a few examples of when the subjunctive mood is used. The key idea is that the subjunctive expresses something that is not definite or certain.

Subjunctive Triggers

In Spanish, certain words and phrases act as triggers for the subjunctive mood. These triggers signal that the subjunctive should be used in the clause that follows. Some common triggers include:

- **Ojalá** (Pronounced oh-hah-LAH) - I hope

- **Es posible que** (Pronounced ehs poh-SEE-bleh keh) - It's possible that

- **Es probable que** (Pronounced ehs proh-BAH-bleh keh) - It's probable that

- **No creo que** (Pronounced noh KREH-oh keh) - I don't think that

- **Temo que** (Pronounced TEH-moh keh) - I fear that

Whenever you see or hear one of these triggers, it's a sign that the verb in the following clause should be in the subjunctive mood.

Examples of the Subjunctive Mood in Use

Let's look at some sentences where the subjunctive mood is used, so you can see how it works in context:

Espero que tengas un buen día. (Pronounced ehs-PEH-roh keh TEHN-gahs oon bwen DEE-ah) - I hope that you have a good day.

In this sentence, "espero" (I hope) triggers the subjunctive, so "tengas" (you have) is used instead of the indicative form "tienes."

Es posible que llueva mañana. (Pronounced ehs poh-SEE-bleh keh YWEH-vah mah-NYAH-nah) - It's possible that it will rain tomorrow.

Here, "es posible" (it's possible) triggers the subjunctive, so "llueva" (it rains) is used instead of the indicative form "llueve."

No creo que ellos vengan hoy. (Pronounced noh KREH-oh keh EH-yohs BEN-gahn oy) - I don't think that they are coming today.

"No creo" (I don't think) triggers the subjunctive, so "vengan" (they come) is used instead of the indicative form "vienen."

Key Points to Remember

1. **Understanding the Subjunctive Mood:** The subjunctive mood is used to express doubts, wishes, emotions, and situations that are not certain or real, unlike the indicative mood, which is used for facts and reality.

2. **Forming the Present Subjunctive:** To form the present subjunctive, start with the yo form of the verb in the present tense, remove the -o ending, and add opposite vowel endings: for -ar verbs, use -e, and for -er/-ir verbs, use -a.

3. **When to Use the Subjunctive Mood:** Use the subjunctive for expressing wishes and desires (e.g., Quiero que), doubts and uncertainty (e.g., Dudo que), emotions (e.g., Me alegra que), and impersonal expressions (e.g., Es importante que).

4. **Subjunctive Triggers:** Words and phrases like ojalá, es posible que, and no creo que act as triggers, signaling that the following verb should be in the subjunctive mood.

5. **Examples in Context:** Understanding how the subjunctive mood is used in sentences, such as Espero que tengas un buen día or No creo que ellos vengan hoy, helps in applying this mood correctly in conversations.

Chapter 36

Expressing Wishes and Desires

In Spanish, there are specific ways to talk about your wishes, hopes, and desires. Whether you want to say what you hope will happen, what you wish for, or what you desire, the language has structures that help you express these feelings. In this chapter, you'll learn how to talk about your wishes and desires using verbs like "querer," "desear," and "esperar." You'll also learn how these verbs often trigger the subjunctive mood, which we talked about in the previous chapter.

Using "Querer" to Express Desires

The verb "querer" is commonly used in Spanish to express a desire or wish. It can mean "to want" or "to love," depending on the context. When you use "querer" to express a desire, it is often followed by another verb in the infinitive form or by a clause that uses the subjunctive mood.

Let's look at some examples:

Quiero comer pizza. (Pronounced kee-EH-roh koh-MEHR PEET-sah) - I want to eat pizza.

In this sentence, "quiero" means "I want," and it is followed by the infinitive verb "comer" (to eat). This is a straightforward way to express a desire to do something.

Here's another example:

Quiero que vengas a mi casa. (Pronounced kee-EH-roh keh BEN-gahs ah mee KAH-sah) - I want you to come to my house.

In this sentence, "quiero" is followed by "que" and the verb "vengas" in the subjunctive mood. The subjunctive is used here because you're expressing a desire for something that is not certain to happen.

Let's look at a few more examples with "querer":

Ellos quieren jugar fútbol. (Pronounced EH-yohs kee-EH-rehn hoo-GAHR FOOT-bol) - They want to play soccer.

¿Quieres que te ayude? (Pronounced kee-EH-rehs keh teh ah-YOO-deh) - Do you want me to help you?

As you can see, "querer" is very versatile and is commonly used to express desires or wishes.

Using "Desear" to Express Wishes

Another verb that is often used to express wishes and desires is "desear," which means "to wish" or "to desire." "Desear" is used similarly to "querer," but it often carries a slightly more formal or stronger sense of wishing for something.

Here's how "desear" is used:

Deseo que tengas un buen día. (Pronounced deh-SEH-oh keh TEHN-gahs oon bwen DEE-ah) - I wish you have a good day.

In this sentence, "deseo" means "I wish," and it is followed by "que" and the verb "tengas" in the subjunctive mood. Again, the subjunctive is used because you're expressing a wish about something that is not certain.

Let's look at more examples:

Deseamos que llueva mañana. (Pronounced deh-SEH-ah-mohs keh YWEH-vah mah-NYAH-nah) - We wish that it rains tomorrow.

Ella desea aprender francés. (Pronounced EH-yah deh-SEH-ah ah-pren-DEHR frahn-SEHS) - She wishes to learn French.

Just like with "querer," you can use "desear" to express a wish, followed by either an infinitive verb or a clause with the subjunctive.

Using "Esperar" to Express Hopes

The verb "esperar" means "to hope" or "to expect." It's used when you want to express a hope or an expectation for something to happen. "Esperar" can also be followed by an infinitive or a clause with the subjunctive mood.

Here's how you use "esperar":

Espero que todo salga bien. (Pronounced ehs-PEH-roh keh TOH-doh SAHL-gah byen) - I hope everything goes well.

In this sentence, "espero" means "I hope," and it is followed by "que" and "salga" in the subjunctive. The subjunctive is used here because you're expressing a hope about something that is not certain.

Here are more examples:

Esperamos que puedas venir a la fiesta. (Pronounced ehs-peh-RAH-mohs keh PWEH-dahs veh-NEER ah lah FYEHS-tah) - We hope you can come to the party.

Ellos esperan ganar el partido. (Pronounced EH-yohs ehs-PEH-rahn gah-NAR el par-TEE-doh) - They hope to win the game.

As you can see, "esperar" is used to express hope or expectation, and it often triggers the subjunctive mood when followed by a clause.

Other Ways to Express Wishes and Desires

In addition to "querer," "desear," and "esperar," there are other expressions in Spanish that can be used to talk about wishes and desires. Some of these include:

- **Ojalá** (Pronounced oh-hah-LAH) - This expression means "I hope" or "I wish" and is often followed by the subjunctive. For example: **Ojalá que no llueva mañana.** (Pronounced oh-hah-LAH keh noh YWEH-vah mah-NYAH-nah) - I hope it doesn't rain tomorrow.

- **Me gustaría** (Pronounced meh goos-tah-REE-ah) - This phrase means "I would like" and is used to express a wish or desire politely. For example: **Me gustaría viajar a España.** (Pronounced meh goos-tah-REE-ah vyah-HAHR ah ehs-PAH-nyah) - I would like to travel to Spain.

- **Quisiera** (Pronounced kee-see-EH-rah) - This is a more polite or formal way of saying "I would like." For example: **Quisiera una mesa para dos.** (Pronounced kee-see-EH-rah OO-nah MEH-sah pah-rah dohs) - I would like a table for two.

These expressions give you different ways to talk about what you wish for, hope for, or desire in various situations.

Using Subjunctive with Wishes and Desires

As mentioned earlier, when expressing wishes and desires that involve uncertainty or things that are not guaranteed, you often need to use the subjunctive mood. Here are a few more examples of how the subjunctive is used with these expressions:

Espero que ganes el concurso. (Pronounced ehs-PEH-roh keh GAH-nes el kohn-KOOR-soh) - I hope you win the contest.

Quiero que mi hermana sea feliz. (Pronounced kee-EH-roh keh mee ehr-MAH-nah SEH-ah feh-LEES) - I want my sister to be happy.

Deseamos que te sientas mejor. (Pronounced deh-SEH-ah-mohs keh teh SYEN-tahs meh-HOR) - We wish that you feel better.

In each of these sentences, the subjunctive is used because the speaker is expressing a desire or hope about something that is not certain.

Key Points to Remember

1. **Using "Querer" to Express Desires:** The verb "querer" is commonly used to express desires or wishes, often followed by an infinitive verb or a clause in the subjunctive mood, such as Quiero que vengas a mi casa (I want you to come to my house).

2. **Using "Desear" to Express Wishes:** "Desear" is another verb used to express wishes or desires, typically in a more formal context. It can also trigger the subjunctive mood, as in Deseo que tengas un buen día (I wish you have a good day).

3. **Using "Esperar" to Express Hopes:** The verb "esperar" means "to hope" and is used to express hopes or expectations. It often requires the subjunctive mood, like in Espero que todo salga bien (I hope everything goes well).

4. **Other Expressions for Wishes and Desires:** Phrases like Ojalá (I hope), Me gustaría (I would like), and Quisiera (I would like) offer alternative ways to express wishes and desires, often in a more polite or hopeful tone.

5. **Subjunctive with Wishes and Desires:** When expressing wishes, hopes, or desires that involve uncertainty, the subjunctive mood is commonly used to convey the idea, as in Espero que ganes el concurso (I hope you win the contest).

Chapter 37

Giving Commands: The Imperative Mood

When you need to tell someone what to do, you use commands, which in Spanish is done using the imperative mood. Whether you're telling a friend to come here, asking someone to stop talking, or giving instructions, the imperative mood is what you use. In this chapter, you'll learn how to form commands in Spanish for different situations, and you'll see how to give both positive and negative commands.

What Is the Imperative Mood?

The imperative mood is used to give orders, make requests, or offer advice. In English, we use commands like "Sit down," "Listen," or "Don't talk." In Spanish, commands are formed differently depending on who you are talking to—whether it's a friend, a group of people, or someone you need to address more formally.

Let's start by learning how to form commands in the imperative mood for different types of situations.

Forming Positive Commands

In Spanish, the way you form a command depends on whether you're talking to someone informally (like a friend) or formally (like a teacher or someone you don't know well). The forms also change depending on whether you're talking to one person or more than one person.

Informal (Tú) Commands

For positive commands when talking to a friend or someone your age, you use the "tú" form. To create the command, simply take the third-person singular form of the verb (the "él/ella" form) in the present tense.

GIVING COMMANDS: THE IMPERATIVE MOOD

Here are some examples:

- **Hablar (to speak): Habla** (Pronounced AH-blah) - Speak
- **Comer (to eat): Come** (Pronounced KOH-meh) - Eat
- **Escribir (to write): Escribe** (Pronounced ehs-KREE-beh) - Write

These commands are used when you're talking to one person you know well. For example:

¡Habla más alto! (Pronounced AH-blah mahs AHL-toh) - Speak louder!

Come tu comida. (Pronounced KOH-meh too koh-MEE-dah) - Eat your food.

Formal (Usted) Commands

If you're talking to someone you don't know well or someone who deserves respect (like a teacher), you use the "usted" form for commands. To form these commands, take the yo form of the verb in the present tense, drop the -o, and add the opposite vowel endings (-e for -ar verbs and -a for -er/-ir verbs).

Here are some examples:

- **Hablar (to speak): Hable** (Pronounced AH-bleh) - Speak
- **Comer (to eat): Coma** (Pronounced KOH-mah) - Eat
- **Escribir (to write): Escriba** (Pronounced ehs-KREE-bah) - Write

For example:

Hable más despacio, por favor. (Pronounced AH-bleh mahs dehs-PAH-syoh por fah-VOR) - Speak more slowly, please.

Coma su cena. (Pronounced KOH-mah soo SEH-nah) - Eat your dinner.

Vosotros/Vosotras Commands (Used Mainly in Spain)

When talking to a group of people informally in Spain, you use the "vosotros/vosotras" form. To form these commands, take the infinitive of the verb and replace the final -r with a -d.

Here are some examples:

- **Hablar (to speak): Hablad** (Pronounced ah-BLAHD) - Speak
- **Comer (to eat): Comed** (Pronounced koh-MEHD) - Eat

- **Escribir (to write): Escribid** (Pronounced ehs-kree-BEED) - Write

For example:

Hablad más alto. (Pronounced ah-BLAHD mahs AHL-toh) - Speak louder.

Comed toda la comida. (Pronounced koh-MEHD TOH-dah lah koh-MEE-dah) - Eat all the food.

Forming Negative Commands

Negative commands (telling someone not to do something) are formed differently. For negative commands, the "tú" form uses the present subjunctive, while "usted," "vosotros/vosotras," and "ustedes" forms also use the subjunctive.

Informal (Tú) Negative Commands

To form a negative "tú" command, take the yo form of the verb in the present tense, drop the -o, and add the opposite vowel endings (-es for -ar verbs and -as for -er/-ir verbs). Don't forget to put "no" before the verb.

Here are some examples:

- **Hablar (to speak): No hables** (Pronounced noh AH-blehs) - Don't speak
- **Comer (to eat): No comas** (Pronounced noh KOH-mahs) - Don't eat
- **Escribir (to write): No escribas** (Pronounced noh ehs-KREE-bahs) - Don't write

For example:

No hables durante la clase. (Pronounced noh AH-blehs doo-RAHN-teh lah KLAH-seh) - Don't speak during class.

No comas eso. (Pronounced noh KOH-mahs EH-soh) - Don't eat that.

Formal (Usted) Negative Commands

For negative formal commands, you use the same form as the positive command but add "no" before the verb. The "usted" form uses the present subjunctive.

Here are some examples:

- **Hablar (to speak): No hable** (Pronounced noh AH-bleh) - Don't speak
- **Comer (to eat): No coma** (Pronounced noh KOH-mah) - Don't eat

- **Escribir (to write): No escriba** (Pronounced noh ehs-KREE-bah) - Don't write

For example:

No hable tan rápido. (Pronounced noh AH-bleh tahn RAH-pee-doh) - Don't speak so fast.

No coma esa comida. (Pronounced noh KOH-mah EH-sah koh-MEE-dah) - Don't eat that food.

Vosotros/Vosotras Negative Commands

The negative commands for "vosotros/vosotras" in Spain are formed by using the present subjunctive form with the opposite vowel ending. Add "no" before the verb.

Here are some examples:

- **Hablar (to speak): No habléis** (Pronounced noh ah-BLEH-ees) - Don't speak
- **Comer (to eat): No comáis** (Pronounced noh koh-MAHEES) - Don't eat
- **Escribir (to write): No escribáis** (Pronounced noh ehs-kree-BAHEES) - Don't write

For example:

No habléis durante la película. (Pronounced noh ah-BLEH-ees doo-RAHN-teh lah peh-LEE-koo-lah) - Don't speak during the movie.

Giving Commands to Groups: Ustedes Commands

If you're giving commands to a group of people, you use the "ustedes" form. For positive commands, use the present subjunctive form of the verb. For negative commands, add "no" before the verb.

Here are some examples:

- **Hablar (to speak): Hablen** (Pronounced AH-blen) - Speak
- **No hablen** (Pronounced noh AH-blen) - Don't speak
- **Comer (to eat): Coman** (Pronounced KOH-mahn) - Eat
- **No coman** (Pronounced noh KOH-mahn) - Don't eat
- **Escribir (to write): Escriban** (Pronounced ehs-KREE-bahn) - Write
- **No escriban** (Pronounced noh ehs-KREE-bahn) - Don't write

For example:

Hablen más despacio. (Pronounced AH-blen mahs dehs-PAH-syoh) - Speak more slowly.

No escriban en la mesa. (Pronounced noh ehs-KREE-bahn en lah MEH-sah) - Don't write on the table.

Key Points to Remember

1. **Understanding the Imperative Mood:** The imperative mood in Spanish is used to give commands, make requests, or offer advice. It varies depending on the formality and the number of people being addressed.

2. **Forming Positive Commands:** For informal "tú" commands, use the third-person singular form of the verb. For formal "usted" commands, use the present subjunctive form. For "vosotros/vosotras" in Spain, replace the final -r of the infinitive with -d.

3. **Forming Negative Commands:** Negative "tú" commands are formed by using the present subjunctive and adding "no" before the verb. The same structure applies for formal "usted" and "vosotros/vosotras" commands, using the appropriate present subjunctive form.

4. **Ustedes Commands:** When giving commands to a group of people, use the "ustedes" form. Positive commands use the present subjunctive, while negative commands add "no" before the verb.

5. **Using Commands Effectively:** Understanding when and how to use different forms of commands is crucial for effective communication, whether you're instructing a friend, giving formal advice, or addressing a group.

Chapter 38

Expressing Feelings and Emotions

Talking about how you feel is an important part of communication, and in Spanish, there are specific ways to express your feelings and emotions. Whether you're happy, sad, excited, or nervous, knowing how to express these emotions in Spanish will help you share what's going on inside with others. In this chapter, you'll learn how to talk about different emotions, how to use the verb "estar" with adjectives to describe your feelings, and how the subjunctive mood can come into play when expressing emotions about others.

Using "Estar" to Talk About Emotions

In Spanish, the verb "estar" (to be) is commonly used when talking about temporary states, including emotions and feelings. When you want to say how you feel, you usually start with "estar" followed by an adjective that describes your emotion.

Let's look at some examples:

- **Estoy feliz.** (Pronounced ehs-TOY feh-LEES) - I am happy.

- **Estás triste.** (Pronounced ehs-TAHS TREE-steh) - You are sad.

- **Está nervioso.** (Pronounced ehs-TAH nehr-VYOH-soh) - He/She/You (formal) are nervous.

- **Estamos emocionados.** (Pronounced ehs-TAH-mohs eh-moh-syoh-NAH-dohs) - We are excited.

- **Están enojados.** (Pronounced ehs-TAHN eh-noh-HAH-dohs) - They/You all are angry.

Notice how the adjective changes depending on who you are talking about. For example, "feliz" (happy) stays the same, but "nervioso" (nervous) changes to "nerviosa" when describing a female.

Here are some common adjectives you can use with "estar" to describe emotions:

- **Contento/Contenta** (Pronounced kohn-TEN-toh/kohn-TEN-tah) - Content, happy
- **Preocupado/Preocupada** (Pronounced preh-oh-koo-PAH-doh/preh-oh-koo-PAH-dah) - Worried
- **Cansado/Cansada** (Pronounced kahn-SAH-doh/kahn-SAH-dah) - Tired
- **Asustado/Asustada** (Pronounced ah-soos-TAH-doh/ah-soos-TAH-dah) - Scared
- **Enamorado/Enamorada** (Pronounced eh-nah-moh-RAH-doh/eh-nah-moh-RAH-dah) - In love

For example, you might say:

Estoy cansado después de la escuela. (Pronounced ehs-TOY kahn-SAH-doh dehs-PWAYs deh lah ehs-KWEH-lah) - I am tired after school.

Ella está preocupada por el examen. (Pronounced EH-yah ehs-TAH preh-oh-koo-PAH-dah por el ehs-SAH-mehn) - She is worried about the test.

These sentences show how "estar" is used to describe emotions that are felt at a particular moment.

Using the Subjunctive with Emotions

When expressing feelings and emotions about someone else, especially when there's a change in subject, the subjunctive mood often comes into play. The subjunctive is used when you're expressing emotions like happiness, sadness, fear, or hope about something that's not certain or about someone else's actions.

Let's see how this works:

Me alegra que estés aquí. (Pronounced meh ah-LEH-grah keh ehs-TEHS ah-KEE) - I'm glad that you are here.

In this sentence, "me alegra" means "I'm glad," and because you're expressing an emotion about something uncertain (whether the person is actually here), "estés" is in the subjunctive mood.

Here are some more examples:

Nos preocupa que ellos no lleguen a tiempo. (Pronounced nohs preh-oh-KOO-pah keh EH-yohs noh YEH-gehn ah TYEM-poh) - We're worried that they won't arrive on time.

Me encanta que me escribas cartas. (Pronounced meh ehn-KAHN-tah keh meh ehs-KREE-bahs KAR-tahs) - I love that you write me letters.

In each of these examples, the emotion triggers the use of the subjunctive mood in the second clause.

Expressing Different Emotions

There are many different emotions you might want to express in Spanish. Let's go through some of the most common ones and how you might use them in sentences:

Happiness (Felicidad)

Estoy feliz porque gané el juego. (Pronounced ehs-TOY feh-LEES por-keh gah-NEH el HWEH-goh) - I'm happy because I won the game.

Me alegra que estés aquí. (Pronounced meh ah-LEH-grah keh ehs-TEHS ah-KEE) - I'm glad that you are here.

Sadness (Tristeza)

Estoy triste porque mi amigo se fue. (Pronounced ehs-TOY TREE-steh por-keh mee ah-MEE-goh seh fweh) - I'm sad because my friend left.

Nos pone tristes que no puedas venir. (Pronounced nohs POH-neh TREE-stehs keh noh PWEH-dahs veh-NEER) - It makes us sad that you can't come.

Anger (Enojo)

Estoy enojado porque rompiste mi juguete. (Pronounced ehs-TOY eh-noh-HAH-doh por-keh rom-PEES-teh mee hoo-GEH-teh) - I'm angry because you broke my toy.

Le molesta que hables tan fuerte. (Pronounced leh moh-LEH-stah keh AH-bles tahn FWER-teh) - It bothers him/her that you speak so loudly.

Fear (Miedo)

Tengo miedo de las arañas. (Pronounced TEHN-goh MEE-eh-doh deh lahs ah-RAH-nyahs) - I'm afraid of spiders.

Temo que no podamos terminar a tiempo. (Pronounced TEH-moh keh noh poh-DAH-mohs tehr-mee-NAR ah TYEM-poh) - I'm afraid that we won't be able to finish on time.

Love (Amor)

Estoy enamorado de ti. (Pronounced ehs-TOY eh-nah-moh-RAH-doh deh tee) - I'm in love with you.

Me encanta que siempre estés conmigo. (Pronounced meh ehn-KAHN-tah keh SYEM-preh ehs-TEHS kohn-MEE-goh) - I love that you're always with me.

Each of these sentences helps you express a specific emotion or feeling in Spanish.

Emotional Reactions

When you react to something emotionally, you might use a verb that reflects your feeling. For example, you might say:

Me sorprende que hayas llegado temprano. (Pronounced meh sohr-PREN-deh keh AH-yahs yeh-GAH-doh tehm-PRAH-noh) - I'm surprised that you arrived early.

In this sentence, "me sorprende" means "I'm surprised," and because it's an emotion about something uncertain (the person arriving early), "hayas llegado" is in the subjunctive mood.

Here are some more examples of emotional reactions:

Nos preocupa que no entiendas la lección. (Pronounced nohs preh-oh-KOO-pah keh noh ehn-TYEN-dahs lah lek-SYOHN) - We're worried that you don't understand the lesson.

Me alegra que estés mejor. (Pronounced meh ah-LEH-grah keh ehs-TEHS meh-HOR) - I'm glad that you're better.

Expressing Preferences with Emotions

You can also use emotions to express preferences or things you like or dislike. For example:

Prefiero que me digas la verdad. (Pronounced preh-FYEH-roh keh meh DEE-gahs lah vehr-DAHD) - I prefer that you tell me the truth.

In this sentence, "prefiero" means "I prefer," and it's followed by the subjunctive "digas" because you're expressing a preference about something that's not certain.

Here are more examples:

Nos gusta que nos ayudes con el proyecto. (Pronounced nohs GOOS-tah keh nohs ah-YOO-dehs kohn el proh-YEK-toh) - We like that you help us with the project.

No me gusta que grites tanto. (Pronounced noh meh GOOS-tah keh GREE-tehs TAHN-toh) - I don't like that you shout so much.

Key Points to Remember

1. **Using "Estar" for Emotions:** The verb "estar" is used to describe temporary emotions and feelings in Spanish, followed by an adjective that matches the subject in gender and number. For example, "Estoy feliz" (I am happy).

2. **Subjunctive with Emotions:** When expressing emotions about someone else or uncertain situations, the subjunctive mood is often used. For instance, "Me alegra que estés aquí" (I'm glad that you are here).

3. **Common Emotional Expressions:** Spanish offers a wide range of adjectives to describe emotions, such as "triste" (sad), "enojado" (angry), and "nervioso" (nervous), which can be used with "estar" to talk about how you feel.

4. **Emotional Reactions:** When reacting emotionally to events or actions, verbs like "sorprender" (to surprise) or "preocupar" (to worry) are used with the subjunctive to express uncertainty or subjectivity. Example: "Me sorprende que hayas llegado temprano" (I'm surprised that you arrived early).

5. **Expressing Preferences with Emotions:** Emotions can also be used to express preferences, likes, or dislikes, often triggering the subjunctive. For example, "Prefiero que me digas la verdad" (I prefer that you tell me the truth).

Chapter 39

Talking About Health and the Body

Talking about your health and the different parts of your body is an important part of any language, including Spanish. Whether you need to explain how you feel, describe a pain, or talk about staying healthy, knowing the right words and phrases will help you communicate effectively. In this chapter, we'll explore vocabulary related to health and the body, how to describe symptoms, and ways to talk about staying healthy.

Basic Vocabulary: Parts of the Body

Let's start by learning some of the most common parts of the body in Spanish. Knowing these words will help you describe where something hurts or what part of your body you're talking about.

- **La cabeza** (Pronounced lah kah-BEH-sah) - The head
- **El ojo** (Pronounced el OH-hoh) - The eye
- **La boca** (Pronounced lah BOH-kah) - The mouth
- **La nariz** (Pronounced lah nah-REES) - The nose
- **El brazo** (Pronounced el BRAH-soh) - The arm
- **La mano** (Pronounced lah MAH-noh) - The hand
- **El estómago** (Pronounced el ehs-TOH-mah-goh) - The stomach
- **La pierna** (Pronounced lah PYEHR-nah) - The leg
- **El pie** (Pronounced el PYEH) - The foot

These are just a few examples, but they're important ones that you'll use often when talking about your body.

Describing Symptoms and How You Feel

When you're not feeling well, it's important to be able to describe your symptoms. In Spanish, you can use the verb "tener" (to have) to talk about having a symptom or "estar" (to be) to describe how you're feeling.

Here are some examples using "tener":

- **Tengo dolor de cabeza.** (Pronounced TEHN-goh doh-LOR deh kah-BEH-sah) - I have a headache.

- **Tienes fiebre.** (Pronounced TYEH-nehs FYEH-breh) - You have a fever.

- **Tiene tos.** (Pronounced TYEH-neh tohs) - He/She has a cough.

- **Tenemos un resfriado.** (Pronounced teh-NEH-mohs oon rehs-free-AH-doh) - We have a cold.

- **Tienen gripe.** (Pronounced TYEH-nehn GREE-peh) - They have the flu.

When using "tener," you're talking about something you "have," like a symptom or condition.

You can also use "estar" to describe how you're feeling:

- **Estoy cansado/cansada.** (Pronounced ehs-TOY kahn-SAH-doh/kahn-SAH-dah) - I am tired.

- **Estás enfermo/enferma.** (Pronounced ehs-TAHS ehn-FEHR-moh/ehn-FEHR-mah) - You are sick.

- **Está mareado/mareada.** (Pronounced ehs-TAH mah-reh-AH-doh/mah-reh-AH-dah) - He/She is dizzy.

- **Estamos bien.** (Pronounced ehs-TAH-mohs byen) - We are fine.

- **Están nerviosos/nerviosas.** (Pronounced ehs-TAHN nehr-VYOH-sohs/nehr-VYOH-sahs) - They are nervous.

Notice how the adjectives change depending on whether you're describing a male or female, and whether you're talking about one person or more than one.

Visiting the Doctor

If you ever need to visit a doctor in a Spanish-speaking country, it's helpful to know how to explain what's wrong. Here are some phrases you might use at the doctor's office:

- **Me duele la garganta.** (Pronounced meh DWEH-leh lah gahr-GAHN-tah) - My throat hurts.

- **Me duelen los ojos.** (Pronounced meh DWEH-lehn lohs OH-hohs) - My eyes hurt.

- **Tengo dolor de estómago.** (Pronounced TEHN-goh doh-LOR deh ehs-TOH-mah-goh) - I have a stomachache.

- **No me siento bien.** (Pronounced noh meh SYEN-toh byen) - I don't feel well.

- **Estoy mareado/mareada.** (Pronounced ehs-TOY mah-reh-AH-doh/mah-reh-AH-dah) - I'm dizzy.

You might also hear the doctor ask you questions like:

- **¿Qué síntomas tienes?** (Pronounced keh SEEN-toh-mahs TYEH-nehs) - What symptoms do you have?

- **¿Desde cuándo te sientes así?** (Pronounced DEHS-deh KWAHN-doh teh SYEN-tehs ah-SEE) - How long have you been feeling like this?

- **¿Dónde te duele?** (Pronounced DOHN-deh teh DWEH-leh) - Where does it hurt?

Knowing how to describe your symptoms in Spanish can make a big difference when you need medical help.

Talking About Staying Healthy

It's also important to talk about ways to stay healthy. Here are some phrases you can use to talk about good health habits:

- **Es importante hacer ejercicio.** (Pronounced ehs eem-por-TAHN-teh ah-SEHR eh-hehr-SEE-syoh) - It's important to exercise.

- **Debes comer muchas frutas y verduras.** (Pronounced DEH-behs koh-MEHR MOO-chahs FROO-tahs ee vehr-DOO-rahs) - You should eat lots of fruits and vegetables.

- **Bebe mucha agua todos los días.** (Pronounced BEH-beh MOO-chah AH-gwah TOH-dohs lohs DEE-ahs) - Drink lots of water every day.

- **Duerme lo suficiente cada noche.** (Pronounced DWER-meh loh soo-fee-SYEN-teh KAH-dah NOH-cheh) - Get enough sleep every night.

- **Evita el azúcar y las grasas.** (Pronounced eh-VEE-tah el ah-SOO-kahr ee lahs GRAH-sahs) - Avoid sugar and fats.

Talking about these habits in Spanish helps you share important information about staying healthy.

Expressing Pain and Discomfort

Sometimes you might need to express that something hurts or that you're feeling discomfort. In Spanish, you can use the phrase "me duele" (it hurts me) followed by the part of the body that's hurting.

Here are some examples:

- **Me duele la cabeza.** (Pronounced meh DWEH-leh lah kah-BEH-sah) - My head hurts.
- **Me duele el estómago.** (Pronounced meh DWEH-leh el ehs-TOH-mah-goh) - My stomach hurts.
- **Me duelen las piernas.** (Pronounced meh DWEH-lehn lahs PYEHR-nahs) - My legs hurt.

If you want to talk about something more general, like feeling sick or tired, you can use "me siento" (I feel) followed by the appropriate adjective:

Me siento enfermo/enferma. (Pronounced meh SYEN-toh ehn-FEHR-moh/ehn-FEHR-mah) - I feel sick.

Me siento cansado/cansada. (Pronounced meh SYEN-toh kahn-SAH-doh/kahn-SAH-dah) - I feel tired.

These phrases are very useful when you need to explain how you're feeling.

Key Points to Remember

1. **Basic Body Vocabulary:** Learn essential body parts in Spanish, like "la cabeza" (head), "el brazo" (arm), and "el pie" (foot), to effectively describe where you feel discomfort or pain.

2. **Describing Symptoms:** Use the verb "tener" for symptoms (e.g., "Tengo dolor de cabeza" - I have a headache) and "estar" to describe how you feel (e.g., "Estoy cansado" - I am tired).

3. **Expressing Pain:** Use "me duele" (it hurts me) to express pain in specific body parts (e.g., "Me duele la garganta" - My throat hurts), followed by the body part that's hurting.

4. **Visiting the Doctor:** Familiarize yourself with common phrases for doctor visits, like "No me siento bien" (I don't feel well) and "¿Dónde te duele?" (Where does it hurt?).

5. **Talking About Health:** Discuss healthy habits using phrases like "Es importante hacer ejercicio" (It's important to exercise) and "Debes comer frutas y verduras" (You should eat fruits and vegetables).

Chapter 40

Travel Vocabulary

Traveling is an exciting way to use a new language. Whether you're visiting a new city, going on a vacation, or exploring a different country, knowing some basic travel vocabulary in Spanish will help you communicate and enjoy your trip. In this chapter, we'll cover essential words and phrases you'll need for traveling, from booking a hotel to ordering food at a restaurant. By the end, you'll be ready to navigate your travels with confidence.

Booking a Hotel

One of the first things you might need to do when traveling is book a hotel. Here are some important words and phrases to help you with this:

El hotel (Pronounced el oh-TEL) - The hotel

La habitación (Pronounced lah ah-bee-tah-SYOHN) - The room

La reserva (Pronounced lah reh-SEHR-vah) - The reservation

El número de confirmación (Pronounced el NOO-meh-roh deh kohn-feer-mah-SYOHN) - The confirmation number

El precio (Pronounced el PREH-syoh) - The price

El desayuno incluido (Pronounced el deh-sah-YOO-noh een-kloo-EE-doh) - Breakfast included

El ascensor (Pronounced el ah-sen-SOHR) - The elevator

Here are some examples of how you might use these words in sentences:

¿Tienen habitaciones disponibles? (Pronounced TYEH-nehn ah-bee-tah-SYOH-nehs dees-poh-nee-BLEHS) - Do you have any available rooms?

Quisiera hacer una reserva. (Pronounced kee-see-EH-rah ah-SEHR oo-nah reh-SEHR-vah) - I would like to make a reservation.

¿Cuál es el precio por noche? (Pronounced KWAHL ehs el PREH-syoh por NOH-cheh) - What is the price per night?

These phrases will help you book a hotel room and ask important questions about your stay.

At the Airport

Airports can be busy and confusing, especially in another language. Knowing some key vocabulary can make your experience smoother:

El aeropuerto (Pronounced el ah-eh-roh-PWEHR-toh) - The airport

El vuelo (Pronounced el BWEH-loh) - The flight

La tarjeta de embarque (Pronounced lah tar-HEH-tah deh em-BAR-keh) - The boarding pass

El equipaje (Pronounced el eh-kee-PAH-heh) - The luggage

La puerta de embarque (Pronounced lah PWEHR-tah deh em-BAR-keh) - The boarding gate

El mostrador (Pronounced el mohs-trah-DOR) - The counter (check-in desk)

El control de seguridad (Pronounced el kohn-TROHL deh seh-goo-ree-DAHD) - Security checkpoint

La salida (Pronounced lah sah-LEE-dah) - The departure

La llegada (Pronounced lah yeh-GAH-dah) - The arrival

Here are some useful sentences for navigating the airport:

¿Dónde está el mostrador de facturación? (Pronounced DOHN-deh ehs-TAH el mohs-trah-DOR deh fahk-too-rah-SYOHN) - Where is the check-in counter?

¿Cuál es la puerta de embarque? (Pronounced KWAHL ehs lah PWEHR-tah deh em-BAR-keh) - Which is the boarding gate?

¿A qué hora sale el vuelo? (Pronounced ah keh OH-rah SAH-leh el BWEH-loh) - What time does the flight leave?

These phrases can help you find your way around the airport and ensure you catch your flight on time.

Getting Around: Transportation

Once you arrive at your destination, you'll need to know how to get around. Here are some transportation-related words and phrases:

El taxi (Pronounced el TAHK-see) - The taxi

El autobús (Pronounced el ow-toh-BOOS) - The bus

El metro (Pronounced el MEH-troh) - The subway

El tren (Pronounced el TREHN) - The train

La estación (Pronounced lah ehs-tah-SYOHN) - The station

El boleto (Pronounced el boh-LEH-toh) - The ticket

La parada (Pronounced lah pah-RAH-dah) - The stop

Some useful sentences for getting around include:

¿Cuánto cuesta el boleto de autobús? (Pronounced KWAHN-toh KWEHS-tah el boh-LEH-toh deh ow-toh-BOOS) - How much does the bus ticket cost?

Necesito un taxi. (Pronounced neh-seh-SEE-toh oon TAHK-see) - I need a taxi.

¿Dónde está la estación de tren? (Pronounced DOHN-deh ehs-TAH lah ehs-tah-SYOHN deh TREHN) - Where is the train station?

These phrases will help you navigate public transportation and find your way to different locations.

Asking for Directions

If you ever get lost or need help finding a place, knowing how to ask for directions is crucial. Here are some important phrases:

¿Dónde está...? (Pronounced DOHN-deh ehs-TAH) - Where is...?

You can use this phrase to ask for the location of just about anything. For example:

¿Dónde está el hotel? (Pronounced DOHN-deh ehs-TAH el oh-TEL) - Where is the hotel?

¿Dónde está el restaurante? (Pronounced DOHN-deh ehs-TAH el rehs-tow-RAHN-teh) - Where is the restaurant?

Here are some more specific phrases to help you ask for directions:

¿Cómo llego a...? (Pronounced KOH-moh YEH-goh ah) - How do I get to...?

¿Está lejos? (Pronounced ehs-TAH LEH-hohs) - Is it far?

¿Puede mostrarme en el mapa? (Pronounced PWEH-deh mohs-TRAHR-meh en el MAH-pah) - Can you show me on the map?

These phrases will help you find your way around a new place and ask for directions if you need them.

Eating Out: Restaurants and Cafés

Trying new foods is one of the best parts of traveling. Here are some key words and phrases you might need when eating out:

El restaurante (Pronounced el rehs-tow-RAHN-teh) - The restaurant

El café (Pronounced el kah-FEH) - The café

El menú (Pronounced el meh-NOO) - The menu

El mesero/la mesera (Pronounced el meh-SEH-roh/lah meh-SEH-rah) - The waiter/waitress

La cuenta (Pronounced lah KWEHN-tah) - The bill

La propina (Pronounced lah proh-PEE-nah) - The tip

El agua (Pronounced el AH-gwah) - The water

Some useful sentences when ordering food include:

- **Quisiera el menú, por favor.** (Pronounced kee-see-EH-rah el meh-NOO por fah-VOR) - I would like the menu, please.
- **¿Qué me recomienda?** (Pronounced keh meh reh-koh-MYEN-dah) - What do you recommend?
- **La cuenta, por favor.** (Pronounced lah KWEHN-tah por fah-VOR) - The bill, please.
- **¿Puedo tener un vaso de agua?** (Pronounced PWEH-doh teh-NEHR oon VAH-soh deh AH-gwah) - Can I have a glass of water?

These phrases will help you order food, ask for recommendations, and handle the bill at restaurants and cafés.

Shopping and Souvenirs

When you're out shopping or buying souvenirs, knowing how to communicate in Spanish can enhance your experience. Here are some key words and phrases:

- **La tienda** (Pronounced lah TYEHN-dah) - The store

- **El mercado** (Pronounced el mehr-KAH-doh) - The market

- **El precio** (Pronounced el PREH-syoh) - The price

- **La talla** (Pronounced lah TAH-yah) - The size

- **El recibo** (Pronounced el reh-SEE-boh) - The receipt

- **¿Cuánto cuesta?** (Pronounced KWAHN-toh KWEHS-tah) - How much does it cost?

- **¿Puedo probarlo?** (Pronounced PWEH-doh proh-BAHR-loh) - Can I try it on?

These phrases will help you navigate shopping experiences, ask about prices, and try on items before you buy.

Emergency Situations

Finally, it's important to be prepared for any emergencies that may arise while traveling. Here are some essential words and phrases:

- **La policía** (Pronounced lah poh-lee-SEE-ah) - The police

- **El hospital** (Pronounced el ohs-pee-TAHL) - The hospital

- **La ambulancia** (Pronounced lah ahm-boo-LAHN-syah) - The ambulance

- **Ayuda** (Pronounced ah-YOO-dah) - Help

- **Estoy perdido/perdida** (Pronounced ehs-TOY pehr-DEE-doh/pehr-DEE-dah) - I am lost

- **Necesito un médico** (Pronounced neh-seh-SEE-toh oon MEH-dee-koh) - I need a doctor

- **¿Dónde está la embajada?** (Pronounced DOHN-deh ehs-TAH lah ehm-bah-HAH-dah) - Where is the embassy?

Knowing these phrases can be crucial if you find yourself in a difficult situation and need assistance quickly.

Key Points to Remember:

1. **Booking a Hotel:** Learn essential phrases for booking and asking about hotel accommodations, like "¿Tienen habitaciones disponibles?" (Do you have any available rooms?).

2. **Navigating the Airport:** Familiarize yourself with airport-related vocabulary such as "El vuelo" (The flight) and useful sentences like "¿Dónde está el mostrador de facturación?" (Where is the check-in counter?).

3. **Getting Around:** Master phrases for using public transportation, including "¿Cuánto cuesta el boleto de autobús?" (How much does the bus ticket cost?) and "Necesito un taxi" (I need a taxi).

4. **Eating Out:** Know how to order food and handle restaurant situations with phrases like "Quisiera el menú, por favor" (I would like the menu, please) and "La cuenta, por favor" (The bill, please).

5. **Handling Emergencies:** Be prepared with essential emergency phrases such as "Ayuda" (Help) and "Necesito un médico" (I need a doctor).

Chapter 41

Expressing Opinions

Being able to express your opinions is an important part of communicating in any language. Whether you want to share what you think about a movie, give your opinion on a school project, or discuss your favorite activities, knowing how to express your thoughts clearly in Spanish will help you connect with others. In this chapter, you'll learn how to express opinions in Spanish, including the key phrases and structures you'll need to know. By the end, you'll be able to share your thoughts and ideas with confidence.

Basic Phrases for Expressing Opinions

When you want to express your opinion in Spanish, there are several key phrases that you can use to start your sentences. Here are some of the most common ones:

- **Creo que...** (Pronounced KREH-oh keh) - I think that...

- **Pienso que...** (Pronounced PYEHN-soh keh) - I believe that...

- **Me parece que...** (Pronounced meh pah-REH-seh keh) - It seems to me that...

- **En mi opinión...** (Pronounced en mee oh-pee-NYOHN) - In my opinion...

- **Opino que...** (Pronounced oh-PEE-noh keh) - I am of the opinion that...

These phrases are all useful ways to begin sharing your thoughts. For example, you might say:

Creo que este libro es muy interesante. (Pronounced KREH-oh keh EHS-teh LEE-broh ehs mwee een-teh-reh-SAHN-teh) - I think that this book is very interesting.

En mi opinión, el chocolate es delicioso. (Pronounced en mee oh-pee-NYOHN el choh-koh-LAH-teh ehs deh-lee-SYOH-soh) - In my opinion, chocolate is delicious.

These phrases help you start your opinion statements in a clear and organized way.

Agreeing and Disagreeing

When you're sharing opinions, it's common to agree or disagree with others. Here are some ways to express agreement or disagreement in Spanish:

Agreeing:

- **Estoy de acuerdo.** (Pronounced ehs-TOY deh ah-KWEHR-doh) - I agree.
- **Tienes razón.** (Pronounced TYEH-nehs rah-SOHN) - You are right.
- **Es verdad.** (Pronounced ehs vehr-DAHD) - It's true.

For example:

Creo que la película es divertida. (Pronounced KREH-oh keh lah peh-LEE-koo-lah ehs dee-ver-TEE-dah) - I think that the movie is fun.

Estoy de acuerdo. (Pronounced ehs-TOY deh ah-KWEHR-doh) - I agree.

Disagreeing:

- **No estoy de acuerdo.** (Pronounced noh ehs-TOY deh ah-KWEHR-doh) - I don't agree.
- **No creo que sea así.** (Pronounced noh KREH-oh keh SEH-ah ah-SEE) - I don't think it's like that.
- **No me parece bien.** (Pronounced noh meh pah-REH-seh byen) - It doesn't seem right to me.

For example:

Pienso que este libro es aburrido. (Pronounced PYEHN-soh keh EHS-teh LEE-broh ehs ah-boo-REE-doh) - I think that this book is boring.

No estoy de acuerdo. (Pronounced noh ehs-TOY deh ah-KWEHR-doh) - I don't agree.

These phrases are helpful when you want to express whether you agree or disagree with someone else's opinion.

Using "Para mí" and "Según yo" for Personal Opinions

Sometimes you want to emphasize that what you're saying is just your personal opinion. In these cases, you can use phrases like "Para mí" (for me) or "Según yo" (according to me).

Here's how you can use these phrases:

Para mí, la música clásica es la mejor. (Pronounced PAH-rah mee lah MOO-see-kah KLAH-see-kah ehs lah meh-HOR) - For me, classical music is the best.

Según yo, deberíamos estudiar más. (Pronounced seh-GOON yoh deh-beh-REE-ah-mohs ehs-too-dee-AHR mahs) - According to me, we should study more.

These phrases add a personal touch to your opinions, making it clear that you're sharing your own perspective.

Expressing Uncertainty

Sometimes, when you're giving your opinion, you might not be completely sure about what you're saying. In these cases, you can use phrases that show uncertainty:

- **No estoy seguro/segura, pero...** (Pronounced noh ehs-TOY seh-GOO-roh/seh-GOO-rah PEH-roh) - I'm not sure, but...

- **Creo que sí, pero...** (Pronounced KREH-oh keh see PEH-roh) - I think so, but...

- **Tal vez...** (Pronounced tahl VEHS) - Maybe...

For example:

No estoy seguro, pero creo que mañana lloverá. (Pronounced noh ehs-TOY seh-GOO-roh PEH-roh KREH-oh keh mah-NYAH-nah yoh-beh-RAH) - I'm not sure, but I think it will rain tomorrow.

Tal vez la respuesta es correcta. (Pronounced tahl VEHS lah rehs-PWES-tah ehs koh-REK-tah) - Maybe the answer is correct.

These phrases help you express your opinion even when you're not completely certain about it.

Connecting Your Ideas

When expressing opinions, it's useful to connect your ideas to make your thoughts clear and easy to follow. Here are some phrases that can help you connect your ideas in Spanish:

- **Además...** (Pronounced ah-deh-MAHS) - Additionally...

- **Por eso...** (Pronounced por EH-soh) - That's why...

- **Sin embargo...** (Pronounced seen ehm-BAHR-goh) - However...

For example:

Me gusta el verano. Además, me encanta nadar en la playa. (Pronounced meh GOOS-tah el beh-RAH-noh ah-deh-MAHS meh ehn-KAHN-tah nah-DAHR en lah PLAH-yah) - I like summer. Additionally, I love swimming at the beach.

Pienso que debemos terminar la tarea. Por eso, voy a empezar ahora. (Pronounced PYEHN-soh keh deh-BEH-mohs tehr-mee-NAHR lah tah-REH-ah por EH-soh boy ah ehm-peh-SAR ah-OH-rah) - I think we should finish the homework. That's why I'm going to start now.

Using these phrases helps you explain your opinions in a more organized way.

Expressing Preferences

Sometimes expressing your opinion means sharing your preferences. Here are some ways to talk about what you prefer in Spanish:

- **Prefiero...** (Pronounced preh-FYEH-roh) - I prefer...

- **Me gusta más...** (Pronounced meh GOOS-tah mahs) - I like more...

- **Me encanta...** (Pronounced meh ehn-KAHN-tah) - I love...

For example:

Prefiero el helado de chocolate. (Pronounced preh-FYEH-roh el eh-LAH-doh deh choh-koh-LAH-teh) - I prefer chocolate ice cream.

Me gusta más el verano que el invierno. (Pronounced meh GOOS-tah mahs el beh-RAH-noh keh el een-VYEHR-noh) - I like summer more than winter.

Me encanta leer libros de aventuras. (Pronounced meh ehn-KAHN-tah leh-EHR LEE-brohs deh ah-ven-TOO-rahs) - I love reading adventure books.

These phrases allow you to express your preferences clearly, helping others understand what you like or enjoy the most.

Key Points to Remember:

1. **Basic Phrases for Expressing Opinions:** Use phrases like "Creo que..." (I think that...), "Pienso que..." (I believe that...), and "En mi opinión..." (In my opinion...) to start your opinion statements clearly.

2. **Agreeing and Disagreeing:** Express agreement with phrases like "Estoy de acuerdo" (I agree) and disagreement with "No estoy de acuerdo" (I don't agree) to share your

stance on others' opinions.

3. **Using "Para mí" and "Según yo":** Add a personal touch to your opinions with phrases like "Para mí..." (For me...) and "Según yo..." (According to me...) to emphasize that you are sharing your perspective.

4. **Expressing Uncertainty:** Use phrases such as "No estoy seguro, pero..." (I'm not sure, but...) and "Tal vez..." (Maybe...) to express opinions with a level of uncertainty.

5. **Expressing Preferences:** Share your likes and preferences with phrases like "Prefiero..." (I prefer...), "Me gusta más..." (I like more...), and "Me encanta..." (I love...), allowing others to understand your tastes.

Chapter 42

The Conditional Tense

The conditional tense in Spanish is a special verb form that you use when you want to talk about what you would do if something were to happen. It's also used to make polite requests or to express wishes and possibilities. In this chapter, we'll learn how to form the conditional tense, when to use it, and how to make your sentences sound more natural in Spanish. By the end, you'll be able to talk about hypothetical situations and express what you would do in different scenarios.

How to Form the Conditional Tense

The conditional tense in Spanish is actually quite easy to form. You start with the infinitive form of the verb (the form you find in the dictionary), and then you add specific endings that are the same for all verbs, whether they end in -ar, -er, or -ir.

Here are the conditional endings:

- **-ía** (Pronounced EE-ah) - I would
- **-ías** (Pronounced EE-ahs) - You would
- **-ía** (Pronounced EE-ah) - He/She/You (formal) would
- **-íamos** (Pronounced EE-ah-mohs) - We would
- **-íais** (Pronounced EE-ah-ees) - You all (in Spain) would
- **-ían** (Pronounced EE-ahn) - They/You all would

To form the conditional tense, simply add these endings to the entire infinitive form of the verb. Here's how it looks with a few verbs:

- **Hablar (to speak):** Yo hablaría (Pronounced yoh ah-blah-REE-ah) - I would speak
- **Comer (to eat):** Tú comerías (Pronounced too koh-meh-REE-ahs) - You would eat

- **Vivir (to live):** Él viviría (Pronounced el vee-vee-REE-ah) - He would live

- **Estudiar (to study):** Nosotros estudiaríamos (Pronounced noh-SOH-trohs ehs-too-dyah-REE-ah-mohs) - We would study

These endings are the same no matter what type of verb you're using, which makes the conditional tense easy to remember and apply.

When to Use the Conditional Tense

The conditional tense is used in several different situations. Let's explore some of the most common uses:

1. Talking About Hypothetical Situations

You use the conditional tense to talk about what you would do if something specific were to happen. For example:

Si tuviera más tiempo, viajaría por el mundo. (Pronounced see too-VYEH-rah mahs TYEM-poh, vyah-hah-REE-ah por el MOON-doh) - If I had more time, I would travel around the world.

Yo compraría una bicicleta nueva si tuviera el dinero. (Pronounced yoh kohm-prah-REE-ah OO-nah bee-see-KLEH-tah NWEH-vah see too-VYEH-rah el dee-NEH-roh) - I would buy a new bike if I had the money.

In these examples, you're imagining a situation and saying what you would do if it were true.

2. Making Polite Requests

The conditional tense is also used to make requests sound more polite. For example:

¿Podrías ayudarme con mi tarea? (Pronounced poh-DREE-ahs ah-yoo-DAHR-meh kohn mee tah-REH-ah) - Could you help me with my homework?

Me gustaría un vaso de agua, por favor. (Pronounced meh goos-tah-REE-ah oon VAH-soh deh AH-gwah, por fah-VOR) - I would like a glass of water, please.

Using the conditional tense in these sentences makes the request softer and more polite.

3. Expressing Wishes or Desires

The conditional tense can also be used to express what you wish would happen. For example:

Me encantaría ir a la playa este fin de semana. (Pronounced meh ehn-kahn-tah-REE-ah eer ah lah PLAH-yah EHS-teh feen deh seh-MAH-nah) - I would love to go to the beach this weekend.

Quisiera tener un perro algún día. (Pronounced kee-see-EH-rah teh-NEHR oon PEH-rroh ahl-GOON DEE-ah) - I would like to have a dog someday.

These sentences show how you can use the conditional tense to talk about what you would like or wish for.

Irregular Verbs in the Conditional Tense

Just like in other tenses, some verbs are irregular in the conditional tense. This means that instead of adding the conditional endings to the infinitive form, the verb changes slightly before you add the endings. Here are some common irregular verbs in the conditional tense:

- **Tener (to have):** Yo tendría (Pronounced yoh tehn-DREE-ah) - I would have

- **Salir (to leave):** Tú saldrías (Pronounced too sahl-DREE-ahs) - You would leave

- **Poder (to be able to):** Él podría (Pronounced el poh-DREE-ah) - He would be able to

- **Hacer (to do/make):** Nosotros haríamos (Pronounced noh-SOH-trohs ah-REE-ah-mohs) - We would do/make

- **Decir (to say/tell):** Ellos dirían (Pronounced EH-yohs dee-REE-ahn) - They would say/tell

These irregular verbs don't follow the regular pattern, so it's important to remember how they change in the conditional tense.

Using "Si" Clauses with the Conditional Tense

One common structure in Spanish is to use "si" (if) clauses with the conditional tense to talk about hypothetical situations. Typically, the "si" clause is in the past subjunctive, and the result clause is in the conditional.

Here's how it works:

Si tuviera un millón de dólares, compraría una casa grande. (Pronounced see too-VYEH-rah oon mee-YOHN deh DOH-lah-rehs, kohm-prah-REE-ah OO-nah KAH-sah GRAHN-deh) - If I had a million dollars, I would buy a big house.

Si fueras presidente, ¿qué harías? (Pronounced see FWEH-rahs preh-see-DEHN-teh, keh ah-REE-ahs) - If you were president, what would you do?

These sentences show how you can talk about what you would do if certain conditions were met.

Expressing Doubts or Uncertainty

The conditional tense is also useful for expressing doubt or uncertainty about something that might happen. For example:

Yo pensaría que es una buena idea, pero no estoy seguro. (Pronounced yoh pehn-sah-REE-ah keh ehs OO-nah BWEH-nah ee-DEH-ah, PEH-roh noh ehs-TOY seh-GOO-roh) - I would think it's a good idea, but I'm not sure.

Ellos creerían en la historia, pero es difícil de probar. (Pronounced EH-yohs kreh-eh-REE-ahn ehn lah ee-STOH-ryah, PEH-roh ehs dee-FEE-seel deh proh-BAHR) - They would believe the story, but it's hard to prove.

This use of the conditional tense helps you express your thoughts while acknowledging some uncertainty or doubt.

Key Points to Remember:

1. **Forming the Conditional Tense:** The conditional tense is formed by adding specific endings (-ía, -ías, -ía, -íamos, -íais, -ían) to the infinitive form of the verb. This structure is consistent across all verb types, making it easy to apply.

2. **Talking About Hypothetical Situations:** The conditional tense is commonly used to describe what you would do in hypothetical scenarios. For example: "Si tuviera más tiempo, viajaría por el mundo" (If I had more time, I would travel around the world).

3. **Making Polite Requests:** Use the conditional tense to make polite requests, softening the tone of your sentences. For example: "¿Podrías ayudarme con mi tarea?" (Could you help me with my homework?).

4. **Expressing Wishes or Desires:** The conditional tense can express wishes or desires, such as "Me encantaría ir a la playa este fin de semana" (I would love to go to the beach this weekend).

5. **Using "Si" Clauses:** Combine the conditional tense with "si" clauses (if clauses) to discuss hypothetical situations, typically using the past subjunctive in the "si" clause. For example: "Si tuviera un millón de dólares, compraría una casa grande" (If I had a million dollars, I would buy a big house).

Chapter 43

Understanding and Using Prepositions

Prepositions are small but important words that help us describe the relationship between different parts of a sentence. In Spanish, prepositions work much like they do in English, but there are some differences in how they are used. In this chapter, we'll learn about some of the most common prepositions in Spanish, how to use them in sentences, and how to make your descriptions more precise.

What Are Prepositions?

Prepositions are words that connect nouns, pronouns, or phrases to other words in a sentence. They often tell us where something is, when something happens, or how things are related to each other. In English, examples of prepositions include "in," "on," "at," "under," and "before." In Spanish, prepositions work in similar ways, but it's important to know the specific words and how to use them correctly.

Common Prepositions in Spanish

Let's start by looking at some of the most common prepositions in Spanish:

- **a** (Pronounced ah) - to, at

- **de** (Pronounced deh) - of, from

- **en** (Pronounced en) - in, on, at

- **con** (Pronounced kohn) - with

- **sin** (Pronounced seen) - without

- **por** (Pronounced pohr) - for, by, through

- **para** (Pronounced PAH-rah) - for, in order to

- **sobre** (Pronounced SOH-breh) - on, over, about

- **entre** (Pronounced EHN-treh) - between, among

- **hasta** (Pronounced AHS-tah) - until, up to

These are just a few examples, but they are some of the most frequently used prepositions in Spanish. Let's explore how to use them in sentences.

Using "a" and "de"

The prepositions "a" and "de" are two of the most common and versatile prepositions in Spanish. Here's how they are used:

"A" (to, at):

"A" is often used to indicate direction, location, or time.

Here are some examples:

Voy a la escuela todos los días. (Pronounced boy ah lah ehs-KWEH-lah TOH-dohs lohs DEE-ahs) - I go to school every day.

Llegamos a las tres de la tarde. (Pronounced yeh-GAH-mohs ah lahs TREHS deh lah TAR-deh) - We arrive at three in the afternoon.

"A" is used to show where someone is going or when something happens.

"De" (of, from):

"De" is used to show origin, possession, or the material something is made of.

Here are some examples:

El libro es de Juan. (Pronounced el LEE-broh ehs deh HWAHN) - The book is Juan's.

Vengo de la tienda. (Pronounced BEHN-goh deh lah TYEHN-dah) - I'm coming from the store.

La mesa es de madera. (Pronounced lah MEH-sah ehs deh mah-DEH-rah) - The table is made of wood.

"De" is very useful for showing where something comes from or who it belongs to.

Using "en" and "con"

Another pair of common prepositions are "en" and "con." These prepositions are used frequently to describe locations, relationships, and how things are done.

"En" (in, on, at):

"En" is used to indicate location or position, similar to how we use "in," "on," or "at" in English.

Here are some examples:

Estoy en la escuela. (Pronounced ehs-TOY en lah ehs-KWEH-lah) - I am at school.

El libro está en la mesa. (Pronounced el LEE-broh ehs-TAH en lah MEH-sah) - The book is on the table.

Vivo en Nueva York. (Pronounced VEE-voh en NWEH-vah YORK) - I live in New York.

"En" is often the go-to preposition when describing where something or someone is.

"Con" (with):

"Con" is used to express being with someone or something, or doing something with someone or something.

Here are some examples:

Voy al cine con mis amigos. (Pronounced boy ahl SEE-neh kohn mees ah-MEE-gohs) - I'm going to the movies with my friends.

Escribo con un lápiz. (Pronounced ehs-KREE-boh kohn oon LAH-pees) - I write with a pencil.

"Con" is straightforward and easy to use whenever you're describing doing something together or using something to do an action.

Using "por" and "para"

"Por" and "para" are two prepositions that can be tricky for English speakers because they both can mean "for." However, they are used in different contexts. Let's break down when to use each one.

"Por" (for, by, through):

"Por" is used to express reasons, duration, and movement through a place.

Here are some examples:

Gracias por tu ayuda. (Pronounced GRAH-syahs pohr too ah-YOO-dah) - Thank you for your help.

Caminamos por el parque. (Pronounced kah-mee-NAH-mohs pohr el PAHR-keh) - We walk through the park.

Estudié por dos horas. (Pronounced ehs-too-DYAY pohr dohs OH-rahs) - I studied for two hours.

"Por" is often used when talking about the reason for something, the amount of time something takes, or moving through a space.

"Para" (for, in order to):

"Para" is used to talk about the purpose or goal of something, deadlines, and destinations.

Here are some examples:

Este regalo es para ti. (Pronounced EHS-teh reh-GAH-loh ehs PAH-rah tee) - This gift is for you.

Necesito el proyecto para el viernes. (Pronounced neh-seh-SEE-toh el proh-YEK-toh PAH-rah el BYER-nehs) - I need the project for Friday.

Voy para la escuela. (Pronounced boy PAH-rah lah ehs-KWEH-lah) - I'm going to school.

"Para" is used when talking about the goal or purpose of an action, the recipient of something, or a destination.

Using "sobre," "entre," and "hasta"

These three prepositions are also commonly used and help you add more detail to your sentences.

"Sobre" (on, over, about):

"Sobre" is used to talk about being on top of something, or when discussing a topic.

Here are some examples:

El cuaderno está sobre la mesa. (Pronounced el kwah-DEHR-noh ehs-TAH SOH-breh lah MEH-sah) - The notebook is on the table.

Leí un libro sobre animales. (Pronounced leh-EE oon LEE-broh SOH-breh ah-nee-MAH-lehs) - I read a book about animals.

"Entre" (between, among):

"Entre" is used to describe something that is between two things or among a group.

Here are some examples:

La pelota está entre las sillas. (Pronounced lah peh-LOH-tah ehs-TAH EHN-treh lahs SEE-yahs) - The ball is between the chairs.

Entre todos, completamos el proyecto. (Pronounced EHN-treh TOH-dohs kohm-pleh-TAH-mohs el proh-YEK-toh) - Among all of us, we completed the project.

"Hasta" (until, up to):

"Hasta" is used to talk about a point in time or space up to which something happens.

Here are some examples:

Vamos a quedarnos hasta las diez. (Pronounced BAH-mohs ah keh-DAR-nohs AHS-tah lahs DYAYS) - We're going to stay until ten.

Corre hasta el final de la calle. (Pronounced KOH-rreh AHS-tah el fee-NAHL deh lah KAH-yeh) - Run to the end of the street.

"Hasta" is useful for talking about limits in time or space.

Key Points to Remember:

1. **Common Prepositions:** Spanish prepositions like a, de, en, con, por, and para are essential for indicating direction, location, possession, purpose, and more. Each preposition has specific contexts in which it is used, making them crucial for clear communication.

2. **Using "a" and "de":** "A" is commonly used to indicate direction, location, or time (e.g., Voy a la escuela - I go to school), while "de" shows origin, possession, or material (e.g., El libro es de Juan - The book is Juan's).

3. **Using "en" and "con":** "En" is used for location or position, equivalent to "in," "on," or "at" in English (e.g., Estoy en la escuela - I am at school). "Con" means "with" and describes doing something together or using something (e.g., Voy al cine con mis amigos - I'm going to the movies with my friends).

4. **Using "por" and "para":** "Por" is used for reasons, duration, and movement through a place (e.g., Caminamos por el parque - We walk through the park), while "para" indicates purpose, deadlines, or destinations (e.g., Este regalo es para ti - This gift is for you).

5. **Using "sobre," "entre," and "hasta":** "Sobre" is used for discussing topics or

describing something on top of another (e.g., El cuaderno está sobre la mesa - The notebook is on the table). "Entre" indicates something between or among (e.g., La pelota está entre las sillas - The ball is between the chairs), and "hasta" is used for limits in time or space (e.g., Vamos a quedarnos hasta las diez - We're going to stay until ten).

Chapter 44

Indirect and Direct Object Pronouns

In Spanish, using object pronouns correctly is an important part of speaking and writing clearly. Object pronouns replace nouns in a sentence to avoid repetition and make your sentences shorter and easier to follow. There are two types of object pronouns: direct and indirect. In this chapter, we'll learn what each of these pronouns is, how to use them, and how they work together in a sentence.

Understanding Direct Object Pronouns

A direct object pronoun replaces the noun that directly receives the action of the verb in a sentence. For example, in the sentence "I see the dog," "the dog" is the direct object because it is what is being seen. In Spanish, instead of repeating "the dog," you can use a direct object pronoun.

Here are the direct object pronouns in Spanish:

- **me** (Pronounced meh) - me

- **te** (Pronounced teh) - you (informal)

- **lo** (Pronounced loh) - him, it (masculine)

- **la** (Pronounced lah) - her, it (feminine)

- **nos** (Pronounced nohs) - us

- **os** (Pronounced ohs) - you all (informal, in Spain)

- **los** (Pronounced lohs) - them (masculine)

- **las** (Pronounced lahs) - them (feminine)

Let's look at some examples of how direct object pronouns are used:

Veo el perro. (Pronounced BEH-oh el PEH-rroh) - I see the dog.

Instead of repeating "el perro" (the dog), you can replace it with the direct object pronoun "lo" (him/it):

Lo veo. (Pronounced loh BEH-oh) - I see him/it.

Here's another example:

Compré la pizza. (Pronounced kohm-PREH lah PEET-sah) - I bought the pizza.

In this case, "la pizza" (the pizza) can be replaced with the direct object pronoun "la" (her/it):

La compré. (Pronounced lah kohm-PREH) - I bought it.

Using direct object pronouns like this helps to avoid repetition and makes your sentences more fluid.

Understanding Indirect Object Pronouns

Indirect object pronouns, on the other hand, are used to replace the noun that is the recipient of the action in a sentence. For example, in the sentence "I give the book to Maria," "Maria" is the indirect object because she is the one receiving the book. In Spanish, instead of repeating "Maria," you can use an indirect object pronoun.

Here are the indirect object pronouns in Spanish:

- **me** (Pronounced meh) - to/for me
- **te** (Pronounced teh) - to/for you (informal)
- **le** (Pronounced leh) - to/for him, her, it
- **nos** (Pronounced nohs) - to/for us
- **os** (Pronounced ohs) - to/for you all (informal, in Spain)
- **les** (Pronounced lehs) - to/for them

Let's look at some examples of how indirect object pronouns are used:

Le doy el libro a María. (Pronounced leh DOY el LEE-broh ah mah-REE-ah) - I give the book to Maria.

In this sentence, "a María" (to Maria) is replaced with the indirect object pronoun "le" (to/for him, her, it):

Le doy el libro. (Pronounced leh DOY el LEE-broh) - I give her the book.

Here's another example:

Les envío una carta a mis amigos. (Pronounced lehs ehn-BEE-oh OO-nah KAHR-tah ah mees ah-MEE-gohs) - I send a letter to my friends.

In this case, "a mis amigos" (to my friends) can be replaced with the indirect object pronoun "les" (to/for them):

Les envío una carta. (Pronounced lehs ehn-BEE-oh OO-nah KAHR-tah) - I send them a letter.

Using indirect object pronouns like this helps to clarify who is receiving the action in a sentence.

Using Both Direct and Indirect Object Pronouns Together

Sometimes, you need to use both a direct and an indirect object pronoun in the same sentence. In Spanish, the indirect object pronoun always comes before the direct object pronoun.

Let's look at an example:

Le doy el libro a María. (Pronounced leh DOY el LEE-broh ah mah-REE-ah) - I give the book to Maria.

If we want to replace both "el libro" (the book) and "a María" (to Maria), we would use "lo" for "el libro" and "le" for "a María":

Se lo doy. (Pronounced seh loh DOY) - I give it to her.

Notice that when you have "le" or "les" before a direct object pronoun like "lo," "la," "los," or "las," the indirect object pronoun changes to "se" to make the sentence easier to say.

Here's another example:

Les envío una carta a mis amigos. (Pronounced lehs ehn-BEE-oh OO-nah KAHR-tah ah mees ah-MEE-gohs) - I send a letter to my friends.

To replace both "una carta" (a letter) and "a mis amigos" (to my friends), we would use "la" for "una carta" and "les" for "a mis amigos":

Se la envío. (Pronounced seh lah ehn-BEE-oh) - I send it to them.

Using both pronouns in this way makes your sentences shorter and avoids unnecessary repetition.

Word Order with Object Pronouns

In Spanish, the placement of object pronouns is important. They usually come before the conjugated verb. However, if there is an infinitive verb (a verb that ends in -ar, -er, or -ir) or a gerund (-ando, -iendo), the pronouns can either be placed before the conjugated verb or attached to the end of the infinitive or gerund.

Here's an example with an infinitive verb:

Voy a darle el libro. (Pronounced boy ah DAR-leh el LEE-broh) - I'm going to give her the book.

Or you can say:

Le voy a dar el libro. (Pronounced leh boy ah DAR el LEE-broh) - I'm going to give her the book.

Both versions are correct, and it's up to you which one to use.

Here's an example with a gerund:

Estoy dándole el libro. (Pronounced ehs-TOY DAN-doh-leh el LEE-broh) - I am giving her the book.

Or you can say:

Le estoy dando el libro. (Pronounced leh ehs-TOY DAN-doh el LEE-broh) - I am giving her the book.

Again, both versions are correct.

Key Points to Remember:

1. **Direct Object Pronouns:** These pronouns replace the noun that directly receives the action of the verb. Common pronouns include me, te, lo, la, nos, os, and los/las. Example: Lo veo (I see him/it).

2. **Indirect Object Pronouns:** These pronouns replace the noun that is the recipient of the action. Common pronouns include me, te, le, nos, os, and les. Example: Le doy el libro (I give her the book).

3. **Using Both Pronouns Together:** When using both direct and indirect object pronouns in the same sentence, the indirect object pronoun comes before the direct object

pronoun. Le or les changes to se when followed by lo, la, los, or las. Example: Se lo doy (I give it to her).

4. **Word Order:** Object pronouns usually come before the conjugated verb. However, with infinitives or gerunds, they can be placed either before the conjugated verb or attached to the end of the infinitive or gerund. Example: Voy a darle el libro or Le voy a dar el libro (I'm going to give her the book).

5. **Clarity and Efficiency:** Using object pronouns helps to avoid repetition and makes sentences shorter and easier to follow, contributing to clearer and more efficient communication.

Chapter 45

The Passive Voice

The passive voice is a way of structuring sentences so that the focus is on the action being done, rather than on who is doing it. In English, we use the passive voice when we say things like "The cake was baked by Maria." In this sentence, the focus is on the cake, not on Maria, who did the baking. In Spanish, the passive voice works similarly, but it's used a bit differently and can be more complex. In this chapter, we'll learn how to form the passive voice in Spanish, when to use it, and how to make your sentences clear and effective.

What Is the Passive Voice?

The passive voice is used when the subject of the sentence is the recipient of the action rather than the one doing the action. This shifts the focus from who is performing the action to the action itself and the person or thing affected by it.

Here's an example in English:

Active voice: Maria baked the cake.

Passive voice: The cake was baked by Maria.

In the passive voice, the action (baking) is emphasized, and the subject (the cake) is what receives the action.

How to Form the Passive Voice in Spanish

In Spanish, the passive voice is formed by using the verb "ser" (to be) followed by the past participle of the main verb. The past participle is a form of the verb that typically ends in -ado for -ar verbs and -ido for -er and -ir verbs.

Here's the basic structure:

Subject + ser + past participle + por + agent (the doer of the action)

Let's look at some examples:

El libro fue escrito por el autor. (Pronounced el LEE-broh FWEH ehs-KREE-toh por el ow-TOR) - The book was written by the author.

In this sentence, "el libro" (the book) is the subject, "fue" (was) is the form of "ser," "escrito" (written) is the past participle, and "por el autor" (by the author) tells us who did the action.

Here's another example:

La canción fue cantada por la cantante. (Pronounced lah kahn-SYOHN FWEH kahn-TAH-dah por lah kahn-TAHN-teh) - The song was sung by the singer.

In this sentence, "la canción" (the song) is the subject, "fue" (was) is the form of "ser," "cantada" (sung) is the past participle, and "por la cantante" (by the singer) indicates who performed the action.

When to Use the Passive Voice

In Spanish, the passive voice is often used in formal writing, such as in newspapers, academic writing, or official documents. It's used less often in everyday conversation, where the active voice or other structures are usually preferred.

However, the passive voice is useful when you want to emphasize the action or when the person who did the action is not important or not known.

For example:

La decisión fue tomada por el comité. (Pronounced lah deh-see-SYOHN FWEH toh-MAH-dah por el koh-mee-TEH) - The decision was made by the committee.

In this sentence, the focus is on the decision and the action of making it, rather than on the committee itself.

Another example:

El puente fue construido en 1892. (Pronounced el PWEHN-teh FWEH kohn-stroo-EE-doh ehn MIL oh-CHOHS-see-EHN-tohs noh-VEHN-tah EE DOHS) - The bridge was built in 1892.

Here, the focus is on the bridge and when it was built, rather than on who built it.

Using "Se" as an Alternative to the Passive Voice

In Spanish, the passive voice is not always the best choice, especially in everyday conversation. Instead, a structure using "se" is often preferred. This structure is called the "se impersonal" or "se pasivo," and it's used to express actions without specifying who is doing them.

Here's how it works:

Se + verb (in third-person singular or plural) + noun

For example:

Se venden libros. (Pronounced seh BEHN-dehn LEE-brohs) - Books are sold.

In this sentence, "se venden" means "are sold," and the focus is on the books, not on who is selling them.

Here's another example:

Se habla español aquí. (Pronounced seh AH-blah ehs-pah-NYOHL ah-KEE) - Spanish is spoken here.

In this case, "se habla" means "is spoken," and the focus is on the fact that Spanish is spoken, not on who speaks it.

Using "se" in this way is more common in Spanish than using the traditional passive voice, especially in everyday language. It's a simpler and more natural way to express passive actions without needing to specify who is doing the action.

Common Mistakes to Avoid

When learning to use the passive voice in Spanish, it's easy to make some common mistakes. Here are a few tips to help you avoid them:

- **Not matching the past participle:** In Spanish, the past participle must agree in gender and number with the subject. For example, "La carta fue escrita" (The letter was written) uses "escrita" to match "la carta" (feminine, singular).

- **Using the passive voice too often:** In Spanish, the passive voice is not used as frequently as in English. It's better to use active voice or the "se" structure in most situations.

- **Forgetting "por" to indicate the agent:** When you do use the passive voice, remember to include "por" to show who performed the action, such as in "El cuadro fue pintado por Pablo Picasso" (The painting was painted by Pablo Picasso).

By keeping these tips in mind, you can avoid common mistakes and use the passive voice correctly and effectively.

Key Points to Remember:

1. **Understanding the Passive Voice:** The passive voice in Spanish focuses on the action being done rather than who is doing it. It's used to emphasize the action or when the doer is not important or unknown. Example: El libro fue escrito por el autor (The book was written by the author).

2. **Forming the Passive Voice:** The passive voice is formed with the verb ser followed by the past participle of the main verb, and often includes "por" to indicate the agent (the doer of the action). Example: La canción fue cantada por la cantante (The song was sung by the singer).

3. **Using "Se" as an Alternative:** The se construction is often used in Spanish as an alternative to the passive voice, especially in everyday conversation. It expresses passive actions without specifying the doer. Example: Se venden libros (Books are sold).

4. **When to Use the Passive Voice:** The passive voice is more common in formal writing, such as in academic texts or news articles. In casual conversation, the se construction or active voice is usually preferred.

5. **Common Mistakes to Avoid:** Ensure the past participle agrees in gender and number with the subject, avoid overusing the passive voice, and remember to use "por" to indicate the agent when necessary. Example: La carta fue escrita (The letter was written), not La carta fue escrito.

Chapter 46

Discussing the Future: Plans and Predictions

Talking about the future is an exciting part of learning a new language. Whether you're making plans with friends, setting goals for yourself, or predicting what might happen, knowing how to discuss the future in Spanish is important. In this chapter, we'll explore how to talk about future events using the future tense, and how to make your sentences sound natural when discussing what you will do or what you think will happen.

Using the Future Tense in Spanish

The future tense in Spanish is used to talk about actions that will happen. In English, we use the word "will" to express the future, like in "I will go to the store." In Spanish, the future tense is formed by adding specific endings to the infinitive form of the verb (the form you find in the dictionary).

Here are the endings you add to the infinitive to form the future tense:

- **-é** (Pronounced eh) - I will
- **-ás** (Pronounced ahs) - You will (informal)
- **-á** (Pronounced ah) - He/She/You (formal) will
- **-emos** (Pronounced EH-mohs) - We will
- **-éis** (Pronounced EH-ees) - You all (informal, in Spain) will
- **-án** (Pronounced ahn) - They/You all will

Let's look at how these endings work with different verbs:

- **Hablar (to speak):** Yo hablaré (Pronounced yoh ah-blah-REH) - I will speak

- **Comer (to eat):** Tú comerás (Pronounced too koh-meh-RAHS) - You will eat

- **Vivir (to live):** Él vivirá (Pronounced el vee-vee-RAH) - He will live

These endings are added directly to the infinitive form of the verb, making it easy to form the future tense. This pattern is the same for all regular verbs, which makes the future tense one of the easier tenses to learn in Spanish.

Talking About Plans

When you want to talk about something you're planning to do in the future, you use the future tense. For example, if you're telling someone about your plans for tomorrow or next week, you can use the future tense to describe what you will do.

Here are some examples:

Mañana, estudiaré para el examen. (Pronounced mah-NYAH-nah, ehs-too-dyah-REH PAH-rah el eh-SAH-mehn) - Tomorrow, I will study for the test.

El próximo año, viajaremos a México. (Pronounced el PROHK-see-moh AHN-yoh, vyah-hah-REH-mohs ah MEH-hee-koh) - Next year, we will travel to Mexico.

Ellos jugarán al fútbol después de la escuela. (Pronounced EH-yohs hoo-gah-RAHN ahl FOOT-bol dehs-PWES deh lah ehs-KWEH-lah) - They will play soccer after school.

In each of these sentences, the future tense is used to talk about plans and intentions. This is a common way to use the future tense when discussing what you're going to do.

Making Predictions

The future tense is also used to make predictions about what might happen. Predictions are guesses or thoughts about what will happen in the future, based on what you know or think will happen.

Here are some examples:

Será un día soleado mañana. (Pronounced seh-RAH oon DEE-ah soh-LEH-ah-doh mah-NYAH-nah) - It will be a sunny day tomorrow.

Habrá mucha gente en la fiesta. (Pronounced ah-BRAH MOO-chah HEN-teh ehn lah FYEHS-tah) - There will be a lot of people at the party.

Ellos ganarán el partido. (Pronounced EH-yohs gah-nah-RAHN el par-TEE-doh) - They will win the game.

Using the future tense to make predictions allows you to express what you think will happen, even if you're not 100% sure.

Irregular Verbs in the Future Tense

While many verbs in Spanish are regular in the future tense, some verbs are irregular. Irregular verbs in the future tense have a different stem that you need to remember, but they still use the regular future endings.

Here are some common irregular verbs in the future tense:

- **Tener (to have):** Yo tendré (Pronounced yoh tehn-DREH) - I will have

- **Salir (to leave):** Tú saldrás (Pronounced too sahl-DRAHS) - You will leave

- **Hacer (to do/make):** Él hará (Pronounced el ah-RAH) - He will do/make

- **Decir (to say/tell):** Nosotros diremos (Pronounced noh-SOH-trohs dee-REH-mohs) - We will say/tell

- **Poder (to be able to):** Ellos podrán (Pronounced EH-yohs poh-DRAN) - They will be able to

These verbs don't follow the regular pattern, so it's important to learn their special stems. However, once you know the stems, you simply add the regular future tense endings.

Using "Ir a" to Talk About the Future

Another way to talk about the future in Spanish is by using the phrase "ir a" (to go to) followed by an infinitive verb. This is similar to saying "going to" in English.

Here's how it works:

Voy a estudiar esta noche. (Pronounced boy ah ehs-too-DYAR EHS-tah NOH-cheh) - I'm going to study tonight.

Vamos a comer pizza para la cena. (Pronounced BAH-mohs ah koh-MEHR PEET-sah PAH-rah lah SEH-nah) - We're going to eat pizza for dinner.

Ella va a escribir una carta. (Pronounced EH-yah bah ah ehs-KREE-beer OO-nah KAHR-tah) - She is going to write a letter.

This construction is very common in conversation and is often used when talking about plans or what is going to happen in the near future.

Expressing Intentions with "Querer"

Sometimes when you're talking about the future, you might want to express your intentions or desires. The verb "querer" (to want) is very useful for this purpose.

Here's how you can use "querer" to talk about what you want to do in the future:

Quiero ser médico cuando sea mayor. (Pronounced kee-EH-roh sehr MEH-dee-koh KWAHN-doh SEH-ah mah-YOHR) - I want to be a doctor when I grow up.

Queremos viajar a España el próximo verano. (Pronounced keh-REH-mohs vyah-HAHR ah ehs-PAH-nyah el PROHK-see-moh beh-RAH-noh) - We want to travel to Spain next summer.

Ellos quieren jugar al baloncesto después de la escuela. (Pronounced EH-yohs kee-EH-rehn hoo-GAHR ahl bah-lohn-SEHS-toh dehs-PWES deh lah ehs-KWEH-lah) - They want to play basketball after school.

Using "querer" allows you to express what you hope to do in the future, adding a personal touch to your plans.

Talking About Future Events with "Cuando"

The word "cuando" (when) is often used in Spanish to talk about future events. When you use "cuando" with a future event, you typically use the present tense after "cuando," even though you're talking about the future.

Here are some examples:

Cuando llegue a casa, te llamaré. (Pronounced KWAHN-doh YEH-geh ah KAH-sah, teh yah-mah-REH) - When I get home, I will call you.

Cuando termine la tarea, jugaré videojuegos. (Pronounced KWAHN-doh tehr-MEE-neh lah tah-REH-ah, hoo-gah-REH vee-deh-oh-HWEH-gohs) - When I finish my homework, I will play video games.

Cuando sea mayor, quiero vivir en la ciudad. (Pronounced KWAHN-doh SEH-ah mah-YOHR, kee-EH-roh vee-VEER ehn lah see-yoo-DAHD) - When I grow up, I want to live in the city.

In these sentences, "cuando" introduces a future event, and the present tense is used after "cuando" even though it's referring to the future.

Key Points to Remember:

1. **Forming the Future Tense:** The future tense in Spanish is created by adding specific endings (-é, -ás, -á, -emos, -éis, -án) directly to the infinitive form of the verb. This applies to all regular verbs. Example: Yo hablaré (I will speak).

2. **Talking About Plans:** Use the future tense to discuss actions or events you plan to do. Example: Mañana, estudiaré para el examen (Tomorrow, I will study for the test).

3. **Making Predictions:** The future tense is also used to predict what might happen. Example: Será un día soleado mañana (It will be a sunny day tomorrow).

4. **Irregular Verbs in the Future Tense:** Some verbs have irregular stems in the future tense, but they use the same future tense endings. Example: Yo tendré (I will have).

5. **Using "Ir a" for Near Future:** The phrase "ir a" followed by an infinitive verb is commonly used to express future actions, similar to "going to" in English. Example: Voy a estudiar esta noche (I'm going to study tonight).

www.ingramcontent.com/pod-product-compliance
Lightning Source LLC
Chambersburg PA
CBHW082337300426
44109CB00045B/2399